Current Research in Ethnomusicology

Edited by
Jennifer C. Post
Middlebury College

A Routledge Series

Current Research in Ethnomusicology

Jennifer C. Post, *General Editor*

Newly Composed Folk Music of Yugoslavia
Ljerka V. Rasmussen

Of Mermaids and Rock Singers
Placing the Self and Constructing the Nation through Belarusan Contemporary Music
Maria Paula Survilla

"Maracatu Atômico"
Tradition, Modernity, and Postmodernity in the Mangue Movement of Recife, Brazil
Philip Galinsky

Songs and Gifts at the Frontier
Person and Exchange in the Agusan Manobo Possession Ritual
Jose Buenconsejo

Balinese Discourses on Music and Modernization
Village Voices and Urban Views
Brita Renée Heimarck

Song from the Land of Fire
Continuity and Change in Azerbaijan Mugham
Inna Naroditskaya

The Cantaoras
Music, Gender, and Identity in Flamenco Song
Loren Chuse

Hanyang Kut
Korean Shaman Ritual Music from Seoul
Maria K. Seo

Baakisimba
The Music and Dance of the Baganda People of Uganda
Sylvia Nannyonga-Tamusuza

Shaped by Japanese Music

Kikuoka Hiroaki and *Nagauta Shamisen* in Tokyo

Jay Keister

ROUTLEDGE
New York & London

Published in 2004 by
Routledge
29 West 35th Street
New York, New York 10001

Published in Great Britain by
Routledge
11 New Fetter Lane
London EC4P 4EE

Routledge is an imprint of the Taylor & Francis Group.

Printed in the United States of America on acid-free paper.

10 9 8 7 6 5 4 3 2 1

Library of Congress Cataloging-in-Publication Data

Keister, Jay.
Shaped by Japanese music : nagauta shamisen in Tokyo / Jay Keister.
p. cm. -- (Current research in ethnomusicology ; v. 10)
Glossary: p.
Includes bibliographical references (p.) and index.
ISBN 0-415-96972-7 (hardcover : alk. paper)
1. Shamisen music--History and criticism. 2. Nagauta--History and criticism. 3. Kikuoka, Hiroaki, 1928-1999. 4. Music--Japan--Tokyo--History and criticism. I. Title, II. Series.
ML1015.S52K44 2004
781.62'956--dc22

2003021588

This book is dedicated
to the memory of Kikuoka Hiroaki (1927-1999),
who taught me about purity through music,
to my parents, John S. (1928-1999) and Josephine J.,
who taught me about harmony through tolerance,
and to my wife, Mami,
who taught me about nature through love.

Contents

Acknowledgments

I wish to thank the following people for helping, either directly or indirectly, to make this book possible:

Rees Archibald, Baba Kazuo, Elaine Barkin, Jane Batson, Amy Catlin, Lindsay Clare, Sue DeVale, Kelly Foreman, Craig Foster, Jonathan Fraser, Fujita Shinzuo, Fukushima Kazuo, Robert Garfias, Hanna Naoki, Hayashi Noriko, Denise Henry, Douglas Hollan, Itasaka Mami, Mr. and Mrs. Itasaka Miki, Katada Kikuyu, Katada Kikusa, John and Josephine Keister, Kikuoka Hiroaki, Kineya Rokuaya, Kineya Yusuke, Kin-san and family, Koizumi Yoshimi, Steve Loza, John Lytton, Grace M, William Malm, Rebecca Maloy, Mochizuki Tahachi, Alan Nagamoto, Nishimura Makoto, Okazaki Yoshiko, Ochi Yoshino, Herman Ooms, Oshio Satomi, Curt Patterson, Janet Pocorobba, Ali Jihad Racy, Helen Rees, Tim Rice, Brenda Romero, Wes Savick, Sugiura Kazuko, Terauchi Naoko, Togi Suenobu, Tokumaru Yoshihiko, Yaiko-san, Yamazaki Kazue, Yokoyama Takako, Ikuko Yuge, Yuriko, Eriko, Tomoko and Noriko.

I would also like to thank the UCLA Center for Japanese Studies, the UCLA Center for Pacific Rim Studies, and the Japan Foundation for their support.

Introduction: The Human Life in the Music

ADVICE TO THE ETHNOMUSICOLOGIST: "STUDY THE HUMAN LIFE IN THE MUSIC"

From March 1997 to December 1998, I was fortunate to have had the opportunity to study *nagauta* music in Tokyo with Kikuoka Hiroaki, a well-known, high-ranking, professional performer, composer, and founder of a music society who passed away in January 1999. Although I made it clear to him from the beginning my position as a researcher of ethnomusicology and that my basic goal was to learn about the current practice of *nagauta*, I was immediately taken in by Kikuoka as a serious student of the music through applied lessons. Being one of Kikuoka's students not only made us both more comfortable in our relationship, but gave me the opportunity to learn the detailed nuances of *nagauta* singing that can best be learned through experiencing direct one-on-one study with a teacher. But this student-teacher relationship that is so central to Japanese performing arts allowed me to learn more than just musical techniques first-hand. Kikuoka shared with me his personal philosophies about music and life that were a constant source of inspiration to me during a difficult period of living in Japan. As is common for many Japanese teachers known by the honorable term of *sensei*, Kikuoka advised me on a wide range of matters, as a father might advise a son.

The one piece of advice from Kikuoka that had the greatest impact on my research in ethnomusicology was directed not only to me, but to ethnomusicologists in general: "If ethnomusicologists want to study the music," he said, "they should study the human life in the music." This advice was the key to understanding how this music, originating in the seventeenth century as accompaniment to *kabuki*, continues to thrive today in modern Japan. The heart of *nagauta* music is not to be found in the extensive repertoire of compositions surviving today in books of notation or preserved on CD recordings, but is embodied in individual performers such as Kikuoka who are lifelong carriers of the tradition, transmitting their experience of the music to students directly through social interaction. Ethnomusicologists should study the human life in music because in Japanese traditional music, as in other traditional arts of East Asia, value is placed less on the external artistic product than it is on the perfection of skills and the mastery of the principles of the genre by individuals.[1] This helps explain why acclaimed master musicians of *nagauta* such as Kikuoka, and his teacher, Yamada Shōtarō,[2] often spoke of having the ability to discern the character and feelings of individual players solely through listening to their performance of the music. *Nagauta* is more than just a repertoire of songs. It is an artistic process or path to be discovered and experienced by the individual musician. "Because musicians create music from life," Kikuoka told me, "music is not first, life is first."

RESEARCH ON *NAGAUTA* AND THE PRACTICE OF ETHNOMUSICOLOGY

Kikuoka's advice to me made me realize the value of such an approach for studying Japanese traditional music and for researching *nagauta* music in particular, considering the literature on the subject. As one of the main genres of music for the *shamisen* (skin-covered, three-stringed, plucked lute), *nagauta* has been the subject of research by both Japanese and Western scholars. The most extensive research of *nagauta* in Japanese is by Asakawa who explains the music's form, poetic structure and history from its origins in the seventeenth century to the present day, including an assessment of how this traditional music is faring in modern Japan and advice for the future (see Asakawa 1974). Asakawa's most substantial work is his detailed catalog and explanation of the repertoire, *Nagauta meikyoku yosetsu* [an explanation of famous *nagauta* pieces] (1991). Detailed analysis of melodic phrases and tonal structure in *nagauta* has been done by Kakinoki (1978, 1975) and Oshio (1999, 1993). Older works by Machida (1924) and Kineya (1932) provide useful descriptions of the music and musicians during the early part of the twentieth century. In a more popular vein is work by Ikeda (2002) that emphasizes an appreciation of the repertoire through the stories and places evoked in the music. *Nagauta* research in English has been largely the domain of one ethnomusicologist, William Malm, who has published extensively on the subject. Malm's early research consisted of a history of the genre and analysis of musical form (Malm 1963). His later research of *nagauta* included an analysis of techniques of word painting (Malm 1978), the development of concert *nagauta* in the nineteenth century (Malm 1994), and an analysis of the influential musician and composer Yamada Shōtarō (Malm 1999).[3] His book, *Six Hidden Views of Japanese Music* (1986), features chapters about the absorption of the music of *nō* drama and folk festivals into *nagauta*, as well as the flexibility of interpretation of pieces by *nagauta* performers.

The historical research and musical analyses of *nagauta* have proven to be invaluable sources for my own study of *nagauta* music and have made tremendous contributions to the large body of literature on Japanese traditional music. Japanese traditional music in general has been extremely well documented, as evidenced in the sheer volume of historical documents and research available in Japanese as well as the growing body of literature in English (see surveys by Simeda 2002, Nelson 2002, and Hughes 1993). Hughes demonstrates that the amount of detailed, descriptive studies that have been done provides numerous possibilities for future research in Japanese music and cites the need for further research of a broad range of topics, including comparative analysis between schools of music, oral mnemonic systems of learning, the *iemoto* (household head) system of transmission in the arts, and aesthetics that are prevalent throughout Japanese music genres (1993). What is evident in reviewing the literature is that although Japanese music has been well documented in terms of its history, form, theory, and performance practice using methodologies commonly associated with historical musicology, Japanese music has not been sufficiently analyzed as an aspect of Japanese culture using methodologies that have become common in ethnomusicology. To understand the experience of *nagauta* — the human life in the music — requires a more focused kind of study.

Ethnomusicology, as defined by Myers, is "the division of musicology in which special emphasis is given to the study of music in its cultural context — the anthropology of music" (Myers 1992:3). Myers's definition of the field is only one of many in a discipline that seems to compel scholars to begin major works with their own definition of ethnomusicology. With almost as many definitions of ethnomusicology as there are ethnomusicologists, it is perhaps impossible to reach consensus on the term ethnomusicology, especially considering the broad range of research interests that are represented in scholarly work. Whether ethnomusicologists study the music of oral or literate traditions, art, folk or popular music, issues such as the origins of music, musical change, or music as symbol, the common feature that comes closest to uniting all this research is the study of music as an aspect of culture. This connection of music and culture was characterized by Alan Merriam as a merging of musicological and anthropological methods of research, which he described as "the objective of ethnomusicology and the keystone upon which the validity of its contribution lies" (Merriam 1964:17). It is curious, however, that studies of Japanese traditional music have tended to shy away from attempts at analyzing music as an aspect of Japanese culture. What is lacking in the literature on Japanese music is an approach to the study of music as a cultural phenomenon and, as such, many research questions commonly asked in ethnomusicology are rarely pursued. What cultural values or social processes are present in Japanese musical performance and composition? What meaning does performing traditional music have for participants in the modern nation of Japan? How is Japanese music symbolic of social organization and cultural values? How does the social practice of Japanese music reinforce and sustain prevailing cultural values? In what ways do musicians support or challenge social organization or cultural values through musical practices?

The absence of such questions seems surprising considering the amount of cultural studies about Japan that Sugimoto refers to as "the Japan phenomenon in the social sciences" (Sugimoto 1997). Since Ruth Benedict's *The Chrysanthemum and the Sword* (1977, originally published in 1946), research in the social sciences has crafted an image of Japanese society around a set of cultural values that have become cliché in their repetition: prioritizing group needs over individual desires, valuing rote memorization over creative originality, the importance of saving face in a shame-based society. The fact that many of these essentialist ideas about Japan have been taken up by the Japanese themselves in their own popular discourse known as *nihonjinron* (literally "Japanese people theory") suggests that perhaps researchers of Japanese music have been wise to avoid simplistic explanations of Japanese music as one aspect of an essentialized cultural portrait.[4] The problem for ethnomusicologists who wish to study the discourse of cultural practices and symbols in the highly codified and historically well-documented world of Japanese traditional music is how to understand music in Japanese culture without constructing totalizing, essentialist models of musical culture that overlook the actual practices of individuals which constitute the human life in the music.

PERSON-CENTERED ETHNOMUSICOLOGY AND THE INTERPRETATION OF MUSIC

One methodological remedy to the problem of creating essentialist models of music cultures that obscure the roles played by individuals in society is the "ethnography of the individual," or the "person-centered" ethnography. First developed by researchers in psychological anthropology, a person-centered approach to ethnography shifts the emphasis away from abstract models of culture, which depict individuals in social or symbolic roles — an "experience-distant" approach — and towards the study of the experience of the individuals themselves — an "experience-near" approach (Kleinman and Kleinman 1991:276).[5] The conventional use of ethnographic data of individuals has been typically based on their "assumed typicality for the community as a whole" in which the individual is depicted as a "passive carrier of tradition" rather than as a "matured and single organism of ideas" (Sapir 1958:509). Whereas conventional ethnography provides a cultural description analogous to a map or aerial photograph of a community, a person-centered ethnography "tells us what it's like to live there" (LeVine 1982:293). This book's focus on the human life in the music is a person-centered study of Kikuoka as a "matured and single organism of ideas," and is part of a recent trend in ethnomusicology of person-centered ethnography that seeks to avoid ethnographies of music that have been described as "cultural-average accounts" (Stock 2001:7). My person-centered approach seeks to avoid the "cultural-average" by telling the story of Kikuoka's career in music, constructing an ethnographic account of his teaching practices, and analyzing his creative strategies as a composer, all in an effort to answer the fundamental question at the center of Tim Rice's re-model of ethnomusicology: "how do people historically construct, socially maintain and individually create and experience music?" (Rice 1987:473).[6]

Ethnomusicological studies that have focused on individuals as the locus of musical construction, maintenance, and creation include studies of Bulgarian music (Rice 1994), Native American Shoshone songs (Vander 1988), Albanian wedding singing (Sugarman 1997), and Chinese music (Stock 1996), to name just a few. In accounting for person-centered studies in ethnomusicology, it is important to distinguish between ethnography and autobiography as translated by ethnomusicologists, such as Frisbie and McAllester's autobiography of a Navajo singer (1978) and Groemer's English translation of the autobiography of Japanese folk musician Takahashi Chikuzan (1999)[7] which is supplemented with extensive musical analysis. Autobiographies such as these provide tremendous amounts of important historical and cultural information unmediated by the ethnomusicologist, but they are not ethnographies in the postmodern sense in that they do not include the experience of an ethnographer. It is precisely this aspect — the subjective presence of the ethnographer in a self-reflexive mode — that has become a hallmark of recent postmodern approaches to ethnography and has served to guard against the creation of cultural-average accounts of essentialized cultural others.

The re-evaluation of the representational stance of the ethnographer in anthropology over the last two decades has led to person-centered ethnographies of music in which the self-reflexive presence of the ethnomusicologist is an integral part of research (Stock 2001:12). The nature of most fieldwork in ethnomusicology as an active, participant-observation experience of performing, learning, and practicing music alongside those one is studying magnifies the presence of the fieldworker to the point that the ethnomusicologist cannot be excluded from the field of view. Ethnomusicologists have thus used their own musical experiences to understand how others experience music (Rice 1994), and even made their own experience of learning music the subject of their study (Bakan 1999). The issue of self-reflexivity has been an area of some debate for fear that we "risk displacing the reader's interest from the people making the music whom we are writing about, to ourselves" (Titon 1997:96). Although I have included myself in the ethnographic setting of this book in chapter two, I do not become the subject of my own research, but instead operate, as Titon suggests, as a "bit player" whose reflections "serve as a kind of interpretation" (ibid.).[8]

The result of postmodern, self-reflexivity in ethnography has been less of a danger to objectivity in the field of ethnomusicology than it has been a benefit to our understanding of music and culture, resulting in more person-centered definitions of the field itself. Titon defines the latest paradigm of ethnomusicology simply as "the study of people making music" (Titon 1997:91) while Bakan defines ethnomusicology as "the study of how music lives in the lives of people who make and experience it, and of how people live in the music they make" (Bakan 1999:17–18). Both of these definitions resonate with Kikuoka's recommendation of "the study of the human life in the music." Considering the image of Japanese traditional music that exists in much of the literature — the time-honored classical music that is enduring and sanctified, yet fragile and static — and the myth of Japanese culture as an island of uniqueness in a globalized world, the time is right for more ethnomusicologists — both Japanese and non-Japanese — to write about their experiences of Japanese music and tell us "what it's like to live there."

But studying the human life in the music requires more than just ethnographic description of the details of a particular musician's methods of musical construction, maintenance and creation. Unlike the raw, unmediated musician's autobiography, the person-centered ethnography requires interpretation on the part of the ethnomusicologist whose presence as a "bit player" gives the researcher a feel for the power of music as it is experienced by musicians. The interpretation of music, not only as a social practice observed by the ethnomusicologist, but as a cultural metaphor that is felt by the ethnomusicologist, becomes particularly important when aspects of music are beyond discourse, that is, unspoken or spoken about in an indirect way. The *nagauta* musicians I encountered during my field research in Tokyo showed little interest in discussing musical meaning or musical form. Kikuoka bristled at some of my intertextual leaps, such as trying to apply aesthetics from Japanese literature to *nagauta*.[9] In the absence of an explicit or literal discourse about meaning, ethnomusicologists look to other aspects of culture to arrive at an interpretation, along the lines of what Geertz calls "thick description" (Geertz 1973). In this approach commonly employed in ethnomusicology, musical and cultural metaphors are public and are thus read as texts by both researchers and culture members, though not necessarily read the same way and consequently subject to different interpretations.

Interpreting music in terms of cultural metaphors should not be developed for the purpose of finding laws that can be used to generate abstract models of music, but specifically to convey the power of the music-making process and giving us a sense of "what it's like to live there." The power of music as a cultural metaphor is perhaps best described in Kingsbury's interpretation of a Western conservatory of music (1988) which shows how music functions as a social force within an enclosed learning environment and becomes the central notion from which value judgments are made. Some of the most influential interpretations in ethnomusicology have come from Feld's research of Papua New Guinean music in which he focused on Kaluli myth as a means of portraying "linkages between sounds, both human and natural, and sentiments, social ethos and emotion" (Feld 1982:15) and developed an aesthetic trope labeled "lift-up-over-sounding" to describe music and other domains of Kaluli culture (Feld 1988). Feld's research, as well as the research of Judith and Alton Becker on notions of time in Javanese music, developed the notion that the major source of symbolic power in music is its "iconicity" or its naturalness which is perceived as being coherent with other aspects of culture (Becker 1981). Such interpretations that emerge naturally out of the researcher's experienced reading of a music culture are not "essentialist," but essential in understanding the richness of music in culture.

The above examples of music as a means of making value judgments, as a linkage of sound, myth (literary legends), and values across cultural domains, and as iconic of cultural organization resonate with the world of *nagauta* inhabited by Kikuoka. Although my interpretation of the cultural metaphors of *nagauta* music draws upon previous analyses of Japanese cultural values and concepts, this developed naturally out of my own experiences of the cultural practice of *nagauta* in a particular time and location. The shaping process of *nagauta* that is the interpretive theme of this book emerged directly out of my lessons with Kikuoka as described in the ethnographic account in chapter two and the coercive forces behind this shaping process became the subject of chapter three. Turning from social analysis to musical analysis, chapters four and five interpret *nagauta* music as a synecdoche of Japanese culture and demonstrate the music's symbolic power, bearing an iconic resemblance to Japanese processes of socialization described in the preceding chapters. My interpretation of the human life in the music involves the symbolic power of music to affect musicians and listeners due to its "naturalness," a quality of musical perception that may not be so easily described or recognized by musicians themselves.

PRACTICE THEORY: *NAGAUTA* AS A SOCIAL FIELD

Particularly useful in analyzing the social aspects of *nagauta* music are the ideas of Pierre Bourdieu, whose practice theory has informed several studies of music and dance to varying degrees (Cowan 1990, Seeger 1987, Sugarman 1993, Turino 1993). Practice theory is especially useful for ethnomusicology as a way of eliciting and understanding personally salient concepts and values for musicians — what is at stake — and observing these concepts and values in action, enabling the ethnomusicologist to study the logic of musical practice.

A starting point for this study is Bourdieu's notion of social fields, which he uses to explain social relations. A field is defined by Bourdieu as:

> a network, or a configuration, of objective relations between positions... [which are] objectively defined, in their existence and in the determinations they impose upon their occupants, agents or institutions, by their present and potential situation in the structure of the distribution of species of power (or capital) whose possession commands access to the specific profits that are at stake in the field (Bourdieu and Wacquant 1992:97).

Simply stated, a field is a system of social positions occupied by individuals or institutions, the nature of these social positions defining the situation for the occupants of the field (Jenkins 1992:85). Bourdieu has given examples of fields such as politics, philosophy, religion, and art, each of which has distinct properties. Each field operates under its own "logic," with the central point of conflict or competition within the field revolving around Bourdieu's notion of capital, or "what is at stake." Avoiding the economic determinism that the term capital implies, Bourdieu broadly defines four different species of capital: economic capital; social capital (highly valued social relations); cultural capital (legitimate knowledge); and symbolic capital (prestige or honor). As an example, the field of academia involves competition not just for economic capital but also for cultural and symbolic capital such as publications in prestigious journals or doctoral degrees from prestigious universities.

This ethnographic study addresses how *nagauta* operates as a social field. As a small, specialized field outside the mainstream, *nagauta* is subject to domination by the economic field — the vast, dominant field of power in society that influences the activity of individuals and institutions within smaller fields. The field of *nagauta* itself is structured by a network of positions (beliefs and opinions, as in "it is my position that… ") that are used by the individuals and institutions within the field in competition for the field's particular forms of capital (economic, social, cultural or symbolic). At the level of the individual, which is the main focus in this study, musicians operating within the field are influenced by what Bourdieu calls habitus, a term that refers to the generating principle behind behavior by which individual agents reproduce the social structure of the given field in which they are situated. In Bourdieu's model, individuals are unaware of habitus as it is deeply embedded at an unconscious level and inculcated through a socializing process that commences in childhood. This notion of a socially informed body plays an important role not only in Japanese performing arts such as *nagauta*, but in other domains of daily life as well.

Although *nagauta* can be studied as a field in itself, it is but one small sub-field within traditional music which is itself a small part of the much larger field of music. Modern Japan is today one of the world's largest markets of commercial music engaged in mass consumption of music from a vast array of Japanese and international performers. Alongside contemporary popular music (all varieties of both Japanese and Western pop), jazz, Western classical music, and world music, pre-twentieth-century traditional Japanese music seems relatively insignificant within this broad commercial field. Genres in the field of traditional music as diverse as *gagaku* (Imperial court music), *sōkyoku* (solo music for *koto*), *honkyoku* (solo music for *shakuhachi*), and *utai* (*nō* drama song), to name just a few, exist as survivals of pre-industrial Japan and have become "markers of the exotic both inside and outside Japan" (De Ferranti 2000:39). While the music for some traditional instruments, such as *koto* (13-stringed zither) and *taiko* (stick-struck, barrel-shaped drums) have undergone a great deal of modernization through the development of new repertoire and instruments, *nagauta* has not undergone any significant, lasting stylistic modifications in the twentieth century.

Unlike commercial music, which depends on a large audience of consumers who may remain relatively passive, traditional forms of Japanese music rely to a great extent on an active audience of amateur hobbyists who take lessons and attend concerts, most of which exist outside the purview of the general public. Whereas the mainstream media maintains a public critical discourse of popular, classical and jazz concerts and recordings, such media discourse for traditional music is confined to a few journals read by professionals and amateur hobbyists. Unlike commercial music, traditional forms are part of a discourse of preservation in which they are valued as "important cultural properties" (*jūyō bunkazai*), a designation given by the Japanese government which regularly bestows titles such as "living national treasure" (*ningen kokuhō*) on musicians who embody and preserve the art form. It is this last aspect of official preservation that maintains the social relevance of the traditional arts and rescues genres such as *nagauta* from complete marginalization into what Marilyn Ivy calls a "vanishing discourse" (1995).

In the sub-field of *nagauta*, preservation is an important aspect of the discourse for many musicians. The conservative, orthodox position in *nagauta* relies on the traditional family lineage system known as *iemoto*, by which the artistic styles and economic power of a few exclusive families are maintained. The unique quality of *nagauta* as performed by a particular family is preserved by generations of musicians who pass down the style, thus maintaining the economic and artistic strength of that family. As will be shown in this book, Kikuoka developed a heterodox position as he felt the need for *nagauta* to become less exclusive in order to maintain its vitality in the modern world and insure its future development. Regardless of one's position about how best the art should be preserved, what is at stake for professional *nagauta* musicians is competition for concert opportunities and acquisition of students by which economic and stylistic power are maintained. For professional musicians, the field of *nagauta* involves competition for the economic capital of concert fees and income from student lessons, as well as the symbolic capital of prestigious honors and special stage names that can be used to increase one's income. For amateur musicians however, what is typically at stake is not economic capital, but symbolic capital such as amateur stage names and licenses that can be used to increase one's social status.

FIELDWORK IN JAPAN: THE LIMITS OF AFFILIATION

In order to understand "what it's like to live there," one must literally "live there" for an extended period of time to conduct ethnography. During 29 months of ethnographic fieldwork in Tokyo from October 1996 to February 1999, I engaged in the kind of participant-observation that has become common practice in ethnomusicology. This consisted of a wide range of activities designed to immerse myself into musical life as much as possible: attending regular music lessons and participating in recitals with several teachers of *nagauta*; regularly attending concert performances; conducting formal and informal interviews with audience members and musicians, both professional and amateur; and observing and participating in daily life in Tokyo.

The difficulty of conducting ethnomusicological fieldwork in Japan over a relatively short time period, as noted by scholars of Japanese studies (Yano 1995; Kondo 1990; Sugimoto and Mouer 1982), needs to be addressed. An outsider roaming freely through society curiously asking questions is typically regarded with suspicion unless the proper connection (*kone*) is made, typically an introduction by a person or institution acting as intermediary. Even with such connections, I found it difficult to penetrate through the polite surface maintained in conversation and behavior that kept me at a distance until a significant amount of time was spent in a particular social group. In order to fully experience Japanese music it was necessary to stay longer in fewer places, which is actually closer to a Japanese person's experience of traditional music.

The nature of social relationships in Japan had a strong influence on setting the parameters of my fieldwork. Establishing affiliations with people led to their having a certain degree of control over my movements because of social obligations and various social alliances. Such limits on affiliation are structurally part of the system of traditional arts. In Japanese music, for example, it is customary for a student to have only one teacher of one instrument. After establishing a relationship with one teacher it is highly inappropriate to roam freely in search of another teacher of the same instrument in the small world of *nagauta*. The teacher-student relationship is intended to be close, personal and exclusive. I was fortunate, however, to have had four different teachers of *nagauta* during my stay, but this was possible only because of important connections, and the fact that these four teachers (of voice, *shamisen*, flute and percussion) were not in direct competition as none of them specialized in the same *nagauta* instrument. These limitations of affiliation also presented challenges in obtaining interviews in that these required some sort of connection through the mediation of a friend or student of the interviewee, thus it was difficult to accumulate a large number of formal interviews. Nevertheless I was able to conduct 21 formal interviews and supplement these with numerous informal conversations that took place around the everyday practice of making music.

In sharp contrast to the constant constraint of affiliation present within the traditional world of *nagauta*, was the relative freedom from those constraints outside that world, especially in the liminal world occupied by the foreigner staying in Japan who is either treated graciously as a guest in spite of their obvious lack of social etiquette or is ignored completely. When not engaged with people in the music world or directly involved in research, I spent a great deal of time traveling around Tokyo teaching English conversation. Not only did this provide a quick and convenient source of funding to subsidize my research, but it was also a method of informal data collection outside the world of traditional music. The free-form nature of these English conversation lessons allowed plenty of opportunity to discuss a wide range of topics, providing an invaluable source for learning various people's opinions about Japanese culture. In some cases, students felt free to express opinions to an anonymous foreigner that they perhaps would not express to friends or family.

MAKING THE PERFECT TEA AND TEACUP: A METAPHOR FOR THE STUDY OF *NAGAUTA*

I would like to begin this study of "the human life in the music" by introducing a metaphor that Kikuoka used extensively in one of our interviews that glosses musical performing, learning, technique, and human life. Kikuoka described the holistic, process-oriented nature of traditional Japanese music as making the perfect "tea and teacup." "Some think that the tea is more important than the outside cup," he explained, "but the Japanese point of view is that everything is equally important: the cup, the lid, the spoon, the plate." Kikuoka described the "teacup" or container of music in this way:

> Making a good container, a perfect cup, takes time. We must maintain a musical instrument, keep the best condition *shamisen* and achieve the proper tuning. After this is taken care of, then people can start playing, otherwise nothing will be properly tuned. Before playing we need so many years. Without mastering basic technique people will not learn the best way and are not able to play. The method is to maintain the *shamisen* and play it. The student learns this method from the teacher little by little.

While the necessity of the teacup is a metaphor for the technique and technology of the *shamisen*, Kikuoka described the "tea" in this way:

> Many people seem to be learning *shamisen* but are only learning technique. Yamada Shōtarō [Kikuoka's teacher] taught the 'inside.' The most important part is inside — the tea. A composer has an imagination or creativity and using this creativity the composer makes music.

Although Kikuoka's metaphor may seem abstract or over-extended, it nevertheless identifies an essence of music that he refers to as "tea" which can be seen as that tradition carried within the individual musician. Kikuoka sees himself as such a carrier of tradition and stated that, whether performing classic *nagauta* pieces or composing new works for the genre, he must capture the spirit of those that came before him.

Kikuoka did not, however, think of his role as one in which he must imitate a past form of music, but described that his main duty was to translate this music of the past into present day Japanese life.

Kikuoka's personal philosophy is not only the key to understanding this performer, composer and teacher, but it also helps one understand the various aspects of *nagauta* music in the twentieth century that are examined in this book. The life story and career of Kikuoka in chapter one demonstrates how *nagauta* developed from a musical accompaniment for kabuki and Japanese classical dance into a concert form in which musicians sought to gain respect for the music independent of theater. This chapter explains Kikuoka's lifelong commitment to making the "perfect teacup" of *nagauta* which included instituting reforms in the social structure of the music that have since affected contemporary performance standards. The more direct way of making the proper "cup" is found in the process of teaching and learning *nagauta* as described in chapter two. This process involves shaping the individual in such a way that the student becomes a suitable carrier of the tradition by learning the necessary appropriate behavior. While the teacher-student relationship is at the center of *nagauta* practice, this relationship is linked to a much broader network of social relations in Japanese society which is examined in chapter three, demonstrating how individuals are shaped through a variety of forces of social coercion present in Japanese society. Chapter four examines how these shaping forces are evident in the structure of *nagauta* composition and performance, depicted lyrically in the music, and reproduced in pre-determined, stereotyped musical phrases. Chapter five locates the human life in the music in Kikuoka's own *nagauta* compositions. An analysis of two of his compositions reveals his strategies for creating works that have a modern musical perspective, yet remain firmly within the boundaries of the tradition.

Kikuoka's personal philosophy blurs the distinction between music and human life in his belief that, in the ideal situation of true artistic achievement, there can be no separation of the two. Following the way of my teacher, I have taken a person-centered approach to *nagauta* in the belief that what matters most is not a repertoire of musical compositions or a series of performances, but the individual human being who is the living embodiment of the music.

Chapter One

A Career in *Nagauta*: Kikuoka Hiroaki

SCARRED BY *SHAMISEN*, SHAPED BY *NAGAUTA*

Shinobu (Figure 1.1) hated the *shamisen* when he was a child. Actually, at first he enjoyed imitating his father's constant singing of *nagauta* and *katōbushi* songs when he was a toddler, but soon Shinobu found himself taking *shamisen* lessons from his father, a stern *nagauta shamisen* player with the professional stage name of Kineya Rokukanji, a name that identified his father as a *nagauta* performer of considerable status. Shinobu was not happy about being forced by his father into hours of daily practice and memorization of through-composed musical compositions that could last up to 30 minutes or even longer. Although *nagauta* notation was a relatively recent invention, Shinobu's father taught him the old-fashioned way of rote memorization because, so his father believed, the best *nagauta* players were the ones with good memory. In fact, his father would rage at young Shinobu whenever he forgot a passage and occasionally threw things in anger. The worst incident was when the adolescent Shinobu was too slow in memorizing a lengthy piece of music and his father threw the weighted *shamisen* plectrum of ivory across the room at his son. His father had actually thrown it to one side, intending only to frighten his son, but Shinobu tried to dodge the projectile, only to move his head directly into the line of fire. The sharp pointed tip of the plectrum struck Shinobu squarely in the forehead, leaving a scar that was visible for the rest of his life.[1]

Although marked for life by the instrument, Shinobu recalled recently that he never actually hated the *shamisen*. *Nagauta* lessons were certainly a burden in his childhood, but he felt that being born at a bad time was what gave him the most hardship. Born into a struggling musician's family in the Tokyo area and raised in an atmosphere of war and sickness in the 1930s was what he really hated about his childhood. After Shinobu's mother died of tuberculosis when he was an infant, he was constantly battling illnesses as a child and missing school for months on end, causing his father and step-mother to worry about their child's future. He also felt the social

Figure 1.1 Kikuoka Hiroaki

pressure of a steadily growing warfare mentality in the 1930s that paralleled the domestic warfare of the constant fighting he remembered in his dysfunctional family. As war in Asia loomed, his boyhood friends talked of becoming proud, decorated soldiers in the Emperor's military, while a horrified Shinobu kept quiet, secretly practicing his *shamisen* at home so as not to appear frivolous or useless during wartime Japan. This "dark" time, as Shinobu described his childhood, was a far cry from the fantasy world of Edo period Japan depicted in classic *nagauta* pieces that the *shamisen* had opened for him. As it turned out, it was the *shamisen*-accompanied songs of *nagauta* — a lyrical world of heroic characters in conflict, seductive ladies in the pleasure quarters, and poetic scenes of the sensuousness of nature — that sparked Shinobu's imagination and eventually became his life's calling.

As a young adult who loved the world of Edo that lived in *nagauta* music, Shinobu came to embrace the *shamisen* and follow in his father's footsteps by making a career as a professional performer. When he went to study *nagauta* professionally at the Tokyo University of Fine Arts he met artists such as Yamada Shōtarō and Kineya Jōkan who became his teachers and main sources of inspiration in his life. The music of *nagauta* that captured the spirit of Edo in his imagination, and his teachers who embodied that spirit as living carriers of tradition, formed a path that Shinobu would follow throughout his career. But as he embarked on that path as a professional-bound student, he discovered something that he felt compromised the purity and beauty of the music he loved — the *iemoto* system. Since the Edo era, this social institution had dominated the world of *nagauta*, valuing blood relationship over talent, compelling musicians to purchase expensive licenses that did not accurately reflect musical skills, and making rich a few high-ranking musicians who financially exploited the many lower-ranking musicians, such as his own father. Along with his teacher, Yamada Shōtarō, Shinobu set out to liberate the music he loved from the *iemoto* system.

The young *nagauta* musician in this story was born Kikuoka Shinobu on December 12, 1927, and changed his name as an adult from Shinobu to Hiroaki.[2] As a professional performer, composer and teacher, Kikuoka Hiroaki was a major figure in the development of concert *nagauta* music in the second half of the twentieth century. Up until his death in January 1999, Kikuoka had been the president of a leading *nagauta* society in Tokyo for 14 years and had been one of Japan's leading performers of *nagauta shamisen*. Throughout his professional career, Kikuoka had witnessed, and played a major role in, the changing currents of the traditional Japanese music scene. Although the modest, unassuming Kikuoka often downplayed his own importance, his lifelong career in music had a direct effect on the social and artistic trends in *nagauta* during the period of his career. His tireless efforts were focused on reforming and developing *nagauta* into what he saw as a more "pure" (*junsui*) form of the music, achieving respectability as a musical form independent of dance and free from the restrictive atmosphere of the Japanese *iemoto* system of artistic transmission.

This first chapter of my subject-centered ethnography of Kikuoka focuses on his experiences as a *nagauta* musician in order to introduce traditional Japanese music as part of a shaping process — a process by which the individual musician shapes, and is shaped by, the world into which he is thrown. Kikuoka's experience of *nagauta* ranges from his personal pleasure of music as an inspiration for his artistic pursuits, to his encounters with traditional organizational structures as maintained through established artistic practices, to his strategies for action within the constantly evolving and socially negotiated construction of modern Japanese society. The shaping of Kikuoka's role as traditional torchbearer, new musical creator, and social reformer, takes place in a time and space of clashing ideologies and changing economic conditions. The narrative of Kikuoka's musical experience and the historical background that informs this narrative as introduced in this chapter constitute one aspect of the human life in the music.

THE TRADITIONAL WORLD OF *SHAMISEN*, KABUKI, AND *NAGAUTA*

The traditional world of *nagauta* that Kikuoka inherited from his father and teachers developed during the Edo period with the rise of the *shamisen* as the main melody instrument accompanying the kabuki theater. The *shamisen* (lit. "three tasteful strings"), is a three-stringed, skin-covered lute derived from two older three-stringed lutes from Asia, the Chinese *sanxian* and the Okinawan *sanshin*, the latter of which was imported from the Ryukyu Islands into Japan in the second half of the sixteenth century. The earliest use of the instrument was probably by blind priests who previously used the *biwa* (wooden, pear-shaped, four-string lute) and found the new instrument equally suitable for their narrative storytelling (Malm 2000:214).[3] The use of the *shamisen* as an accompaniment to singing and storytelling spread quickly throughout Japan as the instrument became central to the development of a number of song genres, many of which eventually came to be used to accompany theater forms that developed during the Edo period.

Genres of *shamisen* music created during Edo are classified into two broad categories according to their vocal style and lyric content. Genres based on narrative storytelling are classified as *katarimono* (narrative songs) and those with more lyrical content are classified as *utamono* (lyric songs), although elements of both storytelling and lyrical poetry are present in most genres. The growth of *shamisen* music during the Edo period is directly linked to the development of kabuki, the main theatrical form that dominated during this time. The narrative genres of *shamisen* music that are still performed in kabuki today include *gidayūbushi* (which came by way of *bunraku* puppet drama), *tokiwazu* and *kiyomoto*. The *shamisen* genre most widely used for kabuki plays and dances is the lyric genre known as *nagauta* (literally meaning "long song") which grew into a repertoire of through-composed song suites that range from 10 to 45 minutes in length and are performed by an ensemble that includes voice, *shamisen*, drums, and flutes. A product of the kabuki theater, *nagauta* is closely linked to kabuki in terms of its historical development and its formal structure.

Kabuki (literally "song, dance, and acting") first appeared at the end of the sixteenth century as a performance of *nembutsuodori*, a Buddhist dance of exorcism, by a Shinto dancer named Okuni. In spite of its origins in religious dance, kabuki quickly evolved into a bawdy collection of dances performed by prostitutes advertising their services until women were banned completely by the Tokugawa government in 1629 (Shively 2002:36). Eventually kabuki became the most popular theater form of the Edo era and had absorbed many other forms of Japanese performing arts. Kabuki became a melting pot of many of the performing arts in existence at the time, including the sophisticated *nō* drama which had been developed and patronized by Japan's ruling warrior class. The popular appeal and growing sophistication of kabuki cut across class divisions, drawing audiences from all four ranks of the government-enforced social hierarchy — from the top-ranking samurai warrior class to the second- and third-ranked farmers and artisans, to the lowest-ranking merchant class (Gerstle 2002:88–89).

As kabuki was typically performed on *nō* stages in its early days, the first music for kabuki was provided by the instruments of the *nō* theater (*nō hayashi*), an ensemble consisting of *nōkan* (transverse flute), *taiko* (stick-struck, barrel-shaped drum), *kotsuzumi* (hourglass-shaped drum played at the shoulder), and *ōtsuzumi* (hourglass-shaped drum played at the hip). By the mid-seventeeth century *shamisen* music had been adopted into kabuki, where its primary theatrical function was to provide musical accompaniment to the dance portions of kabuki performances. Initially short lyric songs (*kouta*) were used, but as kabuki grew in popularity and productions became more elaborate, longer dances were created, for which longer *shamisen* works were needed (Malm 1963:16). In this way, *nagauta* developed as the main supporting music for the dances of kabuki.

Like kabuki, *nagauta* itself became a musical melting pot as it absorbed other music genres. Although classified as a lyric genre, *nagauta* absorbed several narrative genres of *shamisen* music which have since become either defunct or extremely rare in Japan today. Surviving *nagauta* compositions show traces of older styles such as *ōzatsuma*, *itchūbushi*, *katōbushi*, and *gekibushi* (ibid.:17). The most significant in the musical mix of *nagauta* was the influence of the music of *nō* theater. Eventually the *nō hayashi* ensemble of flute and drums began to accompany *nagauta* performance on stage and the instruments became a standard part of the modern *nagauta* ensemble. During the nineteenth century when kabuki was at its height of popularity and its appeal cut across all class boundaries, the incorporation of more stories from the *nō* theater fed a public desire for more sophisticated drama. Many famous *nō* plays were adapted to kabuki and *nagauta* pieces were composed for their accompaniment resulting in more sophisticated lyric poetry and vocal passages that resemble the chant-like voice quality of *nō* vocal recitation. Some of the well-known *nō*-derived kabuki works for which *nagauta* were composed include *Kanjinchō*, *Hashi Benkei*, and *Tsuru Kame*. *Nagauta* also adapted folk music into compositions to suit kabuki theater, such as the boatman's song in the play *Kibun Daijin* (ibid.:18–19). *Nagauta* also came to be augmented by "off-stage music" (*geza*), a variety of percussion, wind and string instruments that are played from behind a stage curtain, unlike the *nagauta* and *nō* ensembles that are played onstage and in full view of the audience.

During the nineteenth century the various art forms contained in kabuki began to expand beyond the professional concert stage through the popularity of lessons and amateur performances. While the practice of kabuki dance outside the professional theater came to be known as *nihon buyō* (Japanese classical dance), *nagauta* also began to develop as an independent art form with the composition of new pieces intended only for concert performance without dance (Malm 2000:231). As these compositions without dance were meant to allow the music to stand on its own, they tended to feature more displays of virtuosity in both the vocal and *shamisen* parts with more extended instrumental interludes. A few of the early compositions of this music have become durable *nagauta* standards that are still performed today, such as *Azuma Hakkei* (1818), *Oimatsu* (1820) and *Aki no Irokusa* (1845), a piece originally without drum accompaniment which may have been a reaction against kabuki dance music (Malm 1963:18). Although *nagauta* never lost its prominent role as dance accompaniment in kabuki, many musicians continued to perform and compose purely concert pieces, some of the more successful pieces resulting in dances being choreographed for them after the fact. It is this concert style of *nagauta* that Kikuoka promoted throughout his professional career.

Apart from a few important compositions at the beginning of the twentieth century, very few compositions since the nineteenth century have had any significant impact on the currently active repertoire of about 130 *nagauta* compositions.[4] Although many new compositions have been and are still being composed by players in the present day, new *nagauta* compositions have not been able to break into the standard repertoire which is dominated by works composed prior to 1912, and rarely do new works have repeat performances following their premieres.[5] The significant new developments in *nagauta* in the twentieth century instead concerned pedagogy and preservation of the pre-twentieth-century repertoire. The development of two different *nagauta* notation systems in the early part of the twentieth century have expanded teaching possibilities and helped preserved the works of what is essentially an oral tradition (ibid.:19). Kikuoka himself was at the center of a significant major development in twentieth-century *nagauta* — the founding of a new *nagauta* society that sought to modernize the social structure of *nagauta* performance and pedagogy. Kikuoka's founding of the *nagauta* society known as Tōonkai defined his historical contribution to the perpetuation of the tradition and is the main focus of this chapter which chronicles his career. The Tōonkai group is known for its high standards of performance and its dedication to both classic and new concert *nagauta* compositions. But what initially set this new group apart from other *nagauta* societies was its fundamental rejection of the dominant social system of the Japanese arts known as *iemoto*.

IEMOTO: THE TRADITIONAL SOCIAL STRUCTURE OF MUSIC

As with other forms of traditional Japanese arts, the transmission of *nagauta* has historically taken place within social organizations known as *iemoto*. The word *iemoto* (literally "head of household") refers to the headmaster of a particular school (*ryu*) of the art form and the term is used today rather loosely to refer to the Japanese social organization of the arts in general. Although the word *ryu* is commonly used to refer to such organizations in the arts, the concept of *iemoto* is rooted in the traditional organization of the Japanese family. The *ie* (literally "house") conception of family refers to the continuity of a family line whose membership ranges from the ancestors and recently deceased, to the currently living heads and successors of the household, to the future descendants (Hendry 1995:24). Although continuity traditionally is intended to be maintained through primogeniture (inheritance by the eldest son), this type of succession is not always the case. Male or female inheritance as well as adoptions may occur. Thus the use of the word *ie* (house) over the word *kazoku* (family) provides insight into the nature of this type of family organization. The *ie* is best understood not as a kinship-based group but as a corporate group holding some kind of property such as a plot of land, a business or an artistic practice (Kondo 1990:122). *Ie* has been described as a "task performance unit" (Pelzel 1970) which is based on work in which "the major aspects of social and economic life are involved" (Bachnik 1983:129) and made up of members who may or may not be biologically related.

Ie in the arts is characterized by the existence of a household head or *iemoto* and a real or virtual family made up of practitioners and teachers of the art. The range of arts which have been organized into such systems since the Edo period is all-encompassing — from performing arts (*shamisen*, *koto*, classical dance, *nō*, kabuki) to visual arts (calligraphy, painting, flower arranging) to ceremonial arts (tea ceremony) and extending even into martial arts and medicine (Ortolani 1969:299). Although there may be differences in structure that vary from group to group, what has come to be known as the *iemoto* system in the arts is characterized by three main characteristics as outlined by Ortolani: 1) a head of the house, or *iemoto*, who holds the exclusive rights of preserving and transmitting the artistic tradition; 2) hierarchical teacher-disciple relationships, such as the relationship between the *iemoto* and the most senior, highest-ranking players, and the relationships between those high-ranking players and their students; 3) a teaching method that entails a private, one-on-one experience of direct, imitative learning from teacher to student. This last point is of central importance in Japanese art in that intellectual or abstract knowledge of the art in the form of a text is considered to be of little use if a student has no access to personal guidance from a teacher (ibid.). The *iemoto* system is so deeply embedded in Japanese society that, in spite of the legal abolishment of the *ie* as a legal unit in the Civil Code drawn up during the Allied Occupation following World War II, the system is still pervasive in the arts (Hendry 1995:27). Because of its negative connotations of feudalism in modern Japan, it is not uncommon for artists to explain that their school is not an *iemoto* system. However, the identifying characteristics of *iemoto* as outlined above are still found in many schools of Japanese music today.

Regarding the first characteristic listed above, traditional music organizations are invariably led by a single master musician who sets the artistic standard to be imitated by all members and grants licenses to perform and teach the music. Licensing is typically done by granting stage names (*natori*) and licenses (*shihan*) to individuals who have achieved the appropriate level of skill, giving the bearer the necessary level of status to participate in professional concert activity or teach the art to others. Stage names in *nagauta* are typically created by combining the last name of the founder of the school with a first name which often includes at least one Chinese character taken from the name of the student's actual teacher. The family name Kineya has been, and continues to be, the most common name in *nagauta shamisen* music with about 30 branches, all claiming a connection to the supposed originator of *nagauta* music, Kineya Kangoro, who performed during the late seventeenth and early eighteenth centuries (Malm 1963:15). Other prominent family names in *nagauta* include Imafuji, Okayasu, Kashiwa, Kineie, Tobaya, Yoshi, Fujita, Maki, Matsuzaki, Matsushima, Matsunaga, Yoshizumi, and Wakayama.

Regarding the second characteristic of teacher-disciple hierarchy, *iemoto* schools of music are structured hierarchically with the *iemoto* at the top, followed by the highest-ranking players taught directly by the *iemoto*. These high-ranking players (*shishō*) are teachers of the lower-ranking members of the school, students who may be planning to become professional musicians, followed by amateur hobbyists.[6] Amateur hobbyists tend to make up the greatest number of members in the school and form an important financial base that is crucial to the survival of the school as money for lessons, licenses and assorted fees flows upward through the teachers to the *iemoto* at the top. The continuance of an *iemoto* organization is made possible only by obtaining a significant number of amateur students who will support the *iemoto* through the payment of lesson fees and an accompanying loyalty (Ortolani 1969:303).

The third general characteristic of *iemoto* systems, direct one-on-one teaching, is the only method in which Japanese music can be learned if a student wishes to learn the music of a particular school. Notated scores in Japanese music, for example, tend to provide only a minimal amount of information and function mainly as a mnemonic device for remembering the work as learned by rote during the lesson. Direct transmission of the music through private lessons with a teacher is at the core of Japanese music and is the preferred method of teachers such as Kikuoka who, although vehemently opposed to an *iemoto* system, maintained this traditional method of teaching.

THE BATTLE FOR JAPANESE MUSIC IN POSTWAR JAPAN: GEIDAI AND TŌONKAI

With the end of World War II the battlefields of the Pacific had fallen silent, but in Allied-occupied Japan, the world of traditional Japanese music that Kikuoka entered when he attended the Tokyo University of Fine Arts had become a cultural battlefield. Under American occupation and ideological influence, ideas of modernity and democracy were becoming increasingly influential in Japan. The Japanese educational system was being modernized and new institutions were being created, such as the new university of fine arts in Tokyo, the troubled founding of which is told by

Kikkawa (1997) and is recounted by Malm (1999) from the perspective of Kikuoka's teacher, Yamada Shōtarō. In the late 1940s plans were being made for the existing Tokyo Music Academy to be absorbed into one single fine arts university to constitute what is now known as Tokyo Geijutsu Daigaku (Tokyo University of the Fine Arts), commonly referred to by the abbreviation Geidai. Concerning traditional Japanese music, there was disagreement as to how to forge the musical future of Japan. The founders of Geidai believed that traditional Japanese music had no place in a modern fine arts university and planned a music program that only included Western classical music composition and performance.

When traditional musicians banded together to protest this omission, they were told that Japanese music had several inherent weaknesses that prevented it from being on an equal level with Western music. The project administrator cited as evidence that Japanese music had no single music theory, could not be taught by a single methodology, was divided into too many competing guilds, and was not capable of raising moral and spiritual character as was Western classical music. Although this last point was clearly ludicrous, the lack of standardization in Japanese music could clearly pose problems in trying to incorporate this music into a modern, regimented university curriculum. Nevertheless, these arguments were unacceptable to proponents of traditional music, and the protest continued until the case appeared before the Civil Information and Education (CIE) office of the American military organization, whose duties included supervising cultural affairs. The CIE sided with the proponents of traditional music and thus Geidai was founded with a faculty of traditional music alongside Western music (Malm 1999:53). Having been one of the last graduates in *nagauta shamisen* from the outgoing Tokyo Music Academy, Kikuoka became one of the first teachers at the newly formed Geidai in 1950.

It was clear to Kikuoka and Yamada that the battle for traditional music at Geidai was only the first victory in a war with foes on two fronts, the modern and the traditional, and they began to lay the groundwork for a new approach to their own discipline of *nagauta*. While they fought for the inclusion of Japanese music in the curriculum, they agreed with their foes that the *iemoto* system was inferior to a more democratic model of music organization. During the late 1950s Yamada and Kikuoka co-founded a new *shamisen* society which was conceived as an alternative to the *iemoto* system and originally designed to try and diminish the influence of *iemoto* in the music world. In 1957 Yamada dropped his stage name and, together with Kikuoka, founded the organization with the name Tōonkai (pronounced in three syllables, like the English words "tow, own"). The first Chinese character *tō* ("east") is an abbreviation of Tokyo Geijutsu Daigaku (Tokyo Fine Arts University), the second character *on* ("sound") is an abbreviation of "music," and the third character *kai* means "association." This name stood not for a family of musicians, but for a democratic organization in which members would vote on policy and elect officers.

Kikuoka boldly mailed out letters to all *nagauta iemoto* in Japan announcing the organization and inviting all *iemoto* and their families to come to Geidai to participate in this new school. Not surprisingly, he received no response. The only member of an *iemoto* family who joined did so out of social obligation because of his ties to Yamada Shōtarō. Also not surprisingly, the acceptance of this group did not come quickly from the umbrella organization, Nagauta Kyōkai, which oversees the activities of all the *iemoto* families. The organization did, however, decide to accept and include Tōonkai one year later due to the strong reputation of Geidai, a reputation built, ironically, on its association with Western, rationalist culture. As one Tōonkai member described it to me, Tōonkai did have a kind of *iemoto*, but not in the form of a person. The modern institution of Geidai functioned as the *iemoto*.

Since the 1950s the Tōonkai organization has had a succession of presidents beginning with the official founder Yamada, followed by Kikuoka after his teacher's death, serving as president from 1985 until his death in 1999. Although this succession from the official founder Yamada to his successor Kikuoka suggests an *iemoto*-type relationship, the Tōonkai president, unlike an *iemoto*, has no absolute artistic power, as style is set by individual teachers within the organization who function independently. But the most radical departure for Tōonkai was the refusal to create stage names for members of the organization, leaving Tōonkai professionals to perform under their real names for concert programs and public appearances. For Kikuoka and Yamada, the stage name was an appellation that could not be trusted as such names were readily available for the wealthy and were seen by them as symbols of the exploitative practices of the *iemoto* system. Wanting to promote a higher quality *nagauta* by valuing merit instead, the gateway into their group, Tōonkai, would be a degree from the Tokyo University of Fine Arts. Gaining a professional membership in Tōonkai today is dependent on success on the entrance exam and graduation from the university in addition to further study at Tōonkai's own institute. This valorization of merit over name was even tested once in an awkward instance when Kikuoka personally gave a failing grade to the teenage son of a senior member of Tōonkai who performed poorly on his *nagauta* entrance exam to Geidai. The young man persisted however, was eventually admitted to Geidai and became a professional Tōonkai musician. Although some ill feelings resulted from this conflict, Kikuoka proved that, within the university ideal of merit, the power of names should make no difference.

THE DEVELOPMENT OF CONCERT *NAGAUTA*: KENSEIKAI AND TŌONKAI

Another important goal of Tōonkai from its beginning was to develop an audience for concert *nagauta* and achieve an independence from the restrictions of dance, which the music originally served. Even today, as many professional musicians will attest, it is difficult for a *nagauta* musician to make a living without playing for dance concerts or for the kabuki theater. Kikuoka and Yamada's Tōonkai was designed to remedy this situation by following in the footsteps of the pioneering group to which Yamada belonged, *Nagauta* Kenseikai, a group founded in 1902 by *nagauta* performers from the kabuki theater who felt constrained by a lack of performance opportunities outside of the dance world and concentrated their efforts on promoting concert *nagauta*. In tracing the roots of Tōonkai, one finds not a family lineage traced in stage names and honorary titles through the activities of an *iemoto* family organization, but rather an ideological lineage traced in progressive and reformist efforts through the activities of *Nagauta* Kenseikai.

In 1895 Kineya Rokushirō III (1874–1956) and Yoshizumi Kosaburō IV left the kabuki theater to found *Nagauta* Kenkyūkai (*Nagauta* Study Society) for the purpose of creating a new *nagauta* without dance and began presenting concerts of traditional and new *nagauta* compositions in Tokyo's new business district (Malm 1999:37). The group's earliest performances were private gatherings for *nagauta* enthusiasts that lost money until the group changed its name in 1902 to *Nagauta* Kenseikai (*Nagauta* Pure Study Society) and subsequently opened its concerts to the public (Machida 1956:410–412). As they gradually began to attract the interest of people outside the insular *nagauta* world, including wealthy patrons, Kenseikai's performances of pure *nagauta* created a boom for concert *nagauta* in the early decades of the twentieth century, in which "expensive vehicles would be lined up outside the theatre and pedestrians would be pushing one another off the sidewalks" (ibid.:412–413). New compositions by group founders Kosaburō, Rokushirō (who became Kineya Jōkan II in 1926)[7] and his student, Yamada Shōtarō beginning in 1931, were a regular feature of these popular performances without dance (Malm 1999:39), making the first half of the twentieth century a high point for concert *nagauta* that has been unparalleled ever since.

Despite wartime problems, Kenseikai held four concerts in 1942 and a concert in 1943, in which Kineya Jōkan II performed before his death in December. Traditional music activity slowed down near the end of the war and by 1944 all major traditional theaters were closed. Yamada's house was bombed and he lost everything except for two *shamisen* which he had left at NHK studios. During these dark times however, the seeds of something new were being planted. During an allied air raid in May 1945, a group of *nagauta* musicians met and planned to create the *Nagauta* Kokkōkai (*Nagauta* Restoration Society). On December 28, 1945, the group officially began as a performing organization. Their goals were later printed in mimeographed publications of 1947 (*Nagauta* Kenkyū I) and 1957 (*Nagauta* kokkō kai goju kaishi) and are summarized by Malm:

> … to plan the rehabilitation of *nagauta* as a genre of Japanese music, to gather together talented researchers, to abolish outmoded customs, to overcome barriers between different *nagauta* guild [sic], to honor individuality, to do away with gaudy frivolity, to diligently research classical pieces while evaluating and composing new works, and to refine performance skills. (Malm 1999:52–53)

The founding of Tōonkai in the late 1950s took these reforms further by eliminating stage names altogether and, during the 1960s, Tōonkai took the lead in promoting concert *nagauta*. A main thrust of this concert promotion was the creation of new compositions for *nagauta*, which typically get few opportunities for performances in this genre dominated by dance and theater. During the 1960s Tōonkai membership and audience attendance grew steadily as a calendar of four concerts per year developed, each one featuring at least one new *nagauta* composition, many of which were composed by Kikuoka, who composed 31 pieces from 1955 to 1996, quite prolific within a musical genre in which so little value or recognition is given to new compositions. Tōonkai however, had sparked an interest, if only temporarily, for both concert *nagauta* and new works for the genre.

Many older musicians and audience members I spoke with had fond memories of the Tōonkai concerts in the 1960s with sold-out concert halls, enthusiastic performances, and exciting new compositions. This is in sharp contrast to the Tōonkai concerts I witnessed in 1997 and 1998 which had dwindling attendance and an atmosphere that would be described as far from exciting. Tōonkai concerts during this period consisted almost entirely of the standard nineteenth-century repertoire with new compositions relegated to one seemingly obligatory place on the program, typically the second number in a performance of about eight pieces. Comments I received from audience members ranged from a general lack of interest in new compositions to some who feel that the new compositions are merely recycled nineteenth-century *nagauta* that offer nothing new.

As periods of concert activity such as Tōonkai during the 1960s and Kenseikai during the pre-World War II period suggest, a future renaissance of concert *nagauta* is not entirely impossible. It seems to be the case, however, that concert *nagauta* will always be overshadowed by kabuki, its parent and protector in the world of the performing arts. The associative meanings with kabuki performance that are embedded in *nagauta* songs always seem to be present. Concert *nagauta*'s motionless rows of seated musicians in uniform black kimono allows the listener to focus more on the classic melodies and lyrics that easily conjure up images of the well-known, spectacular, and colorful dances that ordinarily take place in front of these musicians on the kabuki stage. With little demand for *nagauta* music without these dances, the economics of the concert marketplace seem to work against the complete independence of concert *nagauta*. As Geidai produces new batches of young players each year, there is perpetual competition for paying jobs, and the poorly attended Tōonkai concerts generate little income for players in comparison with dance and theater jobs. With the continuing presence of dance recitals and kabuki performances that provide high-paying jobs able to sustain professional *nagauta* musicians, there is little motivation to promote concert *nagauta*.

"SEEING THE NUMBERS GO BY:" TŌONKAI RAISING THE STANDARDS

In reflecting on Tōonkai's history, Kikuoka was proudest of the group's musical accomplishments, for it was in matters of musical production, not in reform of organizational structure, that Tōonkai presented the greatest challenge to the *iemoto* system in *nagauta*. Tōonkai's greatest significance in Japanese music is the group's contestation of what constitutes appropriate *nagauta*. Depending on one's perspective, Tōonkai can be credited with either raising the standard of *nagauta* performance or standardizing a form of music that has for centuries been produced in a distinctive manner by many different families. Whichever perspective one takes, the Tōonkai style has been influential in the course of *nagauta* in the twentieth century, largely due to its presence in the curriculum of Geidai, dominated by Tōonkai teachers since the founding of the *nagauta* program in the 1950s. With the status of Geidai for support, the standards upheld by Tōonkai have had an effect on the many *nagauta* schools in Japan because of the power of a degree from Geidai to increase the status of any *nagauta* player, even those from *iemoto* families.

As a result, a degree from Geidai today does give a *nagauta* player a certain status similar to an *iemoto* family name and is highly desirable. Thus many players bearing the names of prestigious *nagauta* families have enrolled in the *nagauta* program at Geidai for the additional status of having the degree. All students in the *nagauta* program at Geidai must follow the style as taught by the Tōonkai-affiliated instructors such as Yamada, Kikuoka and their successors such as *shamisen* veteran Ajimi Tōru. Following graduation, however, students from *nagauta* families typically do not join the Tōonkai organization, opting instead to return to their family and remain loyal to its particular style of performance. Following the Tōonkai method for the short time one is enrolled in school is a temporary compromise of the Japanese tradition of loyalty to a single teacher.

Temporarily conforming to the style of another *nagauta* group does not only happen at Geidai. In the concert world, it is not unusual for players from different groups to perform together, although many players would prefer to avoid too much mixing. In any given *nagauta* performance, all players must conform to the style of the lead *shamisen* player. If a Tōonkai player is performing under an *iemoto*, that player must defer to any stylistic preferences of that *iemoto*. In spite of these kinds of compromises, Kikuoka expressed to me that he was nevertheless pleased with the influence of Tōonkai on the sound of *nagauta* in general, which is largely due to the influence of teaching through the Geidai program.

Kikuoka felt that performance standards of modern *nagauta* have been raised, as evident in both *shamisen* and vocal technique of *nagauta* performers all over Japan. He cited well-executed, precision *shamisen* techniques, particularly at fast tempos, and accuracy of vocal pitches with clearly enunciated lyric phrases as the hallmark of Tōonkai's sound. Of the many concerts I observed in Tokyo this high standard was certainly maintained in Tōonkai performances. Conversely, at the annual *Nagauta* Kyōkai concert in Tokyo, which features performances by many *nagauta* families, including Tōonkai, some of the performances by *iemoto*-led groups lacked the melodic and rhythmic cohesiveness in unison *shamisen* playing and unison singing that can be clearly heard in Tōonkai. Critical remarks along these lines were commonly mentioned by players and advocates of the Tōonkai style with whom I spoke. Amateurs affiliated with Tōonkai often made disparaging remarks about other groups' unstable *shamisen* rhythms and "mumbled" (*mogu mogu*) singing rendered incomprehensible by excessive vocal stylization.

However, not everyone was in agreement that the Tōonkai style was an improvement in the sound of *nagauta*. Critics of the Tōonkai sound claimed that the fast tempos of Tōonkai *shamisen* were perfect to the point of sounding mechanical and thus lacked feeling. One top Tōonkai *shamisen* player who plays instrumental sections at breakneck tempi was disparagingly dubbed by some concertgoers as *denki mashin* ("electric machine"). For some listeners, the clearly enunciated, unison singing of the Tōonkai chorus was equivalent to a lack of character or just simply uninteresting. In an interview with one *nagauta* singer from an *iemoto* family, I was not surprised to hear similar criticism of the Tōonkai sound. This performer, like many young *nagauta* players today who come from *iemoto* families, studied the Tōonkai style at Geidai, but returned to his family without joining the organization. His criticism of Tōonkai's style was that it was too predetermined and did not allow for individual expression. Considering that individual expression is not typically valued in *nagauta*, especially not in an *iemoto* family, I interpreted his comments to mean that Tōonkai style did not allow for the style of expression favored by his family. Referring to the number notation that is used by Tōonkai, as well as many other schools of *nagauta*, this singer told me that whenever he listened to Tōonkai singers, he could "see the numbers going by."[8]

THE FATE OF TŌONKAI IDEALS

The quality of the Tōonkai group in the present day testifies to the success of Kikuoka's goal of fostering a high-standard, quality *nagauta* music, but the social influence of the stage name as perpetuated through the *iemoto* system ultimately proved too powerful for Kikuoka to defeat. In fact, the stage name wields so much power in Japan that even Kikuoka temporarily adopted a stage name, Kineya Shōichirō, once during the 1950s simply to enable him to appear on the national television network, NHK, which required stage names of its performers at that time. Hastily bestowed upon him by his teacher, Yamada, who also held an infrequently used Kineya name, Kikuoka no longer used the stage name after this particular job and did not need it for subsequent appearances on NHK after the network recognized his status as a Geidai professor.[9] Although Kikuoka was never compelled to use a stage name again, the influence of this practice eventually held sway within his own Tōonkai organization.

Not only had *iemoto* families in *nagauta* appropriated the Geidai degree for bolstering their own status as players, but in recent years the Tōonkai group reneged on Kikuoka's ideal and appropriated the standard *iemoto* practice of using stage names. In 1996, Tōonkai voted democratically to create a stage name to mark members of their group to increase concert opportunities for the players. By prefacing their real names with the characters *tō* and *on*, the group created an *iemoto*-like stage name marking their group in a manner similar to an *iemoto* family. In the Tōonkai subscription concerts I attended in 1997 and 1998, all members were listed with a *Tōon* stage name, including the top *shamisen* player, *Tōon* Kikuoka. This was precisely the situation that Kikuoka and Yamada had worked to oppose for many years. Kikuoka, who was actually still the president of the organization at the time of this policy change, felt powerless to veto this decision due to the overwhelming majority opinion within the organization and instead watched as his ideal *shamisen* society began to swing back to an older, more conservative style of social organization.

Kikuoka often spoke personally about his disillusionment with the society he founded but never made an issue of it publicly. Instead he dutifully served out his presidency until his death. Retired from the university in 1995, Kikuoka spent his final years concentrating on teaching students in his private lesson place. Kikuoka's teaching, part of a long tradition of passing the music from teacher to student in a one-on-one manner, was an entirely separate domain from the politics of Tōonkai and Geidai, a place in which Kikuoka could maintain complete control and easily maintain the purity of *nagauta* that he had always fought for. Ironically, it was Kikuoka's economically secure position as a Geidai professor of *shamisen* — a modern development in the history of traditional Japanese music — that gave him the career-long security that enabled him to maintain his ideal of a more pure form of *nagauta*. Unlike the great *shamisen* players of the nineteenth century, who were dependent on the theater for steady employment performing *nagauta* as background music, Kikuoka's career as a teacher made it easy for him to reject the theater, which is still the main source of high-paying work today for other professionals, and thus he became increasingly alienated from the majority of musicians working in his organization.

Kikuoka's purist focus on teaching and selectivity about performances also cost him in terms of status, as he watched another senior member of Tōonkai, five years his junior, bestowed with Japan's highest honor, Living National Treasure. Among students in Kikuoka's camp, it was the consensus that Kikuoka truly deserved this designation but could never get it because of his reluctance to play *nagauta* as background for music and dance. The kind of high profile performances that get players national recognition by the Ministry of Culture typically involve performing *nagauta* as dance accompaniment to major dance stars at large theaters. Kikuoka rejected not only these kinds of performances, but he was also reluctant to organize high-profile recitals of his own works, which he considered too egotistical and self-promoting. Although his students were upset by this outcome, Kikuoka did not actively seek to win awards that he believed were hollow designations that did not reflect true merit.

As an artist, Kikuoka was elusive and maintained a low profile. He preferred to spend more of his time teaching and composing than performing. The professional performances to which he was most dedicated were Tōonkai's seasonal concerts, considered too low paying and unrewarding by some Tōonkai players who made their living playing much higher paying jobs accompanying dance. Some of Kikuoka's greatest contributions to traditional Japanese music were his activities off-stage for which he received no recognition. Much of his work at the university was focused on the expansion of the upstart traditional music department, always a source of controversy since the postwar fight for traditional music at Geidai. He spent many years lobbying and finally penetrating the bureaucracy of the Education Ministry in order to introduce other traditional music into the program, including overlooked major genres such as *gagaku*, *kiyomoto* and *tokiwazu shamisen* that are still taught today at the university.

CONCLUSION: A LIFE SHAPING, AND BEING SHAPED BY, JAPANESE MUSIC

As a subject-centered ethnography that considers time, place and metaphor as suggested by Rice, this narrative account of Kikuoka's career depicted the musician not as a passive recipient of culture who unconsciously reproduced hegemonic forces, but as an active force in the development of musical tradition as it was negotiated by musicians in modern society. Following the three aspects of Rice's model, Kikuoka's life narrative unfolds over different segments of time spanning the twentieth century, from his childhood in prewar Japan to the postwar occupation to his later years. The places where this narrative occurred are not conceived of in the traditional geographic sense, but in the sense of socially constructed locales that range from the individual — Kikuoka — to the subcultural — organizations such as *iemoto* or Tōonkai — to the national — the Tokyo University of Fine Arts — to the global — the military forces of the Allied occupation. Within these dimensions of times and places Kikuoka was actively involved in the negotiation of musical metaphors, the beliefs that become "the basis for discourses about music, musical behaviors… and strategies for deploying these beliefs and behaviors in self-interested ways" (Rice 2003:163). The metaphors that emerge from this analysis are conceptions of *nagauta* as art and its quality, *nagauta* as social organization, *nagauta* stage names as symbols, and *nagauta* as a commodity (Figure 1.2).

	Individual: Kikuoka's Own Ideas of Reform	**Sub-Cultural: *Iemoto* Families Guarding Tradition**	**National: University Modernization**	**Global: Direct U.S. Influence**
***Nagauta* as Form of Art**	Art should be pure; based solely on merit and skillful performance.	Art should be traditional; based on preservation by exclusive families.	Art should be rational; based on unified (Western) standards.	Art should be national; reflect the character of a nation.
Quality of Nagauta	Quality of music should progress; improvement through unity of style	Quality of music should be maintained in order to reflect family tradition	Quality of playing should meet standard for school admission and graduation	
***Nagauta* Social Organization**	*Nagauta* society should be inclusive, democratic and egalitarian	*Nagauta* society should be exclusive, and maintain family power of *iemoto*	*Nagauta* should be open to all through the modern educational system	
***Nagauta* Stage Names as Symbols**	Stage names conferring status do not reflect skill and should be eliminated	Stage names marking family affiliation are necessary to continue tradition	University degree becomes a new symbol of legitimacy in *nagauta* society	
***Nagauta* as a Commodity**	Pure *nagauta* not a commodity; should not be dictated by the market (e.g., dance performances)	Most musicians depend on *nagauta* as commodity; variety of concert opportunities for income	University begins to graduate musicians; increases market competition	

Figure 1.2 The locations of metaphors of *nagauta* music in twentieth-century Japan

The idea of *nagauta* as a serious form of art (charted in the top row of figure 1.2) became the basis for Kikuoka's mission in life to create a pure form of the music based on merit, no longer compromised by the inequities of the *iemoto* system, and no longer subservient to dance. At the time Kikuoka came of age, the dominant conception of music-as-art found in the subcultural places of individual schools of *nagauta* was one in which art was meant to be preserved and protected by exclusive families. With the creation of a university of fine arts in the postwar period, arts administrators at the national level rejected such "outdated" conceptions of art and embraced a progressive notion of art based on unified standards imported from Western culture. Ultimately, at the global level, an American notion that art should reflect the national character of a country triumphed with the implicit backing of military force. The metaphor of *nagauta* as an art in modern society generates a new debate about the quality of music. Kikuoka's own idea of *improving* quality of the art through a unified performance style directly opposed the *iemoto* idea of *maintaining* quality through particular families' performance styles. Although Kikuoka's ideas may resonate with Western cultural ideas of progress, they were not directly influenced by Western culture, so the global category in figure 1.2 is left blank. His notion of improving the quality of *nagauta* did, however, influence practice on the national level as qualitative standards were set to judge admissions and graduations at the national university.

A similar dynamic occurred at the level of *nagauta* social organization (charted in the second row of figure 1.2) which shows how Kikuoka's democratic and egalitarian ideals resonated with modern values of equality in education at the university level, where degrees are now available to all and *sensei* of *nagauta* serve instead as instructors of the art. *Nagauta* outside the university, however, is still today dominated by traditional subcultural values of social organization as exemplified by the inequality and exclusivity of the *iemoto* system. The most important symbol of this traditional organization was the stage name (charted in the third row of figure 1.2). Much of Kikuoka's struggle for a pure music based on skill was located in his opposition to this powerful symbolic metaphor in the subculture of *nagauta*. Kikuoka was as passionate about the elimination of titles in *nagauta* as other musicians within the *nagauta* subculture were about earning and keeping them. As the modern ideal of a merit-based university degree in traditional music gained acceptance, the symbolism of a Geidai degree came to have enough symbolic power to appeal even to the *iemoto* subculture. When the traditional music program at Geidai began to attract *nagauta* family musicians to earn this new status symbol based on a standard of merit, it appeared as if Kikuoka had won his battle.

At the level of music as a commodity (charted in the fourth row of figure 1.2) the impact of the successful *nagauta* program at the university on the music marketplace is the source of a final, ironic conflict between Kikuoka and musicians within his own organization. The need for increased concert opportunities in a field filling with Geidai graduates led to the demise of Kikuoka's most cherished ideals. The ideal of concert *nagauta* as an art form independent of theater and dance held by Kikuoka and his predecessors became an impractical ideal for Geidai graduates seeking a limited number of paying jobs. In retrospect it seems inevitable that the creation of a new school of truly talented players such as Tōonkai would lead to the creation of their own stage names, giving the bearer a degree of symbolic status and economic advantage in the musical marketplace.

While this model has been useful in mapping out the tensions and conflicts in individual musical experience, the portrait of Kikuoka in this chapter is nevertheless a distanced view pieced together through interviews and conversations with my teacher, whom I only came to know during the final two years of his life. The next step in this subject-centered ethnography is to approach the human life in the music at closer range, as an ethnographer who was present in the life of the individual at a particular time and place. Since I came to know Kikuoka as a student of *nagauta*, the next chapter features an ethnographic account of my own musical experience within Kikuoka's school and thus focuses on the learning process of *nagauta*, while at the same time provides closure to Kikuoka's life story following his disillusionment with Tōonkai. The close-up ethnography of the musical practice of Kikuoka in the final years of his life brings us one step closer to the human life in the music.

Chapter Two

Learning *Nagauta*: An Ethnographic Account of Teacher-Student Relationships

MY FIRST LESSONS WITH KIKUOKA

"Whatever you do, you can't quit," Akiko told me immediately after my first lesson with Kikuoka in March 1997. "Now that he's taken you on as a student, you are *his* student. If you quit, he'll be very disappointed." As Akiko said this to me with a grave tone of warning in her voice, I sensed that not only would Kikuoka be disappointed if I quit, but so would she, and so might others that I would soon come to know in the lesson place. Perhaps most of all, I would be disappointed in myself if I quit studying *nagauta* with Kikuoka. But in less than two years from that time, Kikuoka would die of cancer, leaving no heir to his small school of *nagauta*, and my lessons would come to an end.

Those first few lessons with Kikuoka (Figure 2.1) were a source of tremendous anxiety for me. Although I was familiar with the literature on Japanese music and expected to have challenging experiences doing research in Japan, my training in ethnomusicology had not adequately prepared me for the powerful experience of being adopted by a Japanese *sensei*. While my rite of passage as an ethnomusicologist was not at all the same as what Kikuoka's other students had gone through, after my 22 months of training had ended, I felt as if I had passed through a traditional Japanese lesson process. This process of one-on-one training with the *sensei*, in spite of the ever-present coercive force of conformity to the group, is nevertheless tailored to the individual and results in a personal transformation of the student, which is the primary goal of *nagauta*.

The learning process for me began in March 1997, the first time I was invited to observe a lesson taken by Akiko, one of Kikuoka's long-time students. Having been in Tokyo at that point for only just a few months with no research funds and precious little income from tutoring English conversation, my intention had been only to observe lessons in Japanese music in any situation where this was found acceptable by teacher and student. I was fully aware of the exorbitant fees typically charged by artists

Figure 2.1 Kikuoka Hiroaki instructs the author on the *shamisen.*

of Kikuoka's caliber and knew I did not have the resources to make the regular financial commitment demanded by high-ranking professional Japanese teachers. Accepting these limitations, I was content to sit at the back of the room during Akiko's lesson and take notes.

But knowing that one of my goals as an ethnomusicologist was to participate as well as to observe, Akiko wanted to help. After her lesson she had me leave the lesson room so she could speak with Kikuoka privately. A few minutes later I was called back into the lesson room and she instructed me to sit in front of Kikuoka and that he was going to give me a lesson. "Don't worry about payment," she whispered to me. As I approached Kikuoka for my first lesson, I was immediately struck by an overwhelming feeling of humility, as if I were approaching a king seated on his throne. I sat in the traditional *seiza* position (legs tucked under the hips), an uncomfortable position which I had nevertheless been gradually getting used to, and bowed deeply to Kikuoka who, seated atop a large wooden stool also in *seiza* position, towered above me.

I began my first lesson with a short piece called *Kurokami* ("Black Hair"), a classic short work in the *nagauta* repertoire.[1] Working only from a lyric sheet, I quickly adjusted to Kikuoka's practice of singing one line of the piece, followed by my imitation of this line sung in unison with him, followed by my singing alone by the third time through. Having to sing solo after only two repetitions was quite stressful at first and I felt a sense of relief and accomplishment just having gotten through the first lesson. I found out later from Akiko that she had explained to him that I had no money and begged him to take me on as a student. Kikuoka had agreed not only to teach me on a regular basis, but that he would not charge his usual monthly lesson fee. I explained to Akiko that I felt terribly undeserving of free lessons from a professional of such a high level and that I should pay at least a small fee every month. She told me that Kikuoka refused to accept any payment and was pleased to take me on as his student. She then informed me that I could never quit and that I should be a loyal student only to him for the rest of my life.

I had conflicting feelings at that moment. On the one hand I felt I had broken through a barrier in my research, having obtained accessibility to a great teacher in spite of severe financial constraints. I also had an unexpected and comforting sense of acceptance and belonging, as if I were joining a family, although I knew I would never become a member in the same sense as the other students. On the other hand, my guilty feelings about being a charity case were compounded by the possible strings attached. Becoming locked into the kind of loyal relationship that Japanese tradition demands was a situation that I was cautioned about by one of my faculty advisors back in California. I had fears that perhaps I would become trapped in a way that might limit my ability to meet and learn from other teachers. I came to Japan with an idea that I was going to maintain my independence as a researcher, beholden to no one. I quickly realized, however, that there was no place in this society for such an unfettered individual.

My guilt over this situation grew stronger with my next lesson during which Kikuoka told me that if I only wanted to interview him, then perhaps taking lessons was simply a "waste of my time" — which I understood to suggest that it was a waste of *his* time.[2] Actually Kikuoka wanted to know if I was serious about learning *nagauta* and I assured him that, in addition to interviewing him, I was genuinely interested in learning how to sing to the best of my ability. In retrospect, this challenge for me to become fully absorbed in the music of a single artist and teacher was not only consistent with his personal philosophies about music, as explained in this book's Introduction, but was a way for me to experience Japanese music in as close a manner as possible for a cultural outsider. It occurred to me that to flit freely about Japan, observing, participating and interviewing here and there was an experience-distant approach, but to "limit myself" by vowing loyalty to a single teacher in a specific locale was a key experience-near worldview shared by many in Japan. As an ethnomusicologist, this was my first lesson from Kikuoka about seeking the human life in the music.

This chapter examines the learning process of *nagauta* and the teacher-student relationship that is central to Japanese traditional arts. The learning that took place between Kikuoka and his students was more than simply the acquisition of musical skills, but a process of socializing students into a group dedicated to a singular approach to an art form. This socialization process involved learning the appropriate behavior of polite speech and bodily movement in social interaction with the teacher and others in the group. Such manners of body and speech were also integral to musical production during lessons and student recitals and an important basis for the evaluation of student development. Student recitals in Kikuoka's school were highly formalized events that not only displayed the results of the lesson process but also functioned as a ritualized demonstration of the social order of the group and in some instances, a personal display of one's status or wealth. This chapter ethnographically traces this process of student development in Kikuoka's school through my own experience as a student during 1997 and 1998 which began with lessons in *nagauta* singing, led to my integration into a virtual family of students, and culminated in student recitals.

JAPAN'S LESSON CULTURE AND ITS IMPORTANCE TO *NAGAUTA*

By committing myself exclusively to the *nagauta* of Kikuoka, I had entered into a tradition of learning in art that not only is the foundation of the classical arts of Japan, but is an ongoing tradition of the serious pursuit of hobbies in the present day that has been described as the "lesson culture" (Moriya 1994:43). Many Japanese people today pursue hobbies that involve taking lessons in a wide variety of arts, ranging from the traditional (tea ceremony, flower arranging) to the modern (piano, ballroom dance), in which the course of study is seen as an end in itself rather than as a means to an end. Moriya uses the term *okeiko-goto*, which he translates as "aesthetic pursuit," to refer to these courses of study that are pursued purely as a hobby with no anticipation of practical use. Although Moriya's research focuses on the twentieth-century development of the culture center (*karucha senta*) in Japan, his description of *okeiko-goto* is similar to that of amateur pursuits in Japanese music within an *iemoto*-like system. Participation in Japan's lesson culture is primarily for self-satisfaction and not professional development, in spite of the fact that students typically work towards earning licenses or certificates of advancement (Moriya 1984:106). As was mentioned in the previous chapter, amateurs involved in the aesthetic pursuit of Japanese traditional music provide an important economic foundation within an *iemoto* system and this population must remain stable for the economic stability of the school. *Okeiko-goto* study of Japanese music by amateurs often begins during adulthood which marks the student as a hobbyist, while professionals are typically groomed from childhood.

As a teacher of *okeiko-goto*, Kikuoka was surrounded by hobbyists of the modern lesson culture, in addition to his professional students and associates, at his Tokyo lesson place (*okeikoba*) where all engaged in the aesthetic pursuit of *nagauta*. This aesthetic pursuit was both individualistic, in that one engaged in the learning process largely for the self-satisfaction of personal development, and social, in that the process integrated the student into a network of social relationships within a group. Students of this aesthetic pursuit experienced Kikuoka's *nagauta* through a process of physical and mental embodiment — literally adapting the body and mind to the way of *nagauta*. This notion of adapting the self to the art form is common in Japanese training and contrasts with Western notions of "mastery" of art in which individuals seek to control or subordinate the material to the self (Rohlen 1996:371).[3] The goal of Japanese artistic training is not the perfection of an art object as an end in itself, but the development of the experiencing self as a never-ending, lifelong process, conceived of as a "path" or "way of art" (*geidō*). Training in *nagauta* involves adapting the self to the art in many ways, ranging from ways of sitting while performing, to ways of holding an instrument, to ways of addressing one's teacher. Through such training individuals are inculcated with behaviors that constitute aesthetically correct *nagauta* as well as social behavior by which individuals conform to the group.

The roots of Japan's lesson culture can be traced back to the rise of the middle class during the late seventeenth century and linked to the development of the *iemoto* system. The prosperity of townspeople of this period led to more disposable income, more flexible working hours and thus more leisure time for recreational arts that included lessons not only in the arts of music and dance, but in medicine and gardening as well. The broad range of lessons available today also include cooking lessons and the currently popular foreign language lessons (Moriya 1994:44–45). For performing artists of the Edo era, the craze for taking lessons not only augmented the livelihood of professionals such as kabuki performers but it also created a demand for teachers.

Although the *iemoto* system had existed in older art forms such as *nō* drama prior to the Edo period, the growth of the lesson culture in Edo led to rapid expansion of the *iemoto* system into many areas of the arts. The proliferation of middle-class disciples created a need for *iemoto* to license intermediate teachers for the purpose of teaching the art, and it is at that point that a stratified *iemoto* system came into existence (Ortolani 1969:305). Because an *iemoto* system cannot thrive unless there is a huge base of amateurs, maintaining the stability of the system necessitates that these amateurs do not advance to the professional level. An *iemoto* system is not about economic advancement or the passing down of a profitable craft to the student. Rather, an *iemoto* organization transmits an art that has little resale value.

> When practical craftsmanship is taught to merchants with the prime aim of making money (not of transmitting an art), the teacher does not become an *iemoto*. But an *iemoto* relationship is established when an amateur studies in pursuit of his particular tastes and in order to develop his personal accomplishments. (ibid.:300)

The learning process is integral to the survival of an *iemoto* as sole possessor of the economic capital of art, and as such necessitates limiting its value to self-development for amateurs. Thus the acquisition of skills for personal reasons is offered as the primary goal for amateurs whose participation is required to maintain the system.

Learning traditional music is crucial to the economic survival of the elite musical culture of Japan. In a comparison of European art music to Japanese art music Malm states: "in European-based cultures one could be, and today usually is a passive patron of music. However, the need to be able to perform publicly has never left the Japanese elite" (Malm 1994:299). While European art music depends on consumers who constitute an appreciative but passive audience of concertgoers, Japanese art music depends on a more active group of participants who serve as both audience members and practicing musicians. Compared to the world of Western art music, the Japanese "classical" music of concert *nagauta* is a small, exclusive, *participatory* domain of art. While symphony halls heavily advertise concerts of local, national and international symphony orchestras and concert artists, professional-level *nagauta* receives relatively little promotion in the mainstream media. Whereas Western concert music has a critical journalism to debate standards of artistic quality and public taste in major newspapers, this kind of journalism exists only in specialist journals such as *Hōgaku to Buyō* (Japanese Music and Dance). Professional concert *nagauta* depends heavily on a specialized audience of amateur students, many of whom study *nagauta* with those artists performing at that particular concert. The Tōonkai concert audience, for example, is largely made up of the same familiar faces of students attending each time to watch their teachers perform.

It is not surprising in such an amateur-dependent system that professional performances of concert *nagauta*, such as the seasonal Tōonkai concerts, are relatively few in number compared to the numerous amateur student recitals that occur throughout the year. In the lesson culture of *nagauta*, amateur student recitals (*osaraikai*) take on much greater significance than general public concerts because the student recital is the culmination of the learning process and consequently, as the pinnacle event for the amateur student, the student recital becomes the most expensive part of the learning process with the student paying high concert fees to professional players for their participation. Such performance fees can make student recitals more lucrative for professional musicians than both the low-paying Tōonkai public concerts — derided as "obligatory" by some players — and even higher-paying jobs accompanying dance performances. Thus, the student recital in the present day can be a critical lifeline for the survival of *nagauta* musicians, in addition to its symbolic role as the highest point of achievement in the lesson culture of *nagauta*.

ENTERING THE LESSON CULTURE: LEARNING HOW TO BE JAPANESE, TEACHING HOW TO BE WESTERN

My first lessons in learning to be Japanese actually began, informally at least, shortly after arriving in Japan with my everyday encounters with Japanese people in shops, restaurants and other public places. Simply through observation and interaction I found myself bowing slightly in everyday social exchanges with complete strangers with very little conscious thought. The bow (*rei*), picked up easily and naturally by foreigners without a word spoken, is of the utmost importance in learning one's position in social interactions. Foreigners however, typically do not learn the subtleties of how bowing displays hierarchical relationships, such as the way in which the person in the inferior position stays down longer than the person in the superior position (Hendry 1995:77). But my first exposure to Tokyo's formal "lesson culture" was not as a student of *nagauta* learning to be Japanese, but as a teacher of English conversation teaching others how to be Western. Due to funding limitations and the high cost of living in Tokyo, I subsidized my research by giving lessons in English conversation, one of the most popular kinds of leisure study in Tokyo. In recent years several nationwide companies appeared in Japan that offer English conversation at many different classroom outlets throughout the Tokyo area. In spite of the stagnant economy I witnessed during my years in Japan, the English learning boom showed no signs of slowing down as companies such as the highly visible Nova language school opened outlet schools next to virtually every major train and subway station in the Tokyo area.

While an important part of the lesson process in traditional Japanese music is to learn appropriate Japanese behavior as modeled by a teacher, English lessons conversely tend to emphasize the modeling of Western behavior by a foreign teacher, typically a younger person from North America, Great Britain, or Australia. The importance of learning by imitation is as important in learning foreign language and culture as it is in learning traditional Japanese arts. English conversation schools are fully aware of Japanese ways of learning and this is evident in their teaching methods. During my brief employment as an instructor for a Japanese-owned and operated English conversation school, I was given a set of guidelines for teachers that included an extensive list of common Japanese behaviors which teachers should take care to avoid. Such behaviors included the easily learned bowing to others, and other common behaviors such as sucking air between the teeth when vexed in conversation, and pointing to one's nose instead of one's chest to indicate the self in conversation. As foreigners tend to pick up some of these behaviors after only a brief time in Japan, it becomes necessary to discourage them during teacher training. Furthermore, the guidelines for instructors at this particular school recommended that instructors behave in a manner that would be perceived as Western. This meant behaving in a casual manner that would be unusual in a typical Japanese school such as removing one's jacket during the lesson, sitting on the edge of a table or encouraging students to address the teacher by his or her first name. For this school, learning to be Western meant learning to be informal and casual.

My own formal training in Japanese behavior began in earnest with my first lessons in *nagauta* from Kikuoka. Although I picked up on the details of behavior in social interactions within the lesson place as quickly as in any other Japanese social setting, the goals of this embodied training process and the effect it would have on my own thinking about music was not immediately clear to me. Only by physically experiencing the learning process over time in Kikuoka's lesson place did I develop an understanding of the shaping process of Japanese music. During the first few months of lessons I struggled a great deal with the basic elements of *nagauta* singing that give the music its power. My voice was constantly hoarse because of the wide vocal range and strident voice favored in this genre. *Nagauta* pieces are usually written in a wide range, emphasizing pitches that are extremely high for the male voice. Although tuning of the *nagauta shamisen* is not based on an absolute pitch, thus allowing the singer to find the most comfortable range, ideally there should be no falsetto voice used, so the *shamisen* should be tuned low enough to accommodate the singer in this way, but at the same time tuned high enough to challenge the singer on the highest pitches of the piece. Equally demanding is the full volume vocal delivery with which these upper register songs are meant to be sung. Like Western opera, the strident tone of *nagauta* is meant to convey dramatic power in even the largest theaters.

An even greater difficulty in learning *nagauta* involved vocal rhythm referred to as *fusokufuri* (Figure 2.2), in which the singer changes pitches on the off-beat, away from the stable pulse of the *shamisen* line. As Malm notes, *fusokufuri* "helps one to hear more clearly the syllables of the text, and also creates another line of rhythmic tension that requires release at the cadence" (Malm 1986:43). While the *shamisen* provides a steady duple rhythm, the pitch changes in the vocal part occur at various points between these main beats. The precise point at which the vocal pitches change may vary according to vocalists, but it is clear from listening carefully to professional *nagauta* singers, that it is not desirable to sound as if one is changing pitch at equal rhythmic intervals to the *shamisen*. Experienced *nagauta* vocalists will often change just before or just after the *shamisen* note and not give the impression of voice and *shamisen* interlocking with each other. Although impossible to render precisely in notation, an example of the voice/*shamisen* relationship is seen in Figure 2.

In the two-year period of my lessons with Kikuoka until his death in 1999, I completed lessons in a total of eight *nagauta* pieces, including lengthy and difficult concert pieces such as *Azuma Hakkei*, *Aki no Irokusa*, and *Oimatsu*. Although Kikuoka always

Figure 2.2 An example of the shamisen-vocal relationship known as *fusokufuri*.

asked me what I wanted to learn next, as was his standard practice with most of his students, I always asked him for a recommendation, asking to learn which pieces he considered to be the most important. Not surprisingly, Kikuoka chose the most famous concert pieces over *nagauta* pieces composed originally for dance. Learning how to sing these pieces not only gave me a deep appreciation for the art of *nagauta* and a hands-on experience of the vocal expression involved in the music, but the experience of learning over time enabled me to feel the real force of this music, operating at a subconscious level through a kind of training that is completely holistic in approach.

While the activities involved in this total method of training the voice and the body could be broken down into musical ones — learning proper phrasing and the minute details of vocal embellishments — and social ones — bowing, speaking, and approaching at appropriate times — it is the total integration of musical and social behavior in this training process that constituted the proper shape of *nagauta* music. While my initially hoarse voice was gradually being re-shaped to suit *nagauta*'s strident vocal style, my body and mind were being shaped to fit into a particular school of musicians with Kikuoka at its center. Rice's conception of place in music is important here in that the Japanese *sensei* — as the living embodiment of a musical tradition — constitutes a "locale" of music, an example of Slobin's notion of the individual musician as an "individual music culture" (in Rice 2003:156). Thus, the musical training involved in Kikuoka's lessons involved a total commitment to the teacher as the living embodiment of the art form and the school that is built around him. The boundaries of this particular place, socially constructed around this particular individual, constituted what is referred to in Japanese culture as an "inside" (*uchi*), a place distinguished from the "outside" (*soto*) by social interdependence and relationships of loyalty among its members. Within this "inside" setting of Kikuoka's school, the central social relationship between teacher and student defined *nagauta* music.

Just as my teaching English to Japanese students in the language school was intended to be a transmission of both spoken words and physical behaviors, Kikuoka's teaching, at a much higher level of course, consisted of the transmission of a total art form in sound and behavior. Learning Japanese music was a dynamic learning of relationships, particularly the reciprocal relationship between teacher and student in which the student's total commitment to learning from the teacher is reciprocated by the teacher's total commitment to training and caring for the student. "Now that he's taken you on as a student," as Akiko said, "you are *his* student." My early struggles in dealing with the physical demands of both the sound of *nagauta* vocal production and the social interdependency of *nagauta* led to my understanding — a fully embodied understanding — that the importance of shaping the individual into the proper form through the lesson process is the central element in Japanese music.

"DON'T WORRY ABOUT THE SOUND": EMBODYING THE *KATA* OF *NAGAUTA*

The purpose of these *nagauta* lessons and the method by which this shaping process operated gradually became clear to me in the early months of training in Kikuoka's lesson place. Although I was already familiar with Asian ideas of developing the self through art (see Dewoskin 1992:69), my inclinations as a musician were causing me to forget this and concentrate solely on learning "the notes" in order to work toward the best possible performance. But the physical experience of learning the art of *nagauta* made it clear to me that the best possible performance of a piece of music was not the ultimate desired result in Kikuoka's school. My end-goal, product-oriented approach prevented me at first from realizing just how much Japanese traditional arts emphasize the "form and style of the creative act itself" (Yuasa 1987:99 n.1). I eventually realized that the real object of artistic development was not the song, but the individual self. "Don't worry about the sound," I was told by Kikuoka, "the form is most important." If I focused on the proper form, I was assured by Kikuoka, the proper sound would come later.[4] In *nagauta*, proper form is more than just the best way to achieve the proper sound. Proper form is the ideal shape by which the individual can be made to fit into the form of the group. The goal of Kikuoka's lessons in *nagauta* was not the cultivation of the song, but the cultivation of the self — the process of shaping the individual to fit the art form.

This emphasis on shaping the individual into a proper form is rooted in monastic Zen practices in which learning is based on a similar process of embodiment. Just as silence is valued in the monastic setting, so it is in music learning that verbal instructions are de-emphasized and the form is instead meant to be learned physically, not cognitively.[5] A hallmark of the Japanese teaching method found in all traditional forms, correct imitation of formal patterns allows for a physical shaping process to take place in which the student embodies the artistic form over time, a concept referred to in Zen as "polishing" the self. Yuasa traces this approach in artistic training back to Zeami, the pioneer creator and theorist of *nō* drama:

> … true art cannot be mastered merely through the conceptual understanding, but must be acquired, as it were, through one's body. In other words, it is bodily acquisition by means of a long, cumulative, and difficult process of training (*keiko*). In Zen cultivation, whether one is engaged in seated meditation or in everyday chores, one is instructed to assume a certain 'form' (*katachi*) or posture for meditation, eating, worship, or working in compliance with the monastic regulations. At any rate, Zen corrects the mode of one's mind by putting the body into the correct postures. Zeami seems to understand artistic training in a similar manner. Training, it seems, is a discipline for shaping one's body into a form. (ibid.:104–105)

This type of training that privileges physical execution over cognitive understanding is still practiced today in *nō* and *nagauta* lessons, in which training "defers and subordinates a comprehensive intellectual grasp of the subject to a mastery of specific, practical details necessary for various tasks associated with performance" (Hare 1996:341). Such a "comprehensive intellectual grasp" is sometimes unavailable to *nō* singers who may not know the obscure meanings of the arcane words they chant, so they must rely entirely on the correct execution of the "practical details" as passed down from their teachers. In this training of the details, there is no artistic content for the performer to cognitively "grasp," but instead a surface aesthetic that "grasps" or transforms the performer, shaping the artist into the form of the art itself.

The specific details learned in artistic training consist of patterns of performance behavior commonly referred to as *kata* (form, pattern, or shape): discrete, detailed units of predetermined patterns of action which are pieced together to constitute entire songs, dances, tea ceremonies or karate routines. These formulaic patterns not only structure the music, but also dictate precisely the manner of artistic execution by musicians. At the level of musical structure, *kata* appear as stereotyped patterns, sometimes with specific names, that comprise the musical formulae by which traditional pieces are composed, performed and learned.[6] At the level of musical performance, *kata* appear as formal patterns of behavior in the stage manner of musicians who must carry out all actions with precision and grace.[7] At the level of musical transmission, *kata* patterns are crucial interpersonal behaviors, such as bowing and honorific language, in the relationship between teacher and student that instills the proper decorum for traditional arts. All these stereotyped patterns, the musical phrases, the stage manner and the interpersonal behavior, are expected to be carried out with the utmost grace and elegance at all times and meant to be performed precisely as they were learned from the teacher. In this way, much of Japanese traditional music appears to be predetermined and formulaic, a musical practice often perceived at first by Westerners to be based solely on "form" as opposed to "content." *Kata* is at once a surface aesthetic, a structural principle, and a process by which individuals are integrated into a social group in order to learn, practice, perform and transmit the music of one particular school.

It would be incorrect to think of the behavioral aspects of *kata* as extrinsic to music, as "extra-musical" actions that are simply added to musical performance. On the contrary, as an integral part of musical training, these formal behaviors are at the foundation of musical training, essentially coming before sound. Just as Kikuoka had told me to focus on form instead of sound, other teachers of Japanese music I have had have emphasized the same idea. In my first lessons in *nagauta* drumming in which I struggled to precisely reproduce the distinctive "pon" sound of the *kotsuzumi* drum, my efforts were corrected by my teacher purely through adjustments in body positioning and suggestions as to how to move in the appropriate way at the appropriate time. When I expressed my concern about making the proper sound, I was told not to worry about sound, and that if I concentrated solely on achieving the proper form, the proper sound would eventually come.[8] *Kata* as an essential foundation for behavior comes before art and demonstrates the primacy of shaping the body into the perfect form.

Perhaps the most important aspect of *kata* is that the surface is emphasized as the only way to fully achieve the appropriate act of artistic beauty. Art that proceeds according to this surface aesthetic should in no way be perceived as shallow, in that there are implications of a deeper spirituality for both the practitioner and the observer of the art of *kata*. The practitioner of the art is following the Buddhist teaching that appropriate or "right" action (on the surface) indicates a "right" mind (below the surface), while the observer of the art has the benefit of seeing a concrete surface manifestation of what is essentially abstract and unseen. As Yano describes the spiritual nature of *kata*:

> Working on the external through kata transforms and defines the internal. The two are interrelated parts of the same whole. What is important... is that unlike much Western thought which gives primacy to what is below the surface and behind the mask as somehow truer and more significant, a theory of kata gives the surface its due. The Western hierarchized dichotomy of form (the false) vs. content (the true) dissolves as continuous and interpenetrating parts. Kata is not merely superficial, but profound, content attendant upon form. (Yano 1995:19)

In this sense, the form of the artwork "itself" may be perceived as neutral or transparent. The song that is recreated by the performer is not an end product, but a by-product, a transparent form that allows others, the teacher in particular, to clearly see the "inside" of the individual performer. Kikuoka and his teacher, Yamada, both made claims to be able to determine a person's character by listening to that person perform a particular *nagauta* piece. Such a notion of the power of *kata* to divine personality or shape individual character has led some scholars to extend the term beyond its normal usage in the arts and show how its use in everyday life shapes personality (Henshall 1999:153) and structures emotion (Yano 1995).

Although the exercise of *kata* is a pursuit of perfection, it is hardly an abstract artistic ideal removed from everyday life, but a "functional ideal" that is attainable by all who follow the correct form (Henshall 1999:152). At the base of this functional ideal is the egalitarian notion that perfect form is not the exclusive property of any single person and perfect form can be achieved by anyone who properly practices *kata*. Within the lesson culture however, such egalitarianism exists within a hierarchy as perfect form is embodied solely in the *sensei* to be emulated. Maintaining the focus on a clearly visible, concrete form as embodied by the *sensei* to which one should remain loyal prevents any possible challenge to the teacher based on an abstract ideal form. Students would not, for example, forsake their teacher's way in favor of historical performance practices learned from a book. Rather it is the *sensei* who is the living embodiment of historical performance practice. With *kata* being so singularly embodied, there is no room for passing up or usurping the teacher, only the hope of equaling the teacher in achievement and thus earning the right to carry on the traditional form which, over time, never actually belongs to any one person. At best, the *sensei* is only a temporary carrier of a tradition that appears to be timeless. At one level, *kata* may be seen as the complete sacrifice of individual autonomy to the tradition, but at another level, the pragmatic and attainable nature of *kata* may be seen as individual empowerment as anyone (at least, theoretically) can directly appropriate the tradition.

Not limited to artistic practices removed from everyday life, training the body and mind through *kata* is an extension of a process of socialization that begins in childhood in Japan, long before adults begin their amateur study at Kikuoka's lesson place or any culture center. Shaping of the self is rooted in the child-rearing concept of *shitsuke* (training or discipline), defined by Hara and Wagatsuma as "the putting into the body of a child the patterns of living, ways of conduct of daily life and a mastery of manners and correct behavior" (as translated by Hendry 1986:11). The inculcation of behavior in childhood that Hendry refers to as "becoming Japanese" suggests Bourdieu's notion of *habitus*, a theory of how individuals are culturally shaped by society (Bourdieu 1977). Bourdieu's concept of habitus involves a process of the embodiment of social meanings that begins in childhood with imperatives from parents to sit up straight or be still. This inscription on the body from childhood is carried through adult life and generates within individuals certain "dispositions" by which they interact socially without being fully conscious of their actions. In this sense, by the time fully socialized adults enter the lesson culture as amateur students, they have already "become Japanese" and are already predisposed to embody *kata* through the teaching process. Lacking such a deeply embedded predisposition towards learning by *kata*, my own learning process was perhaps slower than Japanese students, but led me to develop a hyper-awareness of the details that constituted *nagauta* in Kikuoka's lesson place as I learned to "become Japanese" through the embodiment of formal patterns of behavior.

ENTRANCES AND APPROACHES: MAKING A SACRED SPACE IN A COMMON PLACE

The behavior of *kata* on lesson days structured the *okeikoba*, or lesson place, of Kikuoka as more than just a physical place, but a particular locale that was ritually constructed around the individual teacher. Through the repetition of this patterned behavior on a weekly basis, the "inside" (*uchi*) of the lesson place was distinguished from the "outside" (*soto*) in a manner resembling the delineation of sacred space in the Shinto shrine, a place made suitable for the residence of a sacred spirit by regular acts of purification through ritualized human activity. This purification of the inside involves not only actions that keep out pollution, such as removing one's shoes to keep out dirt, but actions that create purity by "polishing the self" through *kata* with its redundancy of social etiquette. It was through this regular enactment of *kata*, with its heightened sense of ordinary behavior within the *uchi*, that I learned the elegance and grace of *nagauta*. Just as in other ritualized arts of purification involving ordinary behavior, such as the tea ceremony,[9] the routine behavior of entering rooms, approaching the teacher, and receiving the lesson, oriented the student within the lesson place and established a sense one's proper place within this school and thus within the tradition of *nagauta*.

The primary *kata* for this series of entrances and approaches to the lesson place was the most ubiquitous Japanese behavior, the bow. The series of bows would commence upon arrival at Kikuoka's house in the Hongo Sanchōme section of Tokyo which served as his lesson place during the years I studied with him. On lesson day the house would be open and students could enter without knocking into the tiny entrance hall (*genkan*) to remove their shoes before stepping up into the *uchi* proper. Typically someone would open the kitchen door and come out to greet them, sometimes Kikuoka's wife, but usually one of his *deshi*, the young students who were currently in the *nagauta* program at Geidai and were bound for professional careers in *nagauta* performance. These *deshi* played an important role in Kikuoka's school, particularly on lesson days when they were expected to be present and assist Kikuoka. Greetings upon entering the house were very formal with the *deshi* getting on their knees and bowing deeply to the guest. In most cases the guest would also get on his/her knees and bow deeply in response. I often felt so compelled to match their bows that after I entered the doorway I always quickly hurried out of my shoes and got to the floor in time for their greeting. Although Kikuoka's reception room was a Western style "living room" with two plush sofas and hardwood floor, everyone behaved in this room as if it were a traditional Japanese style room, avoiding the two sofas and instead sitting on the hardwood floor in traditional *seiza* position. This room's specific purpose on lesson day was for the exchange of greetings and farewells upon entering and leaving and, in spite of its modern, Western appearance, served as the entrance into the *uchi* of Kikuoka's school, marked as a traditional Japanese spot not by furniture or design, but by Japanese-style behavior.

The heart of this home-school of Kikuoka's was the lesson room itself, a Japanese style, 16 *tatami* mat room (each tatami straw mat is approximately 1.76 x 0.88 meters) upstairs on the second floor where Kikuoka spent the entire day teaching a seemingly endless parade of students. Entrance into the lesson room was preceded by first sliding open the wooden door (*shoji*) while sitting in *seiza* position and bowing deeply in the direction of Kikuoka, who sometimes responded with a slight bow if he was not occupied with a student at that moment. The entering student would then slide in on their knees and, if there were other students waiting for lessons, would exchange bows with the other students. Having properly entered the room, the student then took a place on a cushion (*zabuton*) and waited for a lesson. While waiting in the lesson room, movement was always kept to a minimum, maintaining an atmosphere of calm with as little disturbance as possible. Moving about the room was noticeably different within the lesson space as students would make an effort to stay close to the floor, either moving on their knees or, if standing, keeping the knees bent and the head tilted downward. Such posture became even more pronounced whenever the student moved closer in proximity to Kikuoka.

The lesson room was further subdivided into a teaching area and a waiting area, in a way that maintained a large open space around Kikuoka and his teaching. While Kikuoka was teaching students in a spacious and comfortable area 12 *tatami* mats in size, students waited for their lessons in a much smaller area at the opposite end of the room, only four *tatami* mats in size, made even more cramped by a large, low wooden table. Within this tiny waiting area in which, at any given time, a half dozen students might be waiting for their turn, the financial transactions of lessons took place in an almost invisible process of depositing lesson fees into a box with small drawers that was placed on the table. At the beginning of the month students deposited their monthly lesson fees into the drawers using small envelopes that are customarily used in Japan for financial transactions. This common Japanese custom of making payments concealed in envelopes[10] was not insignificant within the context of the *uchi*. By having students discretely slip envelopes into this box of drawers on the student table, Kikuoka was able to distance himself somewhat from the financial remuneration involved in the lesson process and contain this potentially polluting influence in his teaching space.

Just as the main altar is the central location in a Shinto shrine toward which "approaches" are made to convene with a sacred spirit,[11] Kikuoka's position in the lesson space — as the living spirit of *nagauta* — was the central point one approached in learning *nagauta*. Kikuoka, always dressed in kimono on lesson day, sat at the far end of the room on a chair making him considerably higher up than students who typically sat below in *seiza* position before him, giving him a towering, commanding presence. An additional space around the teacher was maintained by a large table positioned immediately in front of Kikuoka that separated him from the student. When one's turn for lesson came up, the student approached the spot where the lessons took place directly in front of Kikuoka, maintaining the floor-oriented posture with slightly bowed head and slightly bent knees so as not to exceed the height of Kikuoka. Dropping to their knees, the student would first acknowledge the student who had just finished a lesson by exchanging bows. Remaining on their knees, the student scooted forward into the lesson spot, bowed deeply, and spoke the polite request phrase of "*onegaishimasu*" (honorific phrase of request), and Kikuoka would respond with a slight bow. The degree of the student bow varied from person to person, but many students executed the deepest, most polite bow, touching the face almost to the floor.

The student then presented a cassette tape to Kikuoka who would place it into the machine to begin the lesson. Kikuoka kept a notebook handy in which he jotted down what students were working on so that he knew where the student last left off in the piece. Many of Kikuoka's regular students studied both *shamisen* and singing with about 20–25 minutes spent on each. During a *shamisen* lesson, Kikuoka would often sit without his *shamisen* and sing the piece while the student played *shamisen*. He stopped students occasionally to make verbal corrections, sometimes picking up his own *shamisen* and demonstrating a particular part. During singing lessons, Kikuoka played *shamisen* and let the student sing alone. As a student worked through a piece, small portions of the piece were introduced at a time. For example, when a student first begins a piece Kikuoka would play and sing the first three pages, then stop at a convenient breaking point in the score. He would then return to the beginning of the piece and sing, lowering the volume of his voice just a bit as the student would sing with him. During this first repeat he corrected major errors but most minor corrections would come out on the second repetition in which the student was expected to sing alone. This slow, methodical, and well-organized process of learning long compositions proved very effective as Kikuoka would not let student progress any further through a piece until they proved that they could perform each phrase or section to his satisfaction.[12]

After only about 20–25 minutes, Kikuoka stopped the tape recorder, indicating that the lesson was over. He returned the tape to the student and made brief remarks, either encouraging or critical about the student's progress, and students were expected to spend time working with this tape from now until the next lesson. Again, the student bowed deeply to Kikuoka, saying "*domo arigatogozaimashita*" (highly polite phrase of thanks), and the student's exit from the lesson place proceeded in the reverse order of the entrance. The exit from the lesson room included complete exchanges of bows with all other students waiting and another exchange of bows downstairs would occur before leaving the house. Upon completion of this entire social regimen the total number of formal bowing exchanges could range anywhere from ten to thirty bows, depending on how many other people were encountered at the house, during what was often three hours in duration, of which no more than 30 minutes consisted of an actual music lesson with the teacher.

Kikuoka's lessons demonstrated the way in which art is socially constructed in a particular place over a particular time period. Compared to the brief time spent in the actual music lesson, the social interaction through physical *kata* constituted the majority of activities in the lesson place, in the same way a visit to a Shinto shrine for a prayer of about 20 seconds takes an entire afternoon devoted to pilgrimage to the sacred spot, or the way in which drinking tea in a tea ceremony becomes only a brief moment of gustatory stimulation within a lengthy ritual of seemingly ordinary activities. As in the tea ceremony, a ritual in which social interaction transforms mundane household practices such as boiling water, serving tea and wiping bowls into an art form, lessons in Kikuoka's school created a similarly heightened sense of awareness of ordinary social interaction within the confines of a small space.[13] Within such a delimited space, the reduction of movement to the mechanics of a ritualized *kata* of entering, approaching, bowing, and greeting heightens one's awareness of the power of social grace and elegance capable in the self, the focus of *nagauta* training.

LOYALTY IN THE *UCHI* OF KIKUOKA: BELONGING AND EXPULSION

As the "outsider" ethnomusicologist I was thrilled to have had the opportunity to experience this transformative learning process of weekly lessons in Kikuoka's school, even though I knew that I would never be granted any position or status of an "insider," much less the equivalent experience of one, as my guilt over the money situation constantly reminded me. But it was partly my guilt over free lessons that further cemented my loyalty to this artist that I nevertheless truly admired. There was, in fact, one moment in time when I felt myself to be participating as a kind of insider in Kikuoka's school and I felt as if I had joined this virtual family for a fleeting moment. But this moment was just as fleeting as Kikuoka's fragile "family" of musicians itself.

As it is customary in Japan as the year draws to an end in December to tie up loose ends by wrapping up unfinished business, taking care to make overdue social calls, or showing appreciation in certain social relationships, an annual event in Kikuoka's school at the end of the year was for students to come to the house and do domestic chores as a sign of appreciation to Kikuoka. Akiko explained to me that this year-end ritual labor was a nice way of showing gratitude to our teacher and invited me to come along on a Saturday in December 1997. But this was not an event that included Kikuoka's majority of amateur student housewives who were not a part of Kikuoka's inner circle of students. Although Kikuoka's many amateur musicians were loyal followers of their teacher, the financial contributions of these paying customers earned them their right to be treated as houseguests within the school and thus they were not present on this ritual day of service to Kikuoka. This was instead a duty to be carried out by Kikuoka's *deshi* (student disciples), the young, professional-bound students of his school who were currently studying *nagauta* at Geidai University.

In fact, it was precisely domestic duties in the household that defined the roles of these young "disciples" of Kikuoka within his school on lesson days. In addition to serving tea to the amateur students upstairs in the lesson room, these students would spend the day taking care of household needs, assisting Kikuoka's wife when she was home and taking over her household duties whenever she left. While Kikuoka was busy teaching the amateur students, these students answered the phone for Kikuoka, relayed messages to him, served him tea and refreshments, and even prepared lunch for him. Although these students clearly belonged to Kikuoka and had studied with him in the past, they were actually not taking lessons during this time of their careers. While studying at Geidai, they were to learn *nagauta* only from their instructors at the University, and not with Kikuoka. When they were at Kikuoka's lesson place, their role was restricted to serving in Kikuoka's household as *uchideshi* (literally "inside student disciple"), a traditional practice of live-in students once very common in Japanese traditional arts. During their tenure at Geidai, these students did not even receive lessons from Kikuoka in return for their labors as their four years of service to him that coincided with their university study was meant to be a sacrifice for their teacher.

These musicians-in-training would eventually leave their "inside student" positions upon graduation from Geidai and were expected to join Tōonkai and work as professional *nagauta* musicians. But even after becoming mature professionals, these students were meant to remain Kikuoka's students for life, as I witnessed many times in the lesson place with the older Tōonkai professionals who also participated in belonging to the school. Although the older professionals who had previously served Kikuoka in this same manner had moved on in their careers and started their own lesson places with their own students, in the context of Kikuoka's *uchi*, they were still his loyal students for life. On a few occasions I even saw a few of these professional players assume household duties when his current young *deshi* were momentarily away from the lesson room. Some of these former "inside students" also felt a great amount of sympathy for their young counterparts engaged in this traditional role.

One student who was not a professional player, but was a part of Kikuoka's inner circle of students was Akiko, who had invited me to come and join her on chores day. Although she graduated from the *nagauta* program at Geidai in the 1970s, Akiko never joined Tōonkai and became a housewife, temporarily leaving the practice of *nagauta*. She told me the story of what happened after only two years of marriage, finding herself divorced and raising two daughters alone in a government housing project with no child support from her ex-husband, an abusive alcoholic and gambler. Feeling she had nowhere to turn in life, Akiko showed up at Kikuoka's door one afternoon holding a child in each arm and begged to be taken back by her teacher. Kikuoka took her in and agreed to resume teaching her, but refused to take any money from her for lessons. Since that time Kikuoka taught her and took care of her, including her into his family as if she were a daughter. After years of Kikuoka's generosity, she insisted on paying him back for his lessons, but he refused all her attempts at repayment, insisting that he did not need the money. He suggested instead that she return his gift of music by teaching *nagauta* to other students which she began to do in her spare time at her own home. "He's been a real father to me," said Akiko.

On the annual year-end chores day, Akiko and I arrived early and stayed for about eight hours doing various tasks. While some of the female students prepared special year-end foods in the kitchen, I carried a number of boxes, wrapped special gift packages that Kikuoka would mail out for the end of the year, and washed his car. I was supposed to share this duty with his top young *shamisen* student at the time, Yamaguchi, but I was instructed to start without him as he was running late. When Yamaguchi arrived and saw me already washing the car, we both were a little embarrassed. At the end of the day I joined Kikuoka, his wife and his young *deshi* for dinner. For the first time since I began studying with Kikuoka, I felt a feeling of belonging in the *uchi*, feeling as if I had become perhaps a little closer than his many amateur housewives who were his paying clients. What I saw that day seemed to be the picture of a well-kept, devoted, virtual kind of "family" in which tradition is maintained and passed on to future generations. However, I later learned that there was an important member of the *uchi* who was missing that day and realized the significance of this student's absence as part of a major problem lurking beneath the surface in Kikuoka's school. This major problem was a structural one, concerning the way in which Kikuoka had configured his school according to his own philosophy about *nagauta*, and ultimately led to the complete dissolution of his school upon his death in 1999.

The main problem of Kikuoka's school, one that Kikuoka no doubt greatly agonized over, was that it actually functioned similar to an *iemoto* structure, the very structure he had so strongly opposed his entire career, yet his was an *ie* that ultimately failed. As many readers may have surmised by this point, Kikuoka's traditionally structured lesson place, in which students demonstrate a loyal commitment to a single artistic way through prescribed behavior towards a single teacher who represents the art itself, is certainly a model of *iemoto* construction. The reciprocal relationship that develops between teacher and student that resembles a father-child relationship is a common characteristic of any *ie* system of the arts. In spite of these similarities, the continuity that is essential to the preservation of an *iemoto* system did not exist for Kikuoka, partly because of the circumstances of his biological family, and partly because of his ideological resistance to traditional *iemoto* practices.

Having no son and only one daughter, who wished to avoid traditional Japanese music completely, Kikuoka's only option would have been the standard *iemoto* practice of "adopting" a top student to become his successor. This would require him, however, to break his ideological stance by adopting one of his students, a Tōonkai professional, and bestowing a name on the student that would identify him or her as the successor of his musical "family." Instead Kikuoka's students were meant to be Tōonkai professionals, independent musicians without stage names binding them to any teacher, expected to create their own schools rather than take over the school of any teacher. Naturally, whenever they were within Kikuoka's domain, these students of Kikuoka maintained their loyal service, but this was limited only to their direct interactions with him. Once outside the *uchi*, his students were independent and, in the case of playing with other *iemoto*, his students were obligated, if only temporarily, to follow the ways of other master musicians. Such a system may have been configured to respect individual freedom as a performing artist in modern society, but it lacked a formula for continuity.

Perhaps Kikuoka's only hope for continuity was the one student who was missing that day in December when I came to the house to do chores. That student, who I will refer to as "K," only months earlier had been Kikuoka's most favored student and was possibly being groomed to take over as his successor, had it not been for his inexcusable betrayal of Kikuoka. The story of Kikuoka and his top student, K, reveals one way in which the committed, reciprocal relationship between benevolent teacher and loyal student can break down, particularly in the competitive market of traditional music in modern Japan. In this case, the complete breakdown of this relationship ended in the most severe form of punishment, the banishment of the individual from the *uchi*. Complete banishment (*hamon suru*) was a rare occurrence in Kikuoka's teaching history, happening only once before to an amateur student, but it had never occurred between Kikuoka and a professional player.

The betrayal of K came as a sudden shock for Kikuoka, as he had been Kikuoka's closest and most trusted young student for many years. K's status within the school was almost that of a live-in student (*uchideshi*), as he moved into the neighborhood very close to Kikuoka's house so that he could help his teacher on a regular basis and was treated, according to Akiko, "like a son." K took care of many duties on lesson days in addition to driving Kikuoka to concerts and recitals. The benefits of being such a devoted top student are numerous, the most important being the economic benefit of having many concert opportunities through the connection with one's teacher. In a recent performance broadcast on NHK in the mid-1990s, K was positioned in the number two *shamisen* spot next to the number one *shamisen* player (*tatejamisen*) Kikuoka, who had carefully chosen this line-up of players. The symbolism of this stage placement publicly indicated K's high status and personal relationship with Kikuoka.

This intimate teacher-student bond was eventually broken, however, when K's betrayal of Kikuoka was discovered in mid-1997. Rumors had circulated for a while that K had been criticizing Kikuoka behind his back, something particularly risky in a society as small and prone to gossip as the *nagauta* world, but the actual betrayal involved K covertly intercepting students from his own teacher. K had received requests from a group of amateurs in his home prefecture to study *shamisen* with his teacher, the renowned Tōonkai *shamisen* player, Kikuoka Hiroaki. Such requests for well-known teachers from Tokyo to travel long distances to give lessons for a worthwhile fee are not unusual. Apparently, K had intercepted these students for himself, telling them that Kikuoka was too busy to teach them and that his teacher recommended his top student teach them. Eventually the group of amateurs contacted Kikuoka on their own and the deception was revealed. Kikuoka immediately summoned K and told him he would no longer be his teacher and that he would have to leave the Tōonkai organization.

The dire implications of such an expulsion from the school are significant, particularly in the case of a student such as K. Unlike some players who maintained dual associations with Tōonkai and with an *iemoto* family, K did not come from a *nagauta* family and was only able to join the professional ranks of *nagauta* players by joining Tōonkai after his graduation from Geidai. As a result of such an expulsion from Tōonkai, K's career in *nagauta* was in danger. His betrayal of Kikuoka, however, was rooted in the economic pressures he faced as a young professional *nagauta* player who lacked affiliation with an *iemoto* and his "public" criticism of Kikuoka expressed a desire to get out from under Kikuoka's over-protective wing. K had been complaining that he was frustrated at having fewer opportunities to perform through his teacher, who maintained a purist dedication to playing only concert style *nagauta*, limiting performance opportunities for all of his close students. Afterward, K seemed pleased to be liberated from the *uchi* of Kikuoka, telling one of the other top students, Yamaguchi, to take over his role as Kikuoka's driver because he no longer wanted to do it. Ironically, on the day of student chores in December when I had felt such a sense of belonging by washing Kikuoka's car with his student Yamaguchi, it turned out that I was doing K's former job.

A few months later I got an update on K from someone I knew who began taking *shamisen* lessons from K at a local culture center. It turned out that K had been very resourceful in rebuilding his new career. After leaving Tōonkai, K had taken a Kineya stage name from one of the many Kineya *iemoto* families that perform in Japan today and was able to find work performing at the famed Kabukiza Theater in Tokyo's Ginza district. Apparently K found a solution to his professional affiliation problem by acquiring, in other words purchasing, a stage name from a reputable *iemoto*. Another student of Kikuoka's, surprised by this turn of events, told me that K was fortunate because he could have significantly damaged his reputation after being rejected by a reputable teacher. That another *iemoto* had been willing to take on a student with a questionable past may have been made easier by the price that K paid for his new stage name.

A NEW APPROACH TO EQUALITY AND HIERARCHY IN KIKUOKA'S SCHOOL

New Year's Day in Japan, the most important holiday on the calendar, is a time for new and auspicious beginnings. In an auspicious move at the beginning of the New Year 1998 that seemed as if it were a response to the recent expulsion, Kikuoka inaugurated a policy change that appeared to be an attempt to bring his "family" of students a little closer together. He placed an announcement on the table in his lesson room listing the number of students who had "quit" during the past year — the recently expelled K being one of them. Because of the reduced number of students Kikuoka decided to merge professional lesson days with amateur lesson days. Whereas previously professionals had come for lessons on a separate day from the amateurs, this policy change allowed amateur students, including myself, to observe lessons at the professional level whenever they occurred. In effect, this policy change which introduced a more equal relationship between professionals and amateurs, was a move further towards Kikuoka's ideal of a pure *nagauta* and brought into play two important aspects of traditional Japanese society that paradoxically co-exist: hierarchy and equality.[14]

Rooted in Confucian teachings about filial piety, hierarchy is an important part of public and private life in Japan and is a central notion of most scholars' models of Japanese society (Smith 1983:48). From an early age children learn their relative ages as an orderly way of resolving problems of sibling rivalry and establishing reciprocal relationships between benevolent seniors and obedient juniors (Hendry 1995:48). Although within any given family this may not necessarily work out so smoothly in actual practice, the awareness of hierarchical relationships are instilled nevertheless and applied to the world outside the family. In establishing social relationships in public, people often first insist on finding out each others ages in order to develop the appropriate hierarchy which can then be marked by politeness levels of speech and other kinds of behavior showing respect. Within a lesson place of the traditional arts members should be aware of who the most senior players are in the hierarchy. To help make this clearer, hierarchy is symbolically displayed in a *nagauta* performance where one's placement on the stage is a public demonstration of one's position in the group, as was demonstrated by K's stage position when performing with Kikuoka. On the new combined lesson days within Kikuoka's lesson place, whenever professionals arrived at the *okeikoba* for an advanced lesson, they were automatically given priority over amateurs who were already there waiting. I would always defer to these professionals whenever they would arrive, just as others did, but often professionals were reluctant to cut in front of others and would courteously urge the lower-ranking students to go ahead.

The value of equality was introduced with this new configuration in Kikuoka's school, simply by bringing together professionals and amateurs, as the *kata* of common courtesy encouraged an equalizing of social relations within a hierarchical context. Just as the aesthetic design of the tea ceremony brought together people of different classes by making them conform to pleasantries in the confines of a small room, Kikuoka's school unified individuals of different ranks through the uniformly applied grace and elegance of common courtesies. Even in social interaction involving

Kikuoka, the highest-ranking member, hierarchy should not create inequality by favoring any one individual's experience within the school. Although the ethnographic account of the lesson place earlier in this chapter gave the appearance of Kikuoka as a kind of living god on high to be worshipped from the lowly position of a student below, the lesson place is similar to a Shinto shrine in the way it elevates humans up to a sacred, purified domain to commune with a particular spirit. In a clearly delineated location and at a particular moment, hierarchy is neutralized by equality, as in the intimate, after-work drinking party gatherings of Japanese businessmen (*sarariman*), in which an employee can, theoretically at least, say anything to the boss. If the proper setting is created, social relations are equalized, even if only temporarily.

All of Kikuoka's efforts from the beginning of 1998 until his death seemed directed towards an equalization of social relations within his school. From that time on, I observed many examples of the well-known aphorism, "the nail that sticks out must be hammered down," a warning that the ego should not be allowed to destroy social harmony. Kikuoka sternly and systematically "hammered down" many professional players and it seemed as if the higher-ranked the professional, the stricter Kikuoka would become during the lesson. The demonstration of another well-known Buddhist concept of always maintaining the "beginner's mind" was also evident in how many professionals were corrected on such basic techniques as finger positioning and even holding the *shamisen* plectrum (*bachi*). This not only reduces the professional to the same level as a beginner, but more importantly, reasserts the overall concern with proper form and shape in the practice of Japanese music. For the rest of that year Kikuoka seemed determined to carry out his reform of *nagauta*, if not in the larger social domain as he did during his career, then at least in the controlled environment of his own school. But Kikuoka did more than just consolidate lesson days for professionals and amateurs. He sought to dismantle some of the standard practices by which concert *nagauta* had been maintained since the Edo period. In order to get closer to realizing his pure form of *nagauta*, he began to reconfigure the student recital, which he saw as a major source of corruption in the *nagauta* tradition.

THE *OSARAIKAI* RECITAL: ONE MILLION YEN FOR 20 MINUTES

I can still recall the day I saw the largest amount of cash I had ever seen in Japan. At that time I was working part-time at an investment bank in the financial district in Tokyo, where one might expect to see a lot of money in one place. But the largest sum of cash I had ever seen was not at all related to any financial dealings of this major bank. The money was instead going straight to an *iemoto*. An American co-worker of mine who had been studying Japanese classical dance for about seven years in one of Japan's most famous schools of *nihon buyō* came to work one day with an envelope stuffed with 10,000 yen notes. "Here is it is," she said ceremoniously, yet with a sigh of resignation as she showed me the envelope, "one million yen going straight to my teacher!" Even though carrying large sums of cash in check-less Japan was common, seeing the equivalent sum of about U.S.$10,000 going to an *iemoto* made me gasp. "I guess I don't really need to buy a car or put a down payment on a house," she added ironically and further justified the expense by explaining that since she did not have children she had to do something with her money in life. She also pointed out that, as her school was reputed to be one of the most expensive in Japan, for this sum of money she had gotten "a bargain from her teacher."

What she was doing with this money was paying fees for a special recital in which she would become a licensed performer of Japanese dance. This ceremonious recital would grant her the distinction of belonging to a certain school of dance, and allow her the privilege to perform or teach the dances of this particular school. Although the money would be paid directly to her teacher, the teacher would use part of this money to pay for hired musicians, rented costumes and assistants to help with make-up and stage support. All of this to receive a stage name (*natori*) that could be listed in concert programs either as a prefix to one's own name or in complete substitution of it. While this enormous fee is common in Japanese classical dance, estimated to be one of the most expensive hobbies in the world, similar sums are also quite common in Japanese classical music when musicians receive similar titles, an important culmination of the learning process.

Such a large sum of money paid to an *iemoto* is not a one-time-only occurrence in the lesson culture of Japanese traditional music. A regular event of the learning process is the *osaraikai*, a general term used for formal student recitals that can also carry a heavy price tag. The term *osaraikai* comes from the verb "*sarau*" (to review) and the noun "*kai*" (meeting) and serves as a kind of ceremonial evaluation of one's progress in lessons. An *osaraikai* performance will consist of a lengthy concert, typically five or six hours long, in which each student of the teacher plays one piece within an ensemble of professional players. In its strictest sense, each *nagauta* piece performed at *osaraikai* should consist of only one student onstage alongside a collection of professionals to whom the student has paid a large sum of money. There may be exceptions in which two or more students might share a piece to keep the cost down but if the onstage ensemble is a mixture of amateur and professional it is technically no longer an *osaraikai*, but rather a *benkyōkai* (study concert), typically a student recital which may be augmented by professional players.

Since its origins in the Edo era, the *osaraikai* has played a crucial role in the development of concert *nagauta*. At the beginning of the nineteenth century *nagauta* was still used primarily as accompaniment to dance on the kabuki stage as played by professionals. But the popularity of kabuki led to performances of music and dance by *geisha* at teahouses in the entertainment district of Edo. The male clientele of the pleasure quarters developed an interest in having women in their own homes learn the music and dance and kabuki musicians and *geisha* began to earn extra money teaching amateurs (Malm 1994:300). In 1820 the first *nagauta* compositions written specifically to be performed as concert music without dance were composed, and works such as *Shakkyō* (Stone Bridge) and *Oimatsu* (Old Pine) contributed to a growing repertoire of concert *nagauta* that would become the standard performance and pedagogical material of the twentieth century. During most of the nineteenth century, however, there was no professional *nagauta* performed independent of kabuki and dance. The development of concert *nagauta* actually began with the *osaraikai* student recital. Since competition for theater jobs was tough for musicians in the capital of Edo, the student recital soon became an important source of money for professional players. But it was clear from the beginning that the *osaraikai* was less of a concert of musical art or entertainment, than an economically necessary event with socially symbolic significance.

Nagauta shamisen player Kineya Eizō describes in a book by Machida (1924) that originally teachers held monthly concerts (*tsukizarai*) in their homes or lesson places that were intimate, informal and inexpensive for students, but as the skill level of amateurs increased, public *osaraikai* concerts were created to show off students in full ensemble. In paying more costly accompaniment fees to *hayashi* musicians as well as *goshugi* (celebratory gift money) to their teachers, students began to compete with each other to show off their wealth (ibid.:14). Eizō was highly critical of this use of *nagauta* for status-seeking that had apparently become so common in the 1920s that he feared for the future of *hōgaku* if this practice were to continue unchecked (ibid.:16). Kikuoka described to me how *osaraikai* became so big that the practice of the split stage was introduced, in which two performances could occur simultaneously on either side of a dividing screen. This awkward practice not only shortened the enormous length of these all-day events, but the split stage was available to some students for a cheaper fee. Kikuoka often laughed at this now defunct practice, imagining the cacophony of sound created by competing groups with only a folding screen between them.

The history of *osaraikai* demonstrates that since the Edo era these events have always functioned more as ritual displays of status than concerts for listening pleasure. Kikuoka agreed with Eizo and Machida that *osaraikai* have done little more than serve as a stage for people to flaunt their money by presenting their daughters on stage in expensive kimono surrounded by high-status musicians. In the twentieth century the *osaraikai* continued to be the most common venue for concert *nagauta* and is today more important than ever as a source of income for professionals in the competitive concert world. The days of crowded stages and screen dividers are gone and today's students each get an undivided stage for their performance, unless they choose some alternative such as sharing a piece with another student enabling them to split the cost of the musicians. However, the costs are still prohibitive, maintaining the recital's exclusivity and its potential for status-making. For the student today, the cost of participating in an *osaraikai* depends on the number of musicians used and their relative status within the *nagauta* music world. As professional musicians are essentially "rented" by the student for the duration of the piece, the fees for a full size *nagauta* ensemble can be exorbitant. For example, if a *shamisen* student uses a full ensemble of two additional *shamisen*, three singers (the number of *shamisen* and singers should be equal) and a percussion unit consisting of the minimum four musicians, the price can easily exceed one million yen (approximately $9,000 U.S.) for the musicians.

Osaraikai in Tokyo today still function as demonstrations by amateur students to their peers in *nagauta* society of their accumulated capital in *nagauta* society, making Bourdieu's notions of capital useful in understanding the social dimensions of these events (see Jenkins 1992:85). On one level the student can display cultural capital (legitimate knowledge) in the form of musical talent simply by playing well in the company of highly skilled professionals. On another level the student can display social capital (various kinds of valued relations with significant others) simply by performing, regardless of skill, with the most well-known and respected musicians in the professional society. This display of social capital translates directly into a display of one's financial capital in that the higher the status of the musician, the more expensive the fee and thus the more impressive the show of wealth. Furthermore, high profile musicians who have achieved the symbolic capital (prestige and social honor) of honorary titles are not even expected to play well for such a low profile event, validating Kikuoka's cynicism toward this event of social exchanges that he felt only contributed to the mediocrity of the art form.

In spite of his criticism of *osaraikai* as nothing but an ostentatious display of status, Kikuoka was conflicted about the practice and felt compelled to continue to present *osaraikai* within his own school. Questioning the *osaraikai* was a complicated issue for him because, as antithetical as it was to Kikuoka, *osaraikai* was the root of concert *nagauta* as it was handed down from Kikuoka's artistic predecessors. In my interviews with Kikuoka he indicated that he wasn't happy about *osaraikai*, but that it was nevertheless a standard practice of *nagauta*. "In Edo times there was only kabuki performance in the theater and *osaraikai*," said Kikuoka. "The first ever concerts were organized by Kineya Jōkan I in the middle of the Meiji period" he added, "and this was the start of pure *nagauta* performance that Tōonkai continues today." Undoubtedly, Kikuoka felt a strong bond to Jōkan I, a founder of concert *nagauta*, because his son, Jōkan II, was his teacher's teacher. *Osaraikai* were the norm in student concert performance and Kikuoka, as president of the Tōonkai organization, felt compelled to offer them. Kikuoka told me that he would have given up *osaraikai* a long time ago, but felt obligated to offer them so that the increasing number of young Tōonkai professionals could survive in the small marketplace for *nagauta* jobs.

From my own observation of, and participation in, Kikuoka's biannual *osaraikai* on a Saturday in October 1997, many Tōonkai musicians benefited from Kikuoka's *osaraikai* as a huge number were hired for the all-day event. Due to the length of *nagauta* pieces and the number of students involved, Kikuoka's *osaraikai*, like those of other high-ranking teachers, was a marathon concert that lasted from about 11:00AM until 7:00PM, with only brief pauses between pieces. Typical of *osaraikai*, Kikuoka's was not promoted to the general public and the audience consisted mainly of the students themselves and their invited friends and families. Attendance at the concert fluctuated throughout the day as few people had neither the interest nor the stamina to watch every single piece. At certain times during the afternoon the nearly empty concert hall resembled the obligatory and often lonely student recitals in American music schools which are a somewhat less sensational Western counterpart to the *osaraikai* recital. What distinguishes the *osaraikai* however is the presence of professional players, many of whom appeared in several pieces throughout the day and were paid for each individual appearance.

The amount of money involved in this particular event is still unknown to me as these matters are meant to be discrete. Students paid all fees to Kikuoka in one lump sum and fees for each musician were not disclosed. In the month before *osaraikai* each student received an envelope from Kikuoka which indicated the total money due, the total cost dependent on which professional musicians were playing on the piece. Students had the choice of requesting certain professional musicians and Kikuoka arranged it for them as long as they could afford the cost. If a student wanted a larger group they could have it if they paid more. Sensing that I was not able to fully participate in the extravagance of this event, Kikuoka gave me a "bargain" rate for my first *osaraikai* performance. For only 25,000 Yen (about US$240) I was able to sing *Gorō Tokimune* (transcribed in Malm 1963), accompanied by just two of his young *deshi* from Geidai on *shamisen* in what was known in *osaraikai* terms as a "throw-away number" (*suteban*) due to its low-status position very early on in this all-day event. As the marathon concert progressed, pieces using larger groups increased, as did performances by many of the "star players" of the Tōonkai *nagauta* organization paid for by amateur students who could afford their fees.

This ritual event of Kikuoka's resembled numerous other *osaraikai* I have attended in Tokyo. Although Kikuoka's name was included in the title of this event, it was the students who were being celebrated on this day. The title "Kikujukai" was created by borrowing the Chinese character *kiku* (chrysanthemum) from Kikuoka's name and combining it with *ju* (congratulation) and *kai* (meeting), marking this as the teacher's congratulations to his students. While students spent the afternoon preparing for their moment on stage, Kikuoka spent the majority of his time behind the stage, assisting students to properly get in place when their performance time came. For some student performances Kikuoka sat below the stage riser with a back-up *shamisen* tuned and ready to hand to the student in the event of a broken string, playing a supporting role to the student that is quite common for a *sensei* during *osaraikai*. The purpose of each performance is to help make the students look and sound their best as they display their skills alongside ranking professional musicians.

The irony of it all is that the sole amateur surrounded by top professional musicians comes off sounding the most amateurish. The imbalance in talent level is noticeable both audibly and visually, especially in the majority of pieces featuring housewives wearing their colored kimono, surrounded by professionals wearing their concert black kimono bearing their family crests (*montsuki*). This public performance in such high-ranking company results in a ritual that mixes individual pride with public shame. Friends and families who come to support their loved ones' efforts are often rewarded with boxed lunches (*obentō*) and other gifts from the student for their attendance. "We're apologizing to them for suffering our poor quality performances," commented one student with a laugh. Any slip-ups during a performance, of which there are many by nervous amateurs, are met with quiet snickering in the mostly student audience and can become the object of teasing afterwards from one's peers.

Judgments of musicality, however, in this ritual of self-indulgence that is the highlight of the lesson process are ultimately of little importance. Even though some students feared his opinion about their performance, Kikuoka suspended judgment for this event as part of this benevolent role as teacher and caretaker of the student. This display of public vanity, legitimized by the individualistic philosophy behind the lesson process, however, is not without a cost to the student. Kikuoka was being celebrated for creating the ultimate fantasy professional concert for the aspiring *nagauta* amateur and a great deal of money was bestowed upon him for providing such an event. Not only did he receive money from the students participating, but also gift money (*goshūgi*) from his other students who chose not to participate, his former students who attended, and by the professional performers hired for the event, expressing their gratitude for this lucrative performance opportunity that he made possible. As the head of this school that keeps these valuable financial and symbolic exchanges afloat, Kikuoka was the central figure towards which the money flowed, just as in any *iemoto* organization.

BENKYŌKAI: KIKUOKA'S IDEAL OF THE LESSON CULTURE

Closer to Kikuoka's ideal of a *nagauta* based purely on skillful performance was his *benkyōkai* or "study concert" that he offered much more often than *osaraikai*, holding the *benkyōkai* once during an *osaraikai* year and twice during the intervening year. While Kikuoka was always critical of the *osaraikai* recital, despite his own financial benefits from the practice, he expressed a great deal of pride in his *benkyōkai*, preferring these concerts more than his own professional recitals. Unlike the *osaraikai* events, professional concert recitals, and performances accompanying dance, the *benkyōkai* involved very little money and very little opportunity for gratuitous displays of social status. For Kikuoka, *benkyōkai* were the only *nagauta* concerts not tainted by such excess and truly focused on the music.[15]

Although structurally similar as day-long marathons of classic concert *nagauta* pieces performed without intermission by a variety of groups, the *osaraikai* and *benkyōkai* serve two very different purposes. Unlike the *osaraikai* in which a single student is nested in a group of professional players that displays status, the *benkyōkai* eliminates the ostentation by presenting pieces by groups of amateurs with a few professional players mixed in. The most significant difference is that while the many professional players who appear at *osaraikai* may belong to other teachers and are invited for their status as professional musicians, the few professional players present at *benkyōkai* are all Kikuoka's senior students and are there, not by invitation of the *sensei*, but by obligation to the *sensei*. The teacher-student relationship that all *benkyōkai* participants have in common levels the hierarchical field and restores Kikuoka's power to judge all the participants within his field of view, thus equalizing professional and amateur within the scope of the *sensei*. Unlike *osaraikai*, in which a fanciful artifice is created that amateurs can effortlessly play alongside professionals at a professional level, the *benkyōkai* eliminates this artifice, presenting the inverse view that all players, regardless of status, are perpetual students who must forever serve, and forever be judged by, the *sensei*, who is the embodiment of the music itself.

Within Kikuoka's school, this authoritarian enforcement of "musical" values in the *benkyōkai* had been a greater source of complaint than the extravagant costs in the *osaraikai*. While the *osaraikai* indulged the student, the *benkyōkai* indulged the *sensei* who was the sole judge of musical quality for this event. During the *benkyōkai*, Kikuoka would sit in front of the stage off to one side and observe every piece of the all-day performance, often making notes to himself. The last "piece" listed in the program was not a piece of *nagauta* at all, but listed in the notes as "*kansō*" (impressions) by Kikuoka. During this brief speech he thanked everyone for participating and proceeded to critique individual performers, sometimes by name if a major mistake was made. Students, both amateur and professional alike, were understandably upset by this practice and some had complained about this harsh treatment. In recent years, however, Kikuoka had lightened up this critique, which was evident in the *benkyōkai* in which I participated, held on July 5, 1998.

After having experienced his *osaraikai* of 1997, I noticed the radically different approach Kikuoka took to his *benkyōkai*, even in the months preceding this summer event. Planning for this event began as early as March when he announced the *benkyōkai* with a notice on the lesson table with a sign-up sheet for students to request what piece they would like to perform. The names of all of Kikuoka's students were listed in three sections consisting of his current 24 amateur students, his 24 professional players, and his five young Geidai *deshi* who were currently serving in his lesson place. No such formal list existed for his *osaraikai* which was done verbally during one-on-one lessons with Kikuoka who would then assign parts and musicians. Whereas preparation for Kikuoka's *osaraikai* focused on preparing only his amateur students for their particular performances, his *benkyōkai* focused on all performers equally, including professionals who attended lessons to prepare their performances for the concert.

In order to prioritize the music, Kikuoka reconfigured the roles of professional musicians and his expectations of them. Professionals were simply expected to show up and do their job for *osaraikai*, but prior to *benkyōkai*, for which they received no money, they were subject to the corrections and admonitions of a stern Kikuoka. During his lessons with his professional students Kikuoka was constantly correcting them, particularly on basic *shamisen* techniques, such as hand position on the neck and ways of holding the plectrum. In correcting one professional player, Kikuoka invoked the Buddhist "beginner's mind" concept, saying "*Shoshin ni kaeru*" ("return to the beginner's heart"). At this level, there were no such distinctions as professional and amateur while Kikuoka was teaching. On a few occasions Kikuoka even altered his usual, traditional approach to the lesson process. While the one-on-one style of lesson was the norm for preparing a single student for *osaraikai*, just prior to *benkyōkai* Kikuoka prepared several pieces by giving a single lesson at once to several members of a group that would be performing together. Kikuoka made it clear that for this event the harmoniousness of the group sound was of greater importance than individual status.

Kikuoka worked further toward a communal harmony by fully disclosing the finances involved in *benkyōkai*. Unlike the more individualistic *osaraikai* in which large sums of money were kept hidden and not spoken of, *benkyōkai* featured full financial disclosure from its inception to its completion. Prior to the concert, participation fees and what they would pay for were made clear to everyone on the initial sign-up sheet. In the weeks following the completion of the *benkyōkai*, a budget statement appeared on the lesson table which listed all expenses and all money collected. The final budget report, a standard practice in all of his *benkyōkai*, showed that this particular concert event went slightly into the red, but Kikuoka had balanced the budget by contributing some of his own money to make up the shortfall, demonstrating the absence of any profit motive behind the event. Placing all financial transactions on the table was Kikuoka's way of maintain his pure ideal of the *benkyōkai* by reducing the polluting influence of money.

Kikuoka's *benkyōkai* of 1998 took place at a theater in the Asakusa district of Tokyo ordinarily used for performances by geisha (*kemban*), his usual location for *benkyōkai* as one of his long-time *shamisen* students was a geisha from Asakusa. Kikuoka used this theater because its large *tatami* mat room created a more intimate setting than the Western style theater he typically used for the more formal *osaraikai*, in addition to the bargain rental fee that allowed him to keep the costs down. The informal, intimate atmosphere of the *kemban* eliminated the professional concert atmosphere that prevailed in the Western-style concert hall as well as helped make the sparseness of the audience less noticeable. Such a setting helped Kikuoka mark his *benkyōkai* as a concert apart from the ostentatious *osaraikai*. Backstage, however, social divisions were maintained by separating amateurs and professionals. With the amateurs sharing one large dressing room while the professionals prepared in separate smaller rooms, there was little informal mixing of the two throughout the afternoon.

As in *osaraikai*, professional and amateur status was clearly marked by kimono design with professionals easily identifiable in their black kimono bearing a family insignia, compared to amateurs wearing other colors. Choice of kimono plays a significant role in Japanese musical performance as personal appearance is often described as having equal importance as the music and certain codes are meant to be followed (see Tsuge 1983). Kimono for men should be quite simple and plain, usually solid colored, darker fabrics accompanied by trousers (*hakama*) in black and white or gray. Women, on the other hand, choose from a wider variety of colors and patterns, but a dress code is followed in which bright colors and dazzling patterns are worn only by younger women compared to the muted colors and subtle patterns worn by middle-aged and older women. This code, however, did not go unchallenged at Kikuoka's benkyōkai as Akiko wore a kimono that was clearly not appropriate of her age group, a bright blue kimono with an embroidered design of brilliantly colored fans, looking very much like a young woman's kimono. Although her explanation for wearing such a kimono was that it was light and cool for a hot summer's day, I sensed that perhaps she was intentionally challenging the dress code.

Kikuoka's role in *benkyōkai*, however, was different from his role in *osaraikai*. Although he again helped students get prepared and set up on stage before the curtain opened, adjusting posture and balancing the space between performers, Kikuoka did not serve as stage assistant behind the performers as he did in *osaraikai*, providing a sense of technical and moral support. For each *benkyōkai* piece, as soon as the stage was set, Kikuoka walked out front and sat at a small table where he took notes throughout the entire day acting as judge and jury for all participants. This was a major cause of stress for some students as it was very easy to see Kikuoka sitting at his desk, watching carefully and judging everyone's playing. Although I felt relaxed in my assignment of singing the *nagauta* piece *Sukeroku*, my two *shamisen* accompanists, one amateur and one semi-professional player, seemed wary of being judged by Kikuoka and nervous about his presence up front. Immediately afterward they critiqued their own individual performances in anticipation of Kikuoka's criticism that would come later. As one professional musician commented to me, *benkyōkai* was much more difficult than *osaraikai* not only because of Kikuoka's judgment, but with the mixing of amateur and professional, every piece becomes less stable and every musician more prone to making mistakes.

As it turned out, the biggest musical "disaster" of that day's program involved a professional *shamisen* player. The piece featured an amateur housewife and a young *deshi* on vocals accompanied by two female professional *shamisen* musicians, one playing the main melody and the other playing a higher counterpoint part (*uwajōshi*). When a string broke on the lead *shamisen* player's instrument, she reached behind and was immediately provided with another *shamisen* by the stage assistant who was seated behind the riser. The problem in this case was that the replacement *shamisen* was not properly tuned as it should have been. The lead player struggled to tune the instrument while attempting to continue playing the piece, but was unable to do it quickly. While the lead player struggled and showed signs of frustration, the other player continued with her counterpoint part. But the problem seemed compounded when the singer, unable to get the proper cue from the incorrectly tuned lead *shamisen*, started on the wrong pitch. This added to the confusion, making it difficult for the lead player to find the correct pitch. After about a minute Kikuoka shouted from his table out front, "*hon-chōshi*" (the most standard *shamisen* tuning of an octave with an intermediate fourth — e.g., B-E-B), and the player recovered her tuning. In spite of the extended confusion, the players had recovered and proceeded to the end without stopping.

According to Kikuoka, this incident revealed poor troubleshooting for a professional player because she was unable to recover quickly. But he added that it was really the fault of the assistant who should always be re-tuning the reserve *shamisen* as the tuning typically changes several times during a single piece. For this particular piece, Kikuoka said he had chosen one of his young *deshi* to be the assistant because the main *shamisen* player was a professional and should not have had to rely on the support of a professional as an assistant. This is because one of the most important functions of the stage assistant at student recitals is to reach up from behind the riser and adjust the tuning of the *shamisen* for struggling students who are unable to adjust it themselves while playing, a practice that professionals do effortlessly. The role of off-stage assistant, although seemingly minor, can be critical, which was demonstrated by this performance.

Kikuoka's critique of that particular piece, as well as others, was heard in the last "piece" of the *benkyōkai*, listed in the program as his "impressions," the moment of judgment dreaded by many musicians in which Kikuoka would stand out front and critique the entire concert. Kikuoka kept his remarks brief, perhaps due to recent criticisms by students that he had been too harsh in the past, but he was particularly critical nevertheless. At first he spoke generally about stage fright, pointing out how amateur players particularly showed nervousness in their playing and how some amateurs make mistakes without even realizing it. Overall, his advice to amateurs was relatively kind, saying that they should relax and enjoy playing *nagauta* because they have chosen it as a hobby, not a profession. In the equalizing spirit of his *benkyōkai*, Kikuoka reserved his harshest criticism for the professional players and his young *deshi*.

His criticism of professionals was especially blunt, saying that they appeared to be out of practice and that he felt they had not taken this concert or their roles in it seriously. As professional players, he insisted, they are expected to always play perfectly and they should feel ashamed at making even the slightest mistake in public. He was even more critical of his young, professional-bound *deshi*, particularly critiquing their roles as off-stage assistants for many of the pieces, and singling out his one student who had not had the reserve *shamisen* tuned properly. Ultimately, he blamed all of his *deshi* collectively for their stage assistant work, claiming that several times amateurs got lost and were relying on them to recover quickly from their mistakes. Kikuoka claimed that the role of stage assistant was the single most important job in a performance, emphasizing the value of interdependent relationships in music, which was a key point in his philosophy behind *benkyōkai*.

After Kikuoka finished his critique, the room was prepared for the customary post-concert dinner. When everything was set, Kikuoka called everyone in to dinner, explaining that he didn't want people to form their usual groups and urged professionals to sit next to amateurs during dinner. This did not happen as people naturally gravitated towards their friends and peers with whom they felt comfortable. About halfway through dinner Kikuoka stood up and made an important announcement to all his students. Explaining very directly that he was tired of the decadence in *nagauta* society, with its value of money and status over musical skill and artistic appreciation, he announced that next year in the autumn of 1999, he would hold his last *osaraikai*. He told everyone in his school that he saw no purpose or need for *osaraikai* in *nagauta* and that he preferred to organize only *benkyōkai*. Although everyone responded with polite and obligatory applause, people seemed stunned and blank-faced at this announcement, particularly the professional musicians. In the absence of *osaraikai*, one supposes that the wealthy housewives could always find other ways to spend their money, while professionals would feel a reduction in this bi-annual source of income. Some amateur students were pleasantly surprised at Kikuoka's announcement. One of my *shamisen* accompanists admired Kikuoka for his bravery in trying to instigate a change that goes against tradition. Akiko was shocked that he expressed such blunt opinions in public saying, "he must really want a change."

Kikuoka's announcement was hardly a spontaneous response to his satisfaction or disappointment with the *benkyōkai* that day, but part of his plan to restructure his teaching that began earlier in the year with the combined lesson days of professionals and amateurs. The changes he instigated in his teaching during 1998 may have been connected to his disillusionment over the betrayal by his top student in 1997, but such disappointments as the loss of his top student and the loss of control over the reactionary swing in his "alternative" *nagauta* organization were all occupational hazards of his lifelong work to reform and purify the music. Kikuoka was certainly not alone in his criticism of current practices in this society as many amateurs I spoke with had also complained that *nagauta* had become corrupted by "business-like" professional musicians who regularly exploited others for money. However, being part of the professional system, Kikuoka felt that his own power to affect change was limited and thus, in the last year of his life, resorted to cleaning and fixing his own house, which was the last area over which he had control. In the last months of his life, Kikuoka continued instigating a new way to promote his ideal *nagauta* society, even though it went against the modern economy of *nagauta* that Tōonkai had helped shape. Sadly, this *benkyōkai* turned out to be Kikuoka's final student recital. When he passed away in January, 1999, his *okeikoba* at his home closed forever.

CONCLUSION: LEARNING FROM KIKUOKA

Just as the first chapter traced Kikuoka's efforts throughout his career to reform *nagauta* by creating an alternative social organization, this chapter has shown how Kikuoka extended these strategies into his teaching domain during the last years of his life. But whereas the formation of the professional organization Tōonkai can be seen as the result of emphasizing Western artistic values of merit and skill over family relationship, Kikuoka's recent efforts towards leveling the various degrees of status among musicians within his own school were based not on modern Western values, but on the traditional Japanese value of equality as a way of maintaining social harmony. The egalitarianism enforced by Kikuoka is an important aspect of belonging in social groups in Japan, in which both hierarchy and equality are able to co-exist. The leveling of the hierarchy through the integration of professionals and amateurs could have only been enabled by a teacher such as Kikuoka, to whom all students within the school shared in indebtedness.

Compared to the heterodoxy of Kikuoka's alternative music society, Kikuoka's lesson place was quite orthodox, even with his efforts at leveling the field. Compared to the many other lesson places I have either participated in or observed in Japan, Kikuoka's lesson place was the most dominated by formality and ritualized training. Nevertheless, the *nagauta* training within Kikuoka's lesson place resembled the predominant educational approach in Japan of training individuals to fit into the social order through formalized behavior. In a study of the ritual aspects of the Japanese school system, Fitzgerald explains how Japanese schools both educate and train through ritualized behavior:

> This institution trains and ritualizes simultaneously, so that students learn the correct behavioral response, including linguistic behavior, across the whole spectrum from purely symbolic behavior (bowing and using respect language to the teacher and to older students) to much more pragmatic behavior (for example, learning skills such as basic mathematics). (Fitzgerald 1993:334)

Following this method, Kikuoka's lesson process simultaneously socialized the individual within the group through ritualized, symbolic behaviors such as bowing and honorific language, while simultaneously allowing the student to develop the skills necessary to perform *nagauta*. But it must be reiterated that in learning a Japanese art such as *nagauta*, it is not easy, nor is it desirable, to separate symbolic social behavior from pragmatic musicianship for these are integrated within the practice of an art that emphasizes elegance and grace in performance. The appropriate symbolic behavior of *kata* is simultaneously social *and* musical as students are told not to worry about sound, as the real concern is with the formal manner in which the individual fits into the group. In this learning ideal it is not the music that is developed, but the individual who is developed through the graceful integration into a musical group.

But the lesson process should not be interpreted as a mere conformity of students to a dominant group norm, as such an interpretation denies the role of individuality in the learning process. The role of the individual within the context of the group should not be thought of as "individualism," which connotes self-assertion and individual rights, but as "individuality," which suggests "the opportunity for an individual to develop his or her own particular talents or character" (Hendry 1992:56). Lacking any opportunities for financial benefit through amateur pursuits, students in the lesson culture are motivated primarily by the personal satisfaction of self-development that takes place in a domain outside the restrictions of their everyday roles as housewives or wage-earners (See Moriya 1994, Moriya 1984 and Mori 1996). In one way, personal satisfaction may be derived, as demonstrated in the *osaraikai* student recitals, from the egoistic gratification of publicly demonstrating one's social status in the context of expensive recital pieces involving high-ranking players that may also indulge one's fantasies of professional musicianship. In another way, aside from status-seeking, an individual's mastery of performing skills within this domain removed from everyday life can become not only a "means of emotional self-expression, but a treasured element of self-identity" (Reischauer 1977:149). The notion that individuals simply conform to a social group misses the true power behind one's development through *kata*. The rote imitation of the teacher, the living embodiment of the tradition, contains a sense of egalitarianism that upholds the idea, in theory at least, that anyone can appropriate the tradition to the fullest of their abilities simply by executing the *kata* correctly.

Such individualistic self-development through *kata* in Kikuoka's lesson place was made possible by the relationship between teacher and student at the center of this artistic way of *nagauta*. While relationship plays a central role in most researchers' models of Japanese society characterized by terms such as "social relativism" or "situational ethics," in this ethnography of the lesson culture I have heeded the recommendations of Bachnik to avoid such objectivist, abstract terms by examining the teacher-student relationship in a particular time and place that includes the presence of the ethnographer (see Bachnik 1998). Following Bachnik's reconfiguration of pairs of terms commonly used to express "outside/inside" such as *soto/uchi* and *omote/ura* as opposite points on a continuum expressing degrees of "insideness," provides valuable insights into the dynamics of a lesson place such as Kikuoka's. Whereas relationships between individuals in a biologically related Japanese family will tend toward a high degree of informal *ura* ("insider") behavior, the relationships in Kikuoka's *uchi* in the behind the scenes moments I witnessed had the same high degree of *omote* (outsider) behavior as relationships that predominated during the formal lessons with amateurs. Without establishing an informal family atmosphere that would constitute a sense of *uchi*, relationships can be tenuous and it was not surprising that Kikuoka's school had terminated at his death.

The sense of *uchi* that was created in Kikuoka's lesson place was not that of an actual family marked by informal *ura* behavior in relationships, but an affiliation group marked by a highly ritualized *omote* behavior that normally defines the polite distance between Japanese people as they encounter one another in public. In this sense, the lesson place is not primarily about creating a virtual family or forming intimate relationships, but about aesthetically creating the proper social behavior that constitutes an ideal Japanese society. The ideal of *nagauta* is to create this fine surface aesthetic of *omote* behavior through graceful and elegant form in a public display. This is not to say, however, that there was no sense of an "inside" to Kikuoka's lesson place as the degree to which an inside was created depended entirely on one's own relationship with the *sensei*. Inside relationships with the teacher varied widely, from the undying loyalty for Kikuoka expressed by Akiko, who felt cared for by her teacher in a time of desperation, to the betrayal by K who felt uncared for in the business of traditional music performance. My own relationship with Kikuoka made me realize to what extent the teacher-student relationship can convey a sense of loyalty, indebtedness, and obligation that cuts through the surface behavior of *kata*.

I learned from Kikuoka more than just techniques and manners of *nagauta* that I continue to rely on today. Having taken me on as a student when I was unable to pay, Kikuoka instilled in me a sense of appreciation, obligation, and debt that went beyond a polite loyalty for a respected teacher. Although his benevolence was typical of the extreme generosity that Japanese hosts often bestow on foreign guests, sometimes to the extent that the guest may become suspicious of the host's expectations, my respect and admiration for Kikuoka as a teacher and an artist deepened as I came to know him over time. Weekly lessons with Kikuoka inspired me to prioritize the development of my *nagauta* performance skills over everything else to the point that my dissertation research topic could only be focused on one thing. When I found myself at Kikuoka's funeral, praying at the side of his casket, vowing to write a book about his career, his teaching and his art, and later helping to place his cremated bones into the funerary urn, I realized to what extent I had become a loyal subject, integrated into his school that would exist only in the memories and the future actions of his students. In retrospect, I realize that I never would have really learned *nagauta* had I not been shaped by Japanese music in this kind of relationship.

Chapter Three

Nagauta as Social Institution: The Shaping Forces of Form

"*SHOGANAI*": TWO CONVERSATIONS WITH MUSICIANS

One afternoon in February of 1998, I got a phone call from Fumiko, a *nagauta* singer and Geidai graduate I had recently met who had invited me to an upcoming concert in which she would be performing *hauta* (short songs associated with *geisha*), a lyrical style of *shamisen* music closely related to *nagauta*. I was really looking forward to seeing her concert, not only for the chance to hear *hauta*, but also because she was one of the few amateur performers I knew who was not affiliated with Tōonkai and followed the way of an *iemoto*-like musical family. I had been expecting to receive a copy of the concert flier on Akiko's home fax machine as I lived without such common everyday items during my stay in Japan. Fumiko had called to apologize for not having sent the fax and hoped that I could still attend her performance. She had decided not to send the fax because she was uncomfortable about Akiko knowing about this concert. I had not realized it at the time, but Fumiko was good friends with one of Kikuoka's young *uchideshi* and she explained to me that this student would also be singing in this concert and was afraid that Kikuoka would forbid her performing if he found out about it. Fumiko had no problem with me attending the concert and seeing this student of Kikuoka's whom I saw regularly at the lesson place. But she was afraid that Akiko would surely tell Kikuoka. "Please feel free to invite your friends to this concert," she explained, "but not if they have any connection to Kikuoka." When I naively told her that I did not think it would be such a big problem, she explained to me that such restrictions had been imposed on her in the past and she had learned to be very careful about who found out about concerts that might be objectionable to one's teacher. After complaining bitterly about this common problem I assured her that I would not say a word about the concert to anyone.

About two months earlier, in December 1997, I was having breakfast at a Tokyo hotel with Kazuo, a retired film producer who had studied *nagauta* since childhood and taught *nagauta* singing in his spare time. Like Fumiko, Kazuo was also very critical about *nagauta* society and spent a great deal of our time together that morning complaining about it. He complained not only of the kind of restrictions that Fumiko had experienced, but also about the greedy, business-like nature of *iemoto* who charge exorbitant fees, steal other teachers' students, and grant concert names to amateurs who are completely lacking in musical skills. Kazuo explained to me that *natori* stage names had been rendered "meaningless" because most people who had them did not deserve them, which was why he did not have one himself. Kazuo's own teacher, Tōonkai singer and co-founding member Nishigaki Yūzō, had told him that he did not need a license to teach, only the necessary skills which he had learned from his teacher. Kazuo hoped that everyone could take such an attitude and that many people without *natori* would start teaching Japanese music without any connection to an *iemoto* until that system was "completely destroyed." He wondered aloud why people have kept this feudalistic system alive for so long. But then, curiously, he smiled and shook his head in resignation, saying that he actually admired the *iemoto* system. He speculated that if musicians had had more freedom, *nagauta* would have disappeared already, finishing off his thoughts with the often heard Japanese phrase "*shoganai*" ("there is nothing that can be done about it").

The resignation of Kazuo and the surreptitious scheming of Fumiko are just two examples of the many musicians I encountered in Tokyo who were extremely critical of the social order of the *nagauta* world and, in some cases, had constant struggles within that social order. In protecting her student friend, Fumiko feared the authoritarian power of the *sensei* and this extended to a distrust of others who served that central power. Although I was not absolutely certain, my feeling was that Kikuoka might not have minded too much that his student participated in this "unsanctioned" concert. But Fumiko's fears of transgressing social boundaries and breaking school loyalties were deeply embedded in this learning culture of *nagauta* that places a premium on maintaining the purity of the school. Kazuo, on the other hand, felt no such constraints as he placed himself outside this system which, like Kikuoka, he resented as a money-making racket of exploitation that was harmful to the original spirit of the music. However, Kazuo's litany of complaints against the feudalistic practices of the *iemoto* system, like others I had heard from *nagauta* musicians, ended in a tone of resignation and acceptance of things as they are. This internalization of the system that encourages the covert activities of musicians like Fumiko and her friends, and leads a musician like Kazuo to tolerate such a system as a necessary evil for the sake of perpetuation of tradition, is a part of what it means to be shaped by Japanese music.

The shaping of individuals by Japanese music, as the ethnographic account of Kikuoka's lesson place in the previous chapter showed, took place in a special environment that facilitated a one-on-one relationship between teacher and student founded on the prescribed behavior of *kata*. Although the lesson culture is driven by individuals seeking the personal satisfaction of self-development, the student participates in an environment of social coercion that is centered on the *sensei* and extends outward through the coercive force of peers and other social institutions. The degree to which the broad forces of social coercion were felt by participants in this music culture became clear in numerous conversations I had with amateur and professional musicians alike. *Nagauta* musicians were much less interested in discussing the finer points of *nagauta* singing, their personal opinions about stylistic preferences or their favorite performers than they were in expressing concerns about the social and economic aspects of the *nagauta* world. When asked to talk about *nagauta* in free format interview situations, informants routinely began to discuss the social organization of *nagauta* which in many cases became personal critiques of Japanese society as a whole. Talk about *nagauta* is talk about Japanese society.

This chapter examines the social world of *nagauta* as a shaping force in Japanese society and, similar to the previous chapter, shows further how relationships are the defining element of this social world. In this chapter I address how *nagauta*'s social world is constructed not only by the teacher-student relationship, but by relationships between peers, relationships between parents and children and relationships between the individual and larger social institutions beyond the boundaries of the lesson place. Despite the appearance of *nagauta* as a relatively obscure traditional form still practiced by a small number of people in modern Japan, this social field exists within the larger field of Japanese culture and as such is subject to similar kinds of social forces and ruled by similar patterns of behavior. Thus the expanded view of the social practice of *nagauta* featured in this chapter demonstrates the extent to which the predetermined, patterned behavior of *kata* is central not only to *nagauta*, but to the construction of individual identities in relation to the group that forms the basis of social life in Japan.

SELF, GROUP, *KATA*, AND SOCIAL COERCION IN JAPANESE SOCIETY

The popular conception of the "group-orientation" and conformity of Japanese people has led to a great deal of over-simplification about Japanese society and the Japanese self. In the most stereotypical view, Japanese people have been depicted as completely lacking all autonomy and ever willing to sacrifice individual selves to the greater good of society. Early social analysis of Japanese society by Westerners, such as Ruth Benedict's landmark study, *The Chrysanthemum and the Sword* (1977, originally 1946), which depicted Japanese people as motivated more by fear of public shame than personal guilt, helped to promote simplistic views of the Japanese individual. Japan has since been depicted as a society in which individuals conform to the dominant needs of orderly groups, the most cited study being Chie Nakane's model of social "frames" in which individuals integrate into particular groups at the cost of individual autonomy (Nakane 1970).

The very notion of individual autonomy itself is problematic in research on non-Western societies. The idea of an idealized self that can be objective and make decisions entirely independent of society is a result of Western rationalist thinking. As a result, non-Western people are often perceived as the opposite of this idealized self. Thus Japanese people have been portrayed as "concrete thinkers, particularistic moralists, situational conformists, unintegrated selves; as intuitive rather than rational, animistic (undivided from their environment), and unable to separate body and mind" (Rosenberger 1992:2). Such conceptions of Japanese people have not only been popular in the West, but have been perpetuated by the Japanese themselves in the form of *nihonjinron* (literally "theory of the Japanese"). This genre of social self-analysis in Japan, which ranges from academic research to pop culture bestsellers, argues for the "uniqueness" of Japanese culture and embraces notions of group-oriented behavior and the Japanese relational self as evidence. Writers of *nihonjinron* gleefully promote a message that Japanese people are the exact opposite of Westerners in that they are nonrational, relational thinkers with a natural instinct for achieving consensus.[1] *Nihonjinron* is thus a classic example of Said's model of a non-Europeanized society that has internalized an "orientalist" discourse about itself (see Said 1979).

Far from being a society of relational selves naturally inclined to consensus, Japanese people have been shaped to a great extent by centuries of political conditioning since the advent of the Tokugawa era in the seventeenth century. Japanese society prior to that time could hardly be described using terms such as "collective" or group-oriented. On the contrary, the chaos and warfare of the thirteenth through the sixteenth centuries can be seen as a result of unchecked, violent self-interest that was finally halted by the strong-arm imposition of a centralized government in the seventeenth century. During the Tokugawa era (1600–1868) law enforcement held groups responsible for the actions of individuals. Conformity in urban areas was ensured by small neighborhood groups made up of the resident families living on each street. The neighborhood group was held responsible for all the individuals within it and the entire group might be punished for the misdeeds of a single individual (Henshall 1999:151–152). This kind of social management has become the norm in today's Japanese schools as children are routinely divided into small operating groups responsible for the actions of each member (ibid.:114).

The enforced political stabilization maintained throughout the Tokugawa era (1600–1868) created a Japanese society based on conformity to state edicts which became the basis of prescriptive behavior according to *kata*. The Tokugawa government enforced conformity through the codification of citizens into four classes (warriors/nobles; peasants/farmers; artisans; merchants) with detailed prescriptions for the behavior of people according to their station.

> Movement between the classes was theoretically banned but in practice was not unknown, though it was difficult. At a more detailed level, there were prescriptions for type and place of work and residence for particular classes. At a finer level still, there were prescriptions for the type of clothing a person of a particular class could wear, the type of present they could give to a child of a particular gender and a particular age, the type of food they could eat, and even where they could build their toilet. (ibid.:151)

Such detailed prescriptive behaviors that constitute model behavior are still found today in all manner of daily activities, including one's performance in the workplace, the carrying out of domestic chores, religious worship and social etiquette. Not limited to artistic practice, *kata* has played an important role in social coercion in Japanese life as knowledge of the appropriate formal behavior for the appropriate situation is essential to being a socially competent individual in Japanese society.

Social control in Japan has been schematized by scholars as working in two ways: in an authoritarian manner in which control moves "from the top down" and in an internalized manner in which order emerges "from the bottom up" (Matthews 1996:24). "Top-down" control is seen in the ways in which individuals are compelled to conform to the group or suffer the consequences, whereas "bottom-up" control depicts Japanese people as consensus-oriented with order emerging from "individuals' internalized cultural molding, which they view as 'natural,' intrinsic to themselves" (Matthews 1996:24). Both types of control are evident in Sugimoto's concept of "friendly authoritarianism" in which power is made visible and highly compelling yet done using positive inducements and congeniality in a top-down fashion, while in a bottom-up way, such an authoritarianism "encourages each member of society to internalize and share the value system which regards control and regimentation as natural, and to accept the instructions and orders of people in superordinate positions without questioning" (Sugimoto 1997:245). Ethnographic research of small businesses in Tokyo by Kondo (1990) demonstrates how individuals "craft selves" in response to both external and internalized coercive forces, ranging from the intimacy of family which compels by sheer emotion, to enforced control of resistant workers in ethics training camps.

I found a wide range of coercive forces at work in the world of *nagauta* in Tokyo. In addition to the direct force of top-down authoritarianism from teachers there is also a great deal of institutionalized coercion in Japanese society that affects musicians. Bottom-up kinds of internalized control are also evident in the lives of many musicians, who typically start to experience coercion from childhood within their own family. Given musicians' internalized understandings of their limits within tradition, the force of authoritarian coercion from above need not be too explicitly overbearing to have an effect. From the musician's own family to the musician's teacher to the musician's peers, coercion is imprinted onto the self through the practice of this tradition that seems to demand an acceptance of things as they have always been. As Akiko would often say with resignation after imagining what *nagauta* would be like if it were one day rid of the status seeking and high fees of *osaraikai* or the business practices of millionaire *iemoto*: "… but this is Japan."

CONTROL BY PARENTS: BIOLOGICAL AND VIRTUAL

The most immediate, influential and perhaps longest-lasting force of coercion in Japanese society, or indeed in any society, is the parent. In Japan however, "parents" are both biological and virtual in the sense that parental roles are often assumed by others outside the family as a person matures in life. One well-known example is the Japanese company as parent in which the employee becomes the "child" to the company "parent" which assumes a caretaking responsibility, ideally for the remainder of the employee's life, though this promise of lifetime security has been in rapid decline since the 1980s. This parent-like caretaking role can also be found in marriages in which the housewife may be seen as assuming a mother role in taking care of the "spoiled son." In similar fashion, the *iemoto* system of *nagauta* provides musicians, both professional and amateur alike, with a virtual parent in the *sensei* whose influence in all musical matters is meant to endure over the student "child" for as long as the student lives.

Prior to the first meeting with one's *sensei*, however, the student's biological parents can be key figures in the path of entry into *nagauta*. In many cases it is the parents who first introduce *nagauta* to the musician as a child. In the traditional ideal of an *iemoto*, the teacher actually is the father who teaches his own child. For children who are not related to an *iemoto*, it may be the parents who introduce the child to an *iemoto* or some other highly regarded teacher, perhaps a relative. Japanese calendrical ritual even includes an auspicious day for the first lesson of a child in some form of traditional art: the sixth day of the sixth month in the sixth year of the child's life, a young age in which the child has little say in the matter. Several of the musicians I spoke with claimed to have started at this age or even earlier, complaining of the strictness and the coercive power of their parents who had forced them into playing music. Kikuoka's father, as was recounted in chapter one, was a professional *shamisen* teacher who introduced him to *nagauta* by singing to him as an infant. As far back as Kikuoka could remember he was singing *nagauta* in imitation of his father. Although his father was his first teacher, Kikuoka's main teacher for life was Yamada Shōtarō, whom he did not meet until his attendance at Geidai in his late teenage years. But the influence of his father was perhaps the greatest in his path to becoming a professional. Kikuoka's recollection of hating *shamisen* as a child and learning to appreciate it as a young adult is commonly expressed by *nagauta* musicians.

In some cases, children are literally adopted by musicians who then assume both parental and musical duties. This was the case with professional *nagauta* musician

Tahachi Mochizuki, who was my teacher of *nagauta* flutes (*nōkan* and *shinobue*). Following the death of his father, Tahachi was adopted by his uncle, a professional *nagauta* flute player who had no heir to succeed him. At first Tahachi learned *shamisen* from his uncle's wife who provided *shamisen* music for her husband's lessons. Tahachi was being trained in *shamisen* not for the purpose of providing music for his uncle's lessons, but as a preparation for taking over his uncle's position. By learning the *shamisen* first, Tahachi was able to get a strong foundation in *nagauta* so that he could move on to studying flute during his high school years. Tahachi remembers hating the flute in particular and hating *nagauta* in general during the years he was "forced" to take flute lessons. He has since, however, come to love playing *nagauta* flute and takes pleasure in performing both the standard repertoire, as well as contemporary music of which he has written many short pieces. In interviews Tahachi referred to his uncle as his "father."

Parents can also just as easily try to prevent the child's involvement in *nagauta* as promote it. An amateur performer of *nagauta* throughout his whole life, Kazuo was forced by his parents into learning *nagauta* as a child primarily because of their concerns about his health. He had been born a very sickly child and his parents feared that he might not have a respectable position in society if he was too sick to attend university. So they thought of *nagauta* as a back-up career and had him "adopted" by his grandmother, a professional player who taught him *shamisen* and singing. But his family only wanted him to be a professional player in the event of his poor health because they disliked and distrusted music societies. Ironically, when he reached high-school age and his health unexpectedly returned to normal, Kazuo had grown to love *nagauta* and considered a professional career. This horrified his family and his grandmother immediately stopped teaching him *shamisen*. Suddenly Kazuo was without a teacher, effectively forcing him out of *nagauta*. He eventually chose a career outside music instead, becoming a notable film producer for Japan's Tōho Film Company, but maintained *nagauta* as a lifelong hobby.

CONTROL BY NAMING: THE MARK OF BELONGING TO A MUSICAL FAMILY

Perhaps the most powerful symbol of belonging to the virtual parent/*sensei* is the stage name (*natori*), which symbolizes adoption by the musical family and marks the musician as belonging to a virtual family. This power of naming in the arts originates in the traditional *iemoto* family system, in which adoption has always been common, making the practice of inheriting names crucial to maintaining an artistic lineage that is not necessarily determined by biological kinship. At the top level of such a system, the name of the *iemoto* should ideally be passed down to the first-born son to continue the main lineage (*honke*), but in many cases a suitable biological heir may not be available and a top student may be adopted. Because this system is defined by the household which maintains an artistic tradition, biological kinship is less important than belonging to the *ie* as marked by inherited names.[2] The *iemoto*, as bearer of the primary name of the lineage which will be passed on to the most worthy successor, is also in charge of granting stage names to players who wish to join the musical family. Professional-bound students typically pay large sums of money to obtain the name not necessarily because it is a status symbol, as is the case with housewives, but because it directly affects ones earning ability as a professional player.

Granting names to young players is also a form of control that is seen as a kind of protection from the influence of competing schools of *nagauta*. This is especially important in the modern age of Tōonkai influence through Geidai. Young players associated with *nagauta* families who enroll in the *nagauta* program at Geidai will be given stage names by their teachers before they enter Geidai. This identifying mark is a reminder that indicates where the student's loyalty should lie during and after their tenure at Geidai. While at Geidai a young student of *nagauta* will be expected to perform according to the standard set by the instructors there, all of whom represent Tōonkai. Naturally, a student must follow the Tōonkai style if he or she expects to pass the program. Having a stage name, however, serves as a reminder of one's membership and one's bond with the family's style which is not to be forsaken. After graduation from Geidai, a student from a *nagauta* family will typically return to the family and its way of performing without joining Tōonkai. This was the case for the professional *nagauta* singer in chapter one, for example, who was encouraged by Kikuoka to join Tōonkai and refused, arguing that the style was too standardized. Had he joined the group, he would also have had to refrain from using his stage name, at least only for participation in Tōonkai concerts, which would amount to turning his back on his biological, musical family. Such students from *nagauta* families are unlikely to abandon stage names in favor of an "outside" group.

The practice of naming is crucial to identifying the student as belonging to only one *sensei* and one artistic way, and is a sign of the singular devotion that is demanded in the traditional arts. Theoretically, a student should have only one *nagauta* teacher to whom he/she is devoted for life. However, in today's lesson culture it is common for students to want to expand his/her *nagauta* abilities by taking up percussion or flute studies, or to learn *nagauta* vocals if only studying *shamisen* and vice versa. If the student wishes to study with another teacher, ideally their primary teacher should dictate with whom the student will study by making a recommendation. As group affiliation and the approval of one's primary teacher is the most important criteria, personally shopping for another teacher is unacceptable. With *shamisen* players and singers grouped together into families it is fairly easy for a *shamisen* student to find a vocal teacher who is acceptable to the *shamisen* teacher as this teacher would ordinarily come from within this same musical family. If *shamisen* or voice students wish to study instruments of the *hayashi* (*nagauta* percussion and flutes), they must go outside the family as *hayashi* musicians are similarly organized into families, but affiliation is also the determining factor. Particular *hayashi* families affiliate with particular *shamisen*/vocal families for the purposes of performing and recording together and students are constrained to move along these lines.

Having more than one teacher on a single *nagauta* instrument is not acceptable among ranking *nagauta* teachers as it invalidates identification through naming and erodes the power of the *sensei*. While I sensed this from the very beginning and did not ever plan to break this rule out of respect for my teachers, an American friend of mine quite naively encountered problems when she went shopping for *nagauta* teachers. My friend already had a weekly lesson with one teacher and wanted an additional weekly lesson with another teacher. She was interested not just in more lessons but in comparing different playing styles, something that had also interested me. But the second teacher she went to rejected her immediately, saying that she would get confused between the two different styles and was very suspicious of this kind of shopping around. The teacher also claimed that she did not want to be "stealing other teacher's students," particularly because she was an amateur performer and not a professional as was the other teacher. In her mind, "stealing" a student would violate the hierarchy of *nagauta* musicians and the singular approach to the art way. Allowing students to follow more than one teacher gives them an ability to choose that weakens a teacher's control and risks introducing impure "outside" techniques into the pure performance space of the teacher's school. For a student to have a mix of performance techniques learned from several sources shows a failure to have followed a particular "way." Only full dedication to the pure sound of one *sensei* gives one the sound of pure *nagauta*. The roots of this notion of single-minded purity can be found in Zeami's ideas about performing arts. As Kawatake translates Zeami's directive: "A person who aims to succeed in this Way of ours should not engage in any other Way" (Kawatake 1990:261).

CONTROL BY PEERS: WATCHDOGS OF FAMILY LOYALTY

Sugimoto (1997) demonstrates the many systems of surveillance built into modern Japanese society, extending from the institutional to the personal. Institutionalized surveillance is most obvious in the numerous police boxes strategically placed at busy intersections throughout Japan, but perhaps even more effective is the more personal type of surveillance that exists among ones peers. Belonging to a group in Japan entails the responsibility of watching out for the others within the group and thus people keep an eye on each other. Watchdog behavior is common in small schools such as Kikuoka's in which people come to know each other through the shared experience of watching each other's lessons on a regular basis and attending the same recitals and concerts. Through a kind of gossip network of surveillance students feel compelled to maintain their loyalty to the *sensei* and the school.

The impetus for watchdog behavior may come directly from above in a suggestion or even a command from the *sensei* who may delegate this responsibility. For example, in the small school of my flute *sensei*, Tahachi Mochizuki, my teacher heard a complaint about one of his students from a *nagauta* drum teacher. Apparently, this student's rude behavior during drum lessons insulted the drum teacher. Rather than deal directly with the offending student, my flute teacher instead asked another of his students to intervene and take care of the matter by admonishing the offending student. Such watchdog behavior among peers is also internalized and often does not require any suggestion from the *sensei*. The sense of belonging within a school entails keeping an eye on every matter and every person within the domain.

All actions of individuals are watched carefully by others because they may be seen as reflecting badly on the group and, most damagingly, on the *sensei*. It is extremely important that one must not make the *sensei* look bad. I first experienced this in Kikuoka's school after I had had enough lessons with him to gain enough confidence in my singing and began to entertain the idea of performing with others outside of the school. When I discussed with two of Kikuoka's students about the possibility of performing *nagauta* with a few amateur performers outside of Kikuoka's school, this was highly discouraged. I was told that my training from Kikuoka was of superior quality and that I was "too good" to be performing with other people. "They don't have the training that you have," I was told. "*Sensei* has trained you and you should respect his teaching. If you perform with someone who is less skilled, it might make *sensei* look bad." It is understood by everyone within the school that students must ask permission of their teacher before participating in any performance outside the school. The fact that many teachers routinely deny such permission, leads students to circumvent these restrictions by keeping outside performances secret from the teacher, as Kikuoka's young *deshi* did in the story recounted at the beginning of this chapter. As Fumiko's story demonstrated, students who do this must be careful of peers who may be "watchdogs" of the school.

CONTROL BY INSTITUTIONS: *IEMOTO* AND BEYOND

For the *nagauta* musician in Japan, institutional control operates most directly and profoundly at the subcultural level of one's own *iemoto*. Although commonly criticized by many Japanese people as extremely outdated in the modern world, *iemoto* nevertheless continues to operate as a respected institution within Japan which gives *iemoto* groups a certain amount of clout and control in public. This power of *iemoto* was evident in the case of Kineya Rokuaya, an amateur *nagauta shamisen* musician who organized her own concerts on a regular basis consisting entirely of amateur players. Rokuaya had been asked by a producer to organize a concert with sponsorship from a Tokyo newspaper. Her group, which she calls Kisenkai, made this an annual event, playing at a venue in central Tokyo for five years until one *iemoto* decided to put a stop to these concerts. Rokuaya explained to me in an interview:

> The producer of the concert asked me to play the concert with my group. Kisenkai is a very small group, not iemoto, and I have no contact with any iemoto so I am independent. This producer asked Kisenkai to play. We played five times, once a year for five years for the Mitsukoshi concert. This made one iemoto very uncomfortable. He pushed the producer and forced him to stop us. The producer was very disappointed. He asked this iemoto the reason why, but the iemoto had no reason. The only reason was that we were independent from iemoto.

The *iemoto* name represents more than just power over the students within its own school. *Iemoto* names legitimize individuals with the status of official Japanese culture. Anyone bearing such a name has the potential to use it with great effect in dealing even with those outside the music world. The national broadcasting network of Japan, NHK, remains committed to broadcasting performances of Japanese traditional arts and reinforces the power of the *iemoto* system by recognizing performers with official stage names. When Kikuoka wanted to participate in NHK broadcasts in the 1950s, he had to adopt a stage name just for this purpose. At that time NHK would not broadcast any *shamisen* performance by musicians without stage names. Although NHK no longer has such restrictions, allowing Tōonkai players, for example, to appear on the network, ironically Tōonkai has adapted to this situation by adopting *iemoto*-like stage names for its players.

Beyond one's own *iemoto*, the *nagauta* musician must sometimes contend with institutional control outside of the field of *nagauta* music. Throughout his career, Kikuoka worked to overcome institutional restrictions and bureaucratic hurdles that stood in his way. As a university professor at Geidai, Kikuoka had to persevere with academic restrictions and the bureaucratic red tape of government ministries as academic programs for Geidai must first be approved by the government. Thus Kikuoka's efforts to expand the traditional music program within the music department at Geidai were kept at bay through a lengthy bureaucratic process. Kikuoka could not go directly to the Ministry of Education, but had to convince the chain of command within Geidai before the university would send a representative to *Monbusho* to get permission to expand its program. Such lengthy bureaucratic processes exercise control by discouraging people from even applying in the first place.[3]

Japanese employers exercise a great deal of control over employees in ways more far reaching than employers in Western companies and this control often extends beyond the workplace. Kikuoka's career as a professor was subject to a certain degree of control from the University as he was required to apply for permission to play all professional concerts not associated with the University. Interestingly, even Kikuoka was not exempt from obtaining permission from above to play concerts "outside the school" and was forced to submit to the higher authority of the educational institution. Although he was never denied permission for any of his activities as a professional musician and he claimed to have never been covert about any performances, he complained of always having to go through the application process. Fear of employer retribution severely curtailed the activities of one amateur *nagauta* student who worked in a government-run institution and complained to me that her employers threatened termination of any employees engaging in outside employment. Although the student was clearly an amateur, she feared the watchdog behavior of peers within her workplace and avoided all discussion of student recitals or any other performances for fear of losing her job.

MALE *SHAMISEN* VERSUS FEMALE *SHAMISEN*: GENDER INEQUALITIES IN *NAGAUTA*

The gender inequalities that permeate Japanese life are also maintained in *nagauta*. The traditional roles of men as wage earners and women as keepers of the domestic areas are reflected in the division of professionals and amateurs. The professional ranks of *nagauta* musicians are dominated by men who have much greater advantages to make a comfortable living from public performing while women have significantly fewer chances to perform in a professional capacity. Whereas the men play starring roles as highly respected musicians, women make up the majority of the ranks of amateur players who are students of the male professionals, many of whom could not maintain their professional activities without the participation of female students (Oshio 2002:765). Gender roles are further reinforced in the concert and rehearsal settings with women typically taking charge of domestic duties such as serving tea and refreshments as well as assisting other performers in dressing and preparations. Although some women have achieved notoriety being born into *iemoto* families lacking a male heir, and have thus become *iemoto* themselves, it is still primarily the men who are favored in *nagauta*.

Male performers are favored at all levels of performance. The highly revered stage of the Kabukiza Theater in Ginza, for example, has always been off-limits to females, a rule that has been well guarded even in the present day. When the *iemoto* of the Tanaka school of drumming, a frequent performer on the Kabukiza stage, passed his *iemoto* position on to his daughter, he had expected, because of the prestige of his own name, that his daughter would be the one who would break the gender barrier at the theater. His assumption was incorrect, and the new female *iemoto* was not allowed on the stage of Kabukiza. Dance recitals, which require musicians for *nagauta* accompaniment, are similarly dominated by male performers as dancers invariably choose the same favorite musicians for their performances. In formal *osaraikai* recitals as well, musicians of high status are sought after by students to participate in their performances. While the majority of students at *osaraikai* are female, the invited performers are chosen for their status and thus males predominate.

The role of women in *shamisen* music, however, has hardly been insignificant. In fact, since the eighteenth century the *shamisen* has been the principal instrument used in *geisha* entertainment, and many *geisha* today still make their living off their *shamisen* prowess.[4] Some geisha musicians are well respected enough as performers to gather a significant number of students. During the Edo era, the *shamisen* became popular as a hobby for daughters of the merchant class as a way of becoming more desirable spouses, but because of its low-class associations with *geisha* and theater daughters of the warrior class tended to study the more high status *koto* with its aristocratic origins in *gagaku* court music (ibid.:764). Although the *shamisen*, like the *koto*, is still an instrument which women can use for self-development and accomplishment, the belief that learning a traditional Japanese art makes them more attractive as spouses has declined since World War II and there is a noticeable lack of younger women among the ranks of students. In recent years more single women are in the work force and thus have less time for expensive hobbies such as music.[5] Today's amateur *nagauta* market is filled with women, mostly over 50 years old and many in their 60s and 70s, reflecting a time when traditional Japanese arts were valued as a legitimate pursuit for women. Many of the older housewives who studied *nagauta* with Kikuoka had some sort of lessons prior to marriage. After marriage however, the study of *shamisen* for personal fulfillment declines in importance and the tasks of caring for household, husband and children take priority. After children have grown up, many housewives have time to rediscover *shamisen* as a hobby.

Among female professionals in the Tōonkai organization, women are segregated from the men organizationally. Female Tōonkai professionals belong to a special branch called Joshi Tōonkai (Women's Tōonkai), which was created in the 1960s after the number of female professionals began to increase in the Tōonkai ranks. In recent years another group was formed for younger female professionals called Joshi Wakate (Young Women's group). The women's groups have their own series of concerts throughout the year, but have often relied on the participation of certain male performers from Tōonkai to attract audience members. However, gender mixing at these concerts has been subject to debate within Tōonkai. Not only have some of the top male members of Tōonkai objected to the mixing of gender at the women's concerts, but some in the women's group felt a similar ambivalence. The organizers of Joshi Tōonkai's thirtieth-anniversary concert in 1997 had originally planned to do the concert without any male participation to show their independence as a women's group, but a decision was made at the last minute to include male performers. I was told by one of the members that it was decided that the participation of the men could help draw more of an audience, but this was perhaps more of a political decision on the part of the organizers who may have feared causing any controversy.

In the competition for professional jobs performing *nagauta*, women are at a distinct disadvantage. Not only is there a longstanding ban against females performing on certain professional stages such as Tokyo's Kabukiza, many professional concerts are organized for men only. According to professional *nagauta* singer and member of Tōonkai, Noriko Hayashi, professional dancers have their favorite performers whom they hire and they invariably choose men. Noriko criticized the current state of *nagauta* as more concerned with the surface of the performance than the true art of the music. She expressed frustration that male musicians of considerably lesser skill are more highly valued and regularly employed than many females with far greater skills. She also described the struggle of several of her female friends who are performers:

> Female players have two lives. After graduation in their 20s they are single and active [playing concerts]. In their 30s they have a long break and get married. But after their 30s their performance opportunities are fewer. Only through friends or neighbors can they get a performing job.

As Noriko explained, this bias against older females is complicated by the elevated status that comes with age. An older, more experienced musician typically commands more money than a younger musician and, as a result, dancers and concert organizers are less likely to pay such fees for an older female, favoring the younger, newly graduated, and more affordable, female performers.

For female amateurs, the situation is not any better. Tōyukai, an amateur wing of Tōonkai, was created in 1978 to grant amateur performers the opportunity to teach *nagauta* in the Tōonkai style. As is typical of the gender imbalance in the traditional arts, the amateur organization of over 100 members is almost entirely female. Although one might assume that amateur teachers would rob Tōonkai professionals of potential students, the high status of male professionals guarantees them a sufficient crop of students who want to learn from top professionals. The most important function of the Tōyukai group is to provide Tōonkai with a strong base of dues-paying amateurs who will regularly attend the concerts and maintain devoted relationships with their teachers. In order to maintain this important amateur base, it is difficult to enforce the exclusivity that gives real clout to the stage names given out by the organization. Although amateur musicians applying to the group must pass a performance exam, a recent surge in membership during the late 1990s led some observers to view the standards of the group with great skepticism, particularly in 1998 when 30 new members were admitted at once to bolster the ranks. Though economically important for Tōonkai, the Tōyukai organization is subordinate and has little independent political power, as explained to me by one committee member since the group's inception who had been very active and vocal in organizing the group. It became clear to her just how little power Tōyukai had when policies were created within the group, only to have them vetoed by the parent organization, Tōonkai, which oversees Tōyukai.

Gender inequality is also clearly demonstrated in segregated performances of *nagauta*. At the amateur level, one might see men and women performing together on stage in formal *osaraikai* recitals, but at the professional level, women are segregated into ensembles identified by the use of the term *joryū* ("in the women's style") (Oshio 2002:765). When I asked performers, including women, why men and women were segregated, instead of complaints about the inequity of the situation, I heard aesthetic validations for the necessity of gender segregation. The most common explanation was that male and female voices don't match, referring to the desired *nagauta* aesthetic of unison singing at the top of the vocal register without resorting to falsetto tone. In actuality however, as *nagauta* was created by males, female ensembles strive for male aesthetic standards, often singing in nearly the same register and trying to imitate male tone color (ibid.). There appears to be no legitimate sonic reason why men and women cannot perform *nagauta* together.

One male professional *shamisen* player I spoke with explained to me that *shamisen* used by women are different from men because *shamisen* makers use thinner skins and stretched the them differently, knowing the instrument would be used by a woman. Such an explanation is highly unlikely, as male and female musicians have many kinds of personal preferences for various kinds of instruments that are not dictated by a desire for "male" or "female" sound quality. Apparently, this professional musician, when confronted by a Westerner asking for a rational explanation to justify gender segregation, felt the need to create a reason that suggests there are male and female instruments. There is an aesthetic idea, however, that supports his explanation: not that there are male and female instruments in themselves, but that a *shamisen* played by a female is essentially a female *shamisen* by virtue of it being played by a female. This is consistent with the idea in traditional Japanese music that the player somehow merges with, or becomes one with, their instrument in a tradition that puts such emphasis on the individual's physical body.

Focus on the body is also connected to the great importance attached to the visual aspects of traditional Japanese performance. Another common reason given for gender separation in *nagauta* was that mixing gender on stage "did not look right." In the unison playing of *shamisen* in a concert setting, all efforts are made to create a uniform aesthetic and this quest for uniformity must extend to the visual aspect as well and nothing must stick out. A female onstage with a male creates an obvious contrast on the surface, and beyond that, begs comparison with a man, an unwanted trait in Japanese society in general. In an embodied musical practice such as *nagauta*, gender is not something that can be easily neutralized by the adoption of Western notions of gender equality. When the focus is on the body as a performing instrument, the gender of the player is something that simply cannot be ignored.

HARMONIZING WITH NATURE: THE ACCEPTANCE OF SOCIAL CONTROL

Considering the varieties of overt social coercion within *nagauta* society, it is not surprising that many Japanese musicians can be quick to articulate and, in many cases, severely criticize, the rigidity of this social system. But in spite of criticisms of the current state of *nagauta* in Japan, social control is largely accepted by musicians as a natural part of Japanese traditional music. Although *nagauta* musicians are aware of alternative Western models of the arts, in which it is perceived that men and women are treated equally, that individuals are evaluated solely on artistic merit, and that individuals are free agents in artistic pursuits, the musicians I encountered tended to draw on the "uniqueness" of Japanese culture in their acceptance of the situation. Though musicians' complaints about the feudalistic system of the arts in Japan were sometimes followed by suggestions for improvement, phrases such as Kazuo's "*shoganai*" ("it can't be helped") or Akiko's "… but this is Japan" often ended such conversations. There was even a feeling on the part of some of the more outspoken musicians that the situation is unchangeable without damaging the art. One musician who always appeared to be vehemently anti-*iemoto* during our interviews credited the system with effectively preserving artistic traditions over the centuries, and even feared what might happen in the future if the *iemoto* system were to vanish completely. I began to wonder what kind of thinking allowed for such cognitive dissonance in the acceptance of traditional values and practices that were perceived as outdated in the modern world.

The predetermined forms of *kata* offer more than just the promise of artistic fulfillment for anyone who follows an art way. The rigidity of model forms of behavior established over centuries by a particular artistic lineage provides followers with the assurance of a tradition that is authentic because it has endured and will continue to endure.[6] Breaking away from established models and the appropriate *kata* introduces an insecurity and uncertainty about the future — a future that is otherwise guaranteed by belonging to a group defined by these formal behaviors that structure relationships between members. To break form is to break relationships and risk the worst-case scenario of banishment from the group. The discomfort of living with the danger of breaking conformity and the feeling of a lack of autonomy is neutralized by the important Japanese values of "nature" (*shizen*) and, what is perhaps Japan's most significant social value, "harmony" (*wa*). The concept of *wa* has the kind of significance for Japanese people that the concept of "freedom" has for American people: an ultimate value towards which every human must strive. Although this notion of harmony contains all the implications of individual capitulation to the group for the greater happiness of society, the negative implications of the loss of individual autonomy are softened by the Japanese concept of nature. This combination of harmony and nature allows Japanese people to continue to justify a social system that may seem rigid in comparison to modern alternatives.

Japanese philosophical and aesthetic conceptualizations of nature have shaped how modern Japanese people view their own society. One of the most influential philosophical works connecting nature and society in Japan in the twentieth century is Watsuji's *Fūdo* (translated as "Climate and Culture") which argues for a kind of climatic determinism of culture in which he generalizes about monsoon, desert and pastoral cultures. Watsuji later revised his theory of how "human nature is rooted in and particularized by various environments" by arguing that "human beings exist in spatial relationships and that human existence is fundamentally relational" (Maraldo 2002:84–85). Watsuji's revision went beyond the geographic determinism of his earlier theory for a more compelling view of the interconnectedness of nature and society:

> Instead, Watsuji sees the concrete place of our existence as the space of interactions between environment and culture. These interactions differ according to specific localities or types of locality but universally collapse any rigid distinction between nature or the natural world and the human world or culture. The two are formed mutually. (ibid.:85)

Although Watsuji universalized his theory, the collapse of any distinction between nature and culture is still consistent with *nihonjinron* ideas of Japanese uniqueness. The interconnectedness of nature and society in Japan, sharply contrasting with Western ideas that maintain a separation between the two, provide ample justification for acceptance of the social order.[7]

Japanese thinking views society as a part of nature that acts according to its laws. As Clammer (1995) points out, the popular belief held by the Japanese that their people have a special relationship with nature, in spite of the nation's alarming record of pollution and environmental destruction, is not to be rejected as a delusion of a *nihonjinron* philosophy of uniqueness, but accepted as a revealing cultural self-understanding (ibid.:60). In this way of thinking, nature and society are not opposites: human society is structured in the way nature is structured. Clammer sees this philosophy of nature as offering a special kind of liberty — freedom *in* nature — that is quite different from the notion of freedom *from* nature that exists in the West.

> Nature in this view is not merely the object of scientific curiosity and manipulation, or more still, something to be overcome — the ultimate Other — but the setting in which human freedom — defined as the achievement of harmonious (people-people and people-nature) social relationships take place. The so-called 'groupism' of the Japanese should be seen in this light: not as a clannish huddling together, but as the reflection of the principle that community is the natural setting for the achievement and realization of human beings (just as it is for most animal species). (ibid.:61)

In this view, society is not only natural, it is nature itself in that it is perceived as operating according to the same principles. Belonging to society is the most natural way of harmonizing with nature.

Clammer's use of the word "freedom" in locating society within nature is a bit misleading as the Japanese word *jiyū* (freedom) has negative connotations of selfishness and disruption of group harmony (Hendry 1992:64). It is perhaps more useful to think in terms of individual agency than freedom, because social harmony in Japan is hardly a passive acceptance of the top-down authoritarian rule of a society in harmony with nature. Acceptance of things as they are coexists with the conscious individual agency involved in personal discipline that offers hope for a kind of transcendence.

> Human life is accepted as transitory, difficult and often tragic and human beings as weak, confused and eternally living in an environment of moral ambiguity. But the human condition can be, if not totally transformed or transcended, at least alleviated, and this can best be done, not by radical individualism or through radical liberty, but through discipline: submission to and mastery of an art, a skill and, at the highest level, of relationships themselves. (Clammer 1995:103)

Thus, an embodied practice such as *nagauta*, which involves submission to a *sensei*, navigation of the system of social relationships within a group, and development of the body in a highly codified performing art, provides a suitable vehicle for achieving this harmony, with the individual playing an active role in the development of society through the development of the self.

Although submitting to a single authoritarian way of art, the individual ultimately achieves a personal mastery, not by conquering nature, but by shaping it through the shaping of the body. As Clammer points out:

> Clearly the body is deeply implicated in the question of nature: it *is* nature, it is the means through which external nature is apprehended through sight, smell, sensations of temperature of the wind and so on, and it participates in nature through activities. It is also highly charged with symbolism and so is as much 'socially constructed' as nature is itself socially constructed: it is not just *there*, it is perceived, manipulated, evolves, is understood cognitively in different ways at different times. (ibid.:69–70).

The authoritarian system of the performing arts does not conquer the individual, so much as the individual submits to 'the way,' a practice of self-discipline that enables the individual to shape the body to be in harmony with society and nature. Such an act of refinement is not passive acceptance, but an active achievement of skills. Thus, Japan's ancient theater form that best articulated the concept of *kata* in the performing arts is called *nō*, which literally means 'accomplishment' or 'talent,' and is not so much about making an artistic product as it is a traditional formula by which individuals can follow the way of accomplishment. The training and recitals of *nagauta,* as taught by teachers such as Kikuoka, constitute a similar way of achievement for individuals as long as the individual *actively* submits to the shaping process which includes a submission to social order.

Tolerance of the objectionable aspects of Japanese society that permeate *nagauta* practice becomes an important part of an individual's artistic achievement and is integrated into the aesthetics of nature that defines traditional Japanese art. As explained by Saito (1997) the appreciation of natural processes in art that appear to be beyond human control, such as cracked tea bowls, painted images of the moon obscured by clouds, and weather-beaten, moss-covered stone lanterns, demonstrates an aesthetics of imperfection and insufficiency that also justifies unpalatable social practices in the traditional arts:

> Many Japanese artistic activities both presuppose and encourage the artists' listening to and submitting themselves to the voice and dictate of the material and subject matter, as well as affirming the various elements of accidents and surprises beyond their control. The attitude toward society, nature, and life as well as artistic work encouraged as virtuous is to acknowledge and accept the given condition *in toto*, even including their painful, difficult, or disappointing aspects, and to appreciate what is given. (ibid.:383)

Thus the exploitation and control of students by professional *nagauta* musicians, the egotistical displays of wealth and status by amateurs, and the social coercion that enables the continuance of practices seen as unfair, decadent or feudalistic are all a part of the art way to which the individual must submit. Although these unpleasant social realities are not aestheticized by participants in the world of *nagauta*, they are nevertheless tolerated as a natural part of Japanese society and this tolerance is understood as a virtue that contributes to the creation of social harmony.

THE MORAL IMPERATIVE OF PURITY IN *NAGAUTA*

Another key Japanese value that helps in understanding the acceptance of the objectionable and submission to social coercion found in the world of *nagauta* is the concept of purity. Rooted in Shinto practices, the dichotomy of purity/impurity in Japanese life has the kind of moral significance that good/evil has in Western culture. The *uchi*, or inside, of the family home or the social group of the school, as was described in the previous chapter, is made pure through everyday practices that either exclude or treat differently things from the outside that are considered impure. Everyday actions of purification in the home such as removing shoes to exclude the outside "dirt" or the extremely formal treatment of guests have their origins in Shinto ritual acts of purification, such as rinsing one's mouth with water before entering a shrine or being blessed by a priest waving a paper wand. Within the context of Shinto, music and dance are also acts of purification in the ritual performance of *kagura*, intended to purify a sacred place for the appearance of a god (*kami*).[8] Despite its secular origins in kabuki, *nagauta*, like other forms of *hōgaku*, when practiced with the serious commitment of the art way, is also an act of purification that demands submission on the part of the musician.[9]

Purification is accomplished through *kata* both in sound production and social behavior. Performers are expected to execute the music in a refined, elegant and graceful manner, avoiding all extraneous movement or sounds that might destroy the harmony of the group, which would destroy man's harmony with nature. Only by maintaining such surface *kata* in performance will the ritual efficacy of purifying a sacred place be achieved, whether it is the Shinto shrine, the concert stage, or the lesson place. Maintaining the purity of the school requires top-down authoritarian rule from the *sensei* and, as all individuals are aware of the detrimental effects of polluting the group, the bottom-up social coercion by one's own peers. Although some individuals may be critical of markers such as stage names or the exclusivity of *iemoto* organizations, such distinctions can be reassuring in the way they orient the individual in Japanese society, making each person aware of their belonging to a certain group. In this sense, maintaining the purity of the inside is not only an aspect of social control, but provides individuals with a sense of belonging and social well-being.

Furthermore, purity is a moral imperative, particularly in the practice of traditional performing arts such as *nagauta* that requires of individuals a commitment to purity on a personal, psychological level, as described by Lebra:

> Purity refers to the absence of selfish motives which is positively demonstrated by sacrificial self-dedication to others or causes; single-minded endeavors at some project; emotional commitment in oblivion of calculated interest; honesty, sincerity, truthfulness, openness, and so on. In the boundless self, purity is identical with emptiness, non-self, nothingness, an unlimited receptor, or a reflector likened to a spotless mirror. (Lebra 1992:117)

The pure, unselfish, single-minded, emotional commitment required by Japanese performing arts, disciplines that require the practitioner to be an empty, unselfish, unlimited receptor of the tradition, is an ideal perfectly in keeping with Shinto ideas of purity and harmony with nature, as well as Buddhist ideas of inner development towards enlightenment. The ideal of the reduction or elimination of the ego in Japanese arts, and in Asian arts in general, is so well-known in the West (particularly in the martial arts) as to sound clichéd today, but nevertheless it continues to influence artistic practice. Qualities of emptiness, unselfishness, or unlimited receptivity were never spoken about in Kikuoka's school, but were clearly valued by Kikuoka and evident in his teaching techniques, his disciplining of students, and the organization of his school.

While purity as an artistic goal was not commonly discussed by the musicians I observed and interviewed, purity as it related to the social world of *nagauta* was a common concern. The *iemoto* system was seen by some as an established institution that has maintained the purity of *nagauta* in the modern age and by others as an outdated institution whose elevated status and "dirty" business practices polluted the purity of the music. Purity was invoked both as a justification of the social order to maintain the status quo and as a need to reform the social order, as in Kikuoka's goal of pure *nagauta*, which combined social reform with the promotion of concert *nagauta* to gain an appreciation for the pure form of the music itself. But the internalization of the moral imperative of purity perhaps best explains the limits of rebellion against the objectionable in the world of *nagauta*, as it is associated more with the act of restraint than with protest. Kikuoka's complaints of the impurities rampant in a "decadent" *nagauta* society led him to actively seek a more pure *nagauta*, but his efforts toward purifying *nagauta* seemed more dictated by subtle restraint than by radical reform, as he never fully abandoned the appropriate behavior that is crucial to maintaining the purity of the art way of *nagauta*. Following the correct *kata* of appropriate surface behavior is ultimately the best way of insuring purity in *nagauta*.

Based on the social behavior in the world of *nagauta* in which Kikuoka inhabited, and the predominate cultural values that were embedded in those behaviors, the analysis of *nagauta* as a social institution in this chapter demonstrates some of the ways in which the lesson culture of *nagauta* is maintained in the modern world, in spite of its appearance as a fragile, out-of-date, and feudalistic practice. Social behavior in *nagauta* cannot be easily explained by simplistic notions of Japanese tendencies towards forming groups, as argued by consensus theories of Japanese society, nor by claims to cultural uniqueness as advocated by *nihonjinron*. Social control and coercion in Japan has a legacy extending back through the Tokugawa era and similar social mechanisms continue to operate in Japan today, particularly in Tokugawa era performing arts survivals such as *nagauta*. Many such sources of social control affect behavior in *nagauta*, ranging from parents and teachers to peers and social institutions. Social control in *nagauta* may come from the top down, in the sense of direct authoritarian rule by a *sensei* or *iemoto*, or it may involve more subtle control from the bottom up, in the sense of indirect control by ones' peers, which perpetuates this system. Seen from this perspective, *nagauta* is but one subcultural example of the larger social system of Japan, which may be tolerated or justified by deeply embedded values of nature, harmony and purity.

Chapter Four

Nagauta as Cultural Document: The Shaping of *Sukeroku*

THE STORY OF SUKEROKU

Sukeroku is a commoner of old Edo, a townsman who frequents the pleasure quarters of Yoshiwara, who is in love with the most beautiful courtesan in all of Japan, the elegant and graceful Agemaki. One day he arrives in the pleasure quarters to visit his beloved, and he begins to arrogantly boast about his male prowess and popularity with all the prostitutes of the pleasure quarters. Sukeroku boldly insults the samurai Ikyū by offering him a pipe which he clutches between the toes of his bare feet. So begins the kabuki play, *Sukeroku*, which so delighted commoners who frequented the theater during the Edo period that the play has become one of the best-loved in the kabuki repertoire and is today still performed annually at the beginning of the year. During the Edo period, the daring of this commoner who challenges samurai in the pleasure quarters was as shocking as it was liberating for the merchant-class audience members who were forced to comply daily to the appropriate *kata* for people of low social status at the time.

But the *Sukeroku* story has an intriguing twist. His true purpose in coming to the pleasure quarters is not simply to compete with a samurai for the attention of his beloved Agemaki nor is it to challenge the rigidity of the Tokugawa class system. It is revealed that he has the more noble purpose of avenging his father who was killed by someone unknown to Sukeroku, but who wields a well-known sword that Sukeroku will be able to identify on sight and learn the identity of his father's killer. Sukeroku's brash insults are meant to lure his enemy out of hiding. It is also revealed, in a fine example of kabuki's way of interweaving historical and contemporary materials, that Sukeroku is actually not a commoner, but the famous warrior Soga Gorō in disguise who, along with his brother Jūrō, sought revenge on their father's killer who possessed the famous sword Tomokirimaru. It turns out that another character whom

Sukeroku encounters in the play is actually his brother Jūrō in disguise and the samurai whom Sukeroku insults turns out to be the Soga brothers' nemesis, Heike general Heinai Zaemon.

While Edo audiences easily understood these transformations and enjoyed this theatergoers' game of "matching worlds from the present with those of the past" (Brandon 1975:14), Sukeroku's double identity is especially significant in that a commoner is able to challenge the restrictions of the prevailing social code, while also possessing the heroic spirit of a samurai.[1] This double identity makes Sukeroku an ideal model of the Japanese self who has balanced the raw forces of nature with the refined qualities of culture. Sukeroku is a simple, unpretentious, individual whose passionate sensuality and single-minded commitment to justice through violent revenge is softened by pure values of sincerity, honesty and truthfulness. The continuing tradition of performing *Sukeroku*, whether performed with actors on the kabuki stage, or without actors in concert *nagauta* performances and *osaraikai* recitals, testifies to the longevity and richness of this character in Japanese culture. When I asked Kikuoka to name his favorite *nagauta* piece, I expected him to choose one of the famous concert works composed independently of theater, such as *Aki no Irokusa* or *Azuma Hakkei*. Without hesitation he said, "*Sukeroku*."

Sukeroku is clearly one of the great icons of the Japanese ideal self and has had a tremendous influence on Japanese culture through annual kabuki performances. During the Tokugawa era, kabuki played a major role in the life of Edo townspeople that rivals today's popular culture of movies and music. Famous actors of the day were emulated in their stylish manners, their clothing, and their style of speaking, while their images were reproduced on colorful woodblock prints and collected by adoring fans. Although kabuki of this period was clearly a sensationalist, popular form of theater compared to the more classical and refined *nō* drama, it was nevertheless driven by the same principles of the shaping forms of *kata* behavior shared by all the fine arts in Japan. Thus, the plays were guided by an aesthetic of realism, in which even the most ordinary actions, such as preparing food, drinking sake or filling a pipe, were emphasized for the purpose of behavioral instruction:

> What is certain is that kabuki had to some extent a didactic purpose. Part of the search for reality was linked with the desire to instruct the audience in good manners and good conduct, be it how to visit a brothel in elegant style, or how a warrior's wife should crush insolence or defend her young mistress from villainy, or the proper way of exacting revenge. (Dunn 1969:23)

Like the everyday actions aestheticized in tea ceremony and the lesson place of *nagauta*, the *kata* of kabuki was meant to instruct through ideal models of behavior. But kabuki today, like its traditional counterparts, has become marginalized as a remnant of premodern culture and has lost its instructive influence over the masses. The story of Sukeroku that shaped the culture of the townspeople of old Edo seems to have little relevance in today's Japan.

Are the plays and songs of Sukeroku nothing more than historical remnants of Edo culture that are only of interest to a select few aficionados of kabuki and *nagauta* such as Kikuoka? As my ethnographic account of the lesson culture and the coercive forces of *nagauta* suggests, *nagauta* compositions such as *Sukeroku* would seem to function more as neutralized vehicles for the learning process of the individual than as musical settings of legendary stories that are appreciated as art objects. In the context of the lesson culture, the musical compositions of *nagauta* are transparent forms used for the evaluation of student development and for the display of an elegant social order of graceful individuals belonging to a seamless group. In speaking with musicians, the significance and meaning of *nagauta* compositions from another era seemed to be of little concern for amateurs and professionals in Kikuoka's lesson place who were occupied with the musical and social demands of the art of *nagauta*. So significant was the social order of the *nagauta* world that discussions of musical details, such as approaches to vocal phrasing, the difficulty of executing certain *shamisen* passages, or traits of particular melodies, were eclipsed by concerns about the social order as explained in the previous chapter. In trying to find out what was at stake for *nagauta* musicians within the lesson culture of Kikuoka's lesson place, I initially found little relevance in studying the meanings inherent in eighteenth- and nineteenth-century musical compositions that seemed arbitrary in current practice.

Discovering that the ways in which musical practice is constructed as a social order was the central issue for *nagauta* musicians does not mean that analysis of *nagauta* should be limited to social behavior and cultural concepts of nature, harmony or purity. Viewing art as a social institution can include the analysis of musical forms that may have a similar shape and construction as that of the social order. In the case of *nagauta*, it is not particularly fruitful, nor is it an easy task, to maintain a separation between social behavior and musical structure. It is not that appropriate behavior and the correct *kata* within the context of a social group headed by a *sensei* is inseparable from the music, it literally *is* the music. Thus, the discourse among *nagauta* musicians in this ethnography seems to be the inverse of the discourse among musicians at the Western music conservatory in Henry Kingsbury's ethnography (1988). Whereas Kingsbury's research suggests that when musicians talked about "the music" (e.g., the appropriate performance of scores by Beethoven or Mozart), they were actually talking about each other, my research suggests that when *nagauta* musicians talk about each other, they may actually be talking about the music.

In this sense, *nagauta* compositions can themselves be studied in search of the social ordering principles of appropriate behavior and *kata* that exist in musical practice. *Nagauta* should be analyzed not only as a social institution, but also as a cultural document. In an article on Japanese dance, Valentine (1982) takes a similar approach:

> Viewing art as a social institution is often contrasted with an interpretive approach to art as a cultural document: the two alternatives may even be taken to be irreconcilable. Yet… features of dance organization involved in the compartmentalization of dance must be taken into account when attempting to generalize on a performance's social and cultural significance, and such organizational features may themselves function as documents, in that they are both derivative and indicative of the wider social structure. (ibid.:270)

Similarly, features of *nagauta* musical organization and structure must be taken into account when attempting to understand music's social and cultural significance. Performing arts such as Japanese music and dance may exist as social institutions that structure human behavior, but the iconic cultural documents they produce may also contribute to perceptions of what is considered natural — and hence, beyond discourse — in Japanese life. This chapter focuses on *nagauta* as a cultural document: specifically how performance and composition are shaped by the same aesthetics that inform the social institution of *nagauta*. The social order that characterizes the lesson culture of *nagauta* is evident in the seamless visual order of concert performances, the combination of contrasting timbres in the *nagauta* ensemble, the ambiguity of fragmented *nagauta* lyrics, the stereotyping of emotional expression, and in the patterned structure of *nagauta* compositions. A musical analysis of the *nagauta* composition *Sukeroku* reveals how this music symbolically shapes this well-known Japanese icon.

THE SEAMLESS VISUAL ORDER OF CONCERT PERFORMANCE

Performances of concert *nagauta*, like other genres of Japanese *hōgaku*, are presented in a highly standardized way, displaying a visual image of social order that rarely varies in its ritualistic presentation. The staging and placement of musicians in concert performance presents a stately tableau of performers facing the audience in orderly rows similar to the elaborate doll displays of Japan's annual *hinamatsuri* doll festival. Performances invariably take place on a stage dominated by long risers covered with a bright red cloth set up in front of a backdrop of traditional Japanese folding screens. The arrangement of the players in this type of staging is structured according to the hierarchy of performers in the group. *Shamisen* players are seated on the stage-right half of the elevated platform and vocalists are seated on the stage-left half. The players of the *hayashi* instruments (drums and flutes) are seated on the stage floor in front of the elevated platform. The elevation of the *shamisen* players and vocalists is significant in that they are considered to be the most important musical unit in *nagauta*, while the lesser important (at least from a *nagauta* point of view) *hayashi* instruments are seated at the lower level.

At a typical Tōonkai professional concert performance, hierarchy is marked by the seating arrangements with the inside positions of *shamisen* and vocalist reserved for the leaders, often followed in rank order, according to seniority or in the order of a teacher's favored students, as was explained in chapter two in which Kikuoka's top student was seated immediately to his left. Seating order is also pre-determined for *hayashi* musicians with *taiko*, *ōtsuzumi*, *kotsuzumi*, and flute arranged from stage right to stage left respectively. In the case of multiple *kotsuzumi* players, hierarchy may be determined by the senior player sitting to the right of the others. The minutiae of such staging, such as the appropriate types of background folding screens and the precise measurements of the red carpet, are so important that Kikuoka taught a special class at Geidai dedicated to this subject.

The overall effect is that of a static frieze, framed by the proscenium of the stage. The stage curtain typically remains closed until the piece is about to begin, then opens to reveal all players seated in their proper order with no extraneous movement. This manner of presentation also avoids any awkward entrances or exits as all performers sit in *seiza* position, with legs tucked under the hips. This sitting position cuts off leg circulation and can quickly become extremely uncomfortable, even for many Japanese people, after only a few minutes. Rather than allowing the audience to witness the awkward display of players crawling out of their positions after the conclusion of a piece that could last as long as 30 minutes, the curtain closes while all are still seated and, in many cases, while the last notes of the piece are still sounding.

The black kimono, worn by professional male and female performers alike, create uniform anonymity necessary to insure that no one "nail" ever sticks out. In most professional performances, as mentioned previously, mixing of gender is avoided, further enforcing a sense of uniformity. Careful, controlled, and almost completely rigid stage manner is required of all musicians and any extraneous movements are violations of this orderliness. The power of any accidental extraneous movements is heightened in such an orderly atmosphere, sometimes creating a tension that is felt by the audience. One such performance I witnessed, in which a kotsuzumi drummer struggled for several minutes to suppress a cough during a very quiet and dramatic percussion section known as *shishimai* (lion dance), only to end in an awkward coughing fit, was a clear violation of this orderliness. Although one fellow audience member was sympathetic, he criticized the performer for not being prepared for such an incident and having a throat lozenge available. The visual orderliness of *nagauta* performance, like the lesson process, demands a similar physical and mental concentration from the player and further contributes to shaping players to the tradition by conforming musicians to a single, seamless group.

NAGAUTA AS A HARMONY OF UNIQUELY INDIVIDUAL PARTS

In contrast to the seamlessness of the visual presentation of concert performances, the sound of *nagauta* reveals a variety of disparate parts that have been fashioned into a single style yet, in a significant way, leaves some of the "seams" showing. As explained in chapter one, *nagauta* developed within the theatrical genre of kabuki and shares a similar eclecticism of its parts. Just as kabuki absorbed various genres of performing arts that preceded it, such as *nō* drama, *nagauta* also absorbed other types of *shamisen* music, as well as the instruments of *nō*. Many *nagauta* compositions contain traces of older *shamisen* styles, such as *ōzatsumabushi*, *katōbushi*, *gekibushi*, which may be evident in particular phrases or small sections of a piece. With the exception of the powerful *ōzatsumabushi shamisen* patterns, melodic references to older *shamisen* genres and fragments of songs are noticeable only to veteran players and *nagauta* aficionados.

Much more obvious to the untrained ear, however, is the use of the *nō* drums and flute, which have entrances designed to introduce a new section of music by changing the overall character of the sound. Although the *kotsuzumi/ōtsuzumi* pair of drums often play kabuki-derived patterns that match the *shamisen* rhythm, the combination of *taiko* drum and *nōkan* flute play *nō*-derived patterns which are noticeably "out-of-sync" with the *shamisen* phrases. This out-of-sync tension, which Malm refers to as a "sliding doors" effect (Malm 1986:42–43), is not released until the end of a musical movement when all instruments play simultaneous cadences. An even stronger conflict is heard in the pitches of the *nōkan*, a flute which is not tuned to the *shamisen* and thus plays an entirely independent, dissonant melody that is synchronized only with the *taiko* drum. Such a jarring juxtaposition of sounds in *nagauta* allows the *nō hayashi* instrumentation to retain its distinctive sound, conjuring the atmosphere of *nō* while enhancing the drama of the *nagauta* piece. The final climactic movement of *nagauta* pieces typically features all of the instruments playing dense patterns simultaneously, creating a dissonant accumulation of sound. The density of the final passage is also increased by the more frequent use of drum calls (*kakegoe*) shouted by the musicians of the *nō hayashi*, which also have no relation to the vocal melody.

The diverse mix of sounds that constitute the sound of the full *nagauta* ensemble demonstrates the Japanese ideal of "natural" harmony as it occurs musically. Not to be confused with Western functional harmony, which is non-existent in traditional Japanese music, Japanese social harmony (*wa*) brings together sonically conflicting parts with a respect for their musical origins. Although the *nō* percussion and flute unit has been made to conform to the rhythmic structure of *nagauta*, the "natural" sound of *nō* is kept intact. In a similar manner, certain vocal sections of *nagauta* pieces are adapted from earlier *nō* drama, but the vocal part remains clearly in a *nagauta* style, only suggesting its *nō* origins.[2] But the overall "natural" sound is achieved by maintaining the original relationships and sound within each musical unit — *kotsuzumi/ōtsuzumi*, *taiko/nōkan*, and *shamisen*/vocal. This respect for the essential or natural characteristics of the original sound is important in Japanese aesthetics in which a successful work of art should "facilitate the audience's appreciation of the material used and the subject matter depicted" (Saito 1998:551). The resulting heterogeneous sound texture of all these units performing together is historically layered, much like the kabuki play Sukeroku is historically layered with its simultaneous character references from different historical periods.

Such a "harmonic" coexistence of distinctly individual parts in *nagauta* can be understood in reference to Nakane's model of Japanese society as being based on "frame" relationships rather than more Western "attribute" relationships, which is applied to Japanese music by Tokumaru (1991). For example, employees of a university can think of themselves and others around them as having certain attributes (e.g., deans, professors, students, staff employees) or think of themselves as belonging within certain frames (e.g., belonging to a particular department or belonging to the particular university). Whereas musicians in an attribute society see themselves as connected more by the attribute of being a musician than by the frame in which they belong, musicians in a frame society see themselves connected more by the frame of their affiliation group than by any common attributes with other musicians outside their social frame.

The large-scale, progressive musical developments that cut across groups in Western culture over long historical periods is the result of attribute-oriented musicians, while the co-existence of many individual schools with individual styles originating at different points in history and existing in perpetuity in Japan is the result of frame-oriented musicians. Thus, while the West can experience a revival of baroque music, for example, no such revivals exist in Japan, where musical forms such as *gagaku* or *nō* have been perpetuated since their inception by the simultaneous existence of groups over time (Tokumaru 1991:140; also see De Ferranti 2000:1). In the history of *nagauta*, the *nō hayashi* musical unit, bounded by its "frame," was introduced into the "frame" of *nagauta* and, with the creation of some additional rhythmic patterns, was incorporated into a new frame in which the two ensembles currently coexist. But the *hayashi* groups of musicians have always maintained a great degree of autonomy within their own frame, complete with separate performance names for musicians, training schools and social structure. In this way, *hayashi* percussion and *shamisen*/vocal music are able to co-exist within the single frame of *nagauta* by virtue of their separate frames. Furthermore, these associations according to frame also account for the wide range of variation heard in the same *nagauta* composition as performed by different combinations of schools. The performance of any given *nagauta* composition is a compendium of arrangements by vocalists, *shamisen* players, *hayashi* and offstage musicians, each of whom play according to the dictates of their particular school.[3]

THE AMBIGUOUS LYRICAL PATH OF *NAGAUTA*

The foundation of *nagauta* is the song (*uta*), a kind of lyric poetry sung with *shamisen* accompaniment. A survival of the popular kabuki theater of the eighteenth and nineteenth centuries where it is still heard today, *nagauta* lyrics reference the stories and dances depicted on the kabuki stage in their supporting role as musical accompaniment.

However, unlike the text and action of kabuki plays, which often dramatize the value of self-sacrifice of one's personal desires (*honne*) for the fulfillment of one's social obligations (*giri*), and the tragedies of the enforced regimentation of social classes, the lyric poetry as heard in concert *nagauta* provides a much less didactic, non-narrative version of the life and times of Edo. Rather than tell a story, *nagauta* lyrics function more as poetry that captures the mood of the situation with fragmented images of scenery, characters and vague references to any sort of plot. When used as a series of interludes during the course of a kabuki drama, *nagauta* provides indirect lyrical imagery that merely alludes to the story and augments the more direct commentary of the actors. When used as accompaniment to dance pieces, which typically have no commentary by actors, the lyrical imagery of *nagauta* may be represented visually by the dancers. But the most ambiguous setting for *nagauta* lyrics is found in concert performances without dance or theater in which the focus is no longer on the play, but instead on poetic, lyrical imagery that illuminates the complexity of human feelings as it is brought to life by the music.

Concert *nagauta*, shorn of the didactic drama of kabuki, conveys beauty and drama in the indirect and subtle way of Japanese *waka* and *haiku* poetry in which expressions of beauty and sadness are contained in concrete imagery. Unlike most other forms of *shamisen* music used in kabuki, which are classified as narrative genres (*katarimono*), *nagauta* is classified as a lyric genre (*utamono*), resembling Japanese lyric poetry. Lacking any clear narrative, *nagauta* lyric verse presents images of nature and the newly developing urban life in the city of Edo as metaphors for mood or character, typically with an ambiguity of subject and without direct comment from an author-narrator. Similar to *waka* poetry, these images are strung together in brief stanzas that employ various combinations of lines consisting of 5 and 7 syllables. However, unlike the short forms of Japanese poetry, the verses of a complete *nagauta* piece as presented in its concert version are strung together into an extended song that, although more fragmentary than thematic, allows for a kind of metaphorical development to take place.

Most *nagauta* lyrics follow a general six-part form based on kabuki dance form that varies depending on the piece (Malm 1963:34–36). The opening section (*oki*) sets the scene with an image of nature that establishes the tone for the piece, for example a haunted depiction of nature to indicate a ghost story. The second section (*michiyuki*), which typically introduces a character (the actor) into the lyrics, continues to avoid any kind of narrative, thus rendering the character as simply another element in a landscape of imagery. The *nagauta* piece unfolds through the next two sections (*kudoki* and *taikoji*) as a series of scenes involving images of nature, the city or personages, in which a plot never actually develops. The imagery, however, becomes gradually more charged, such as in love scenes suggesting sexuality or fight scenes suggesting violence. The fifth section (*chirashi*) is the climax of the composition and typically involves a change to more pious imagery that may invoke Japanese gods or the emperor, often serving as a prayer for good fortune. The sixth section (*dangire*) is the shortest, usually only a repeat of the last line of the previous section, which serves as a kind of exclamation point providing closure in the work, emphasizing the religious goal of the lyrical path of *nagauta*. As a whole these sections constitute a work that take the listener on a path that typically ends in a sanctified, religious atmosphere. What illuminates these poetic fragments, delineates and develops these sections, and provides the shape of this spiritual path are the stereotyped patterns of vocal and *shamisen* melody.

NAGAUTA SONGS AS *KATA*: STEREOTYPED PATTERNS AND THE SHAPE OF EMOTION

Analyzing the musical structure of *nagauta* compositions reveals a use of musical *kata* similar to the use of physical *kata* in the social domain. Like the collection of stereotyped patterns of behavior that individuals rely on in various social situations of music-making, the building blocks for *nagauta* compositions are also a set of stereotyped musical patterns. *Nagauta* compositions are almost entirely through-composed and do not develop thematically in the manner of Western classical music compositions. Instead, *nagauta* is based on various combinations of four kinds of melodic patterns: 1) melodies absorbed from many defunct *shamisen* genres; 2) *ōzatsuma* patterns (a subset of the first category) that consist of 48 stereotyped phrases used for heightened speech sections; 3) repertoire-wide leitmotives that signify special moods, places or people; and 4) standard melodic procedures without any known historical connection. It is this last category that makes up the majority of *nagauta* compositions (Malm 1963:213–214).[4] The existence of such stereotypical patterns in *nagauta* has a practical purpose in that it aids in the memorization of lengthy, through-composed *nagauta* pieces.[5]

The stereotyped patterns of *shamisen* music clearly mark the six-part kabuki form of *nagauta* lyric poetry and aid the listener in identifying the sectional development of the piece. The endings of sections are characterized by points of repose in which drum patterns resolve and pitches stabilize around a pitch center. This bears a similarity to classical Japanese dance (*nihon buyō*) with its characteristic stopped moments in which the dancer freezes in a pose. Endings of sections follow stereotypical patterns so that changes to new sections are easily recognizable by listeners. The endings of *nagauta* pieces follow such stereotypical patterns so consistently that members of the audience begin to applaud and the stage curtain begins to close before the piece is completely finished.

Although a familiarity with the narrative basis of a given *nagauta* piece may enhance a listener's appreciation of the song, no prior knowledge of the story is needed to appreciate *nagauta*'s programmatic, musical evocation of beautiful, poetic imagery. The series of lyric images strung together in a *nagauta* piece makes the music highly suitable for accompanying Japanese dance, described by Valentine as an art of momentary poses strung together by movements (Valentine 1998:267). Like Japanese dance, an appreciation of *nagauta* is not dependent on the listener's ability to follow a story, only the moment-to-moment appreciation of fleeting, poetic images. With only the thinnest thread of narrative to follow, the listener is left with fragments of poetic images that are meant to stimulate the senses and the emotions.

The fragmented, lyric nature of *nagauta* produces an ambiguity in the music that contributes to its emotional affect. In the absence of an easy-to-follow narrative, the focus of listening is instead on brief poetic phrases that are given a highly dramatic and emotional treatment by the vocalist. In Kikuoka's school, learning how to sing is a matter of learning the correct *kata* — execution of the precise vocal phrasing that will make the lyric poetry come to life. According to Kikuoka, if the vocals are properly done, the sights, sounds and smells of the scenery will be felt, the characters will come to life, and the audience will be able to feel the emotions expressed at certain critical moments of the piece. In my lessons, it was particularly those moments of emotional expression that Kikuoka spent a great deal of time teaching me. Kikuoka's opinion was that these moments were the most critical in a *nagauta* song and they were also the most difficult to learn because the details of their expression were not indicated in the notation and could only be learned directly from a teacher.

Learning from Kikuoka how to sing properly involved knowing which words receive special emphasis through the use of slight microtonal pitch movement up or down, special embellishments such as glissando or grace notes, timbral modification of the voice, and other subtle vocal techniques not indicated in the notation.[6] These vocal techniques were not improvised and were very specifically determined in lessons given by Kikuoka, who had learned these details from his teachers. In Kikuoka's school, there was an appropriate *kata* for the emotional words or phrases in any given *nagauta* song and it is these finer points of singing that distinguish the singing in Kikuoka's school from the many other *nagauta* musical guilds in Japan. Just as in daily life, in which there may be an appropriate *kata* for dealing with a particular situation, *nagauta* consists of appropriate *kata* for particular phrases. The presence of such precisely determined *kata* serves as a stabilizing force in the music, protecting it from being overdone by any expressiveness on the part of the vocalist. Although expression of emotion is valued in *nagauta,* it is a highly codified expression of emotion through *kata* that maintains a respect for the subject matter depicted, which is an important aesthetic quality in Japanese classical arts.

Kikuoka's more traditional approach can be contrasted with a more modern form of music that operates according to similar principles. Yano's (2002) study of *enka* popular music details how this form is structured according to prescribed, predetermined patterns, but *kata* in this music serves as a structural foundation that enables the emotional expression of the individual. The ideal of singing *enka* music, according to Yano, is for the singer to somehow transcend the *kata* upon which the song and its performance practice is based and express one's own individuality or originality (*kosei*). Such spectacular displays of emotion should ideally inspire tears in the audience who are made to feel *natsukashii* (sentimental) and the actual tears of the singer become a key type of *kata* to achieve this effect (ibid.:120–121). Such displays of actual tears on stage by a singer are meant to be seen as authentic expressions of emotion as described by Yano:

> This ultimate embodiment of emotion becomes proof of her merit, involvement, and vulnerability. As she reaches within, to a personal reservoir of pain and tears, she also reaches out to tap that common reservoir within members of the audience. Tears, and the suffering they display, become an irresistible link between singer and audience. (ibid.:121)

Such displays of raw emotion have no place in a classical art such as *nagauta*. Emotion in *nagauta* remains in its codified state and any emotional feelings on the part of audience members is a private experience, not a public spectacle. Such emotional distancing may account for *nagauta*'s lack of a broad appeal in a modern Japan in which *enka*, even though identified with middle-aged and older generations, is still immensely popular. As a classical art-way of *hōgaku*, *nagauta* demands that a disciplined, cool demeanor be maintained at all times and followers of the art generally understand this aesthetic value of the smooth surface. When discussing favorite *nagauta* singers in the Tōonkai group with one of Kikuoka's students, I commented that I enjoyed one particular singer because of his "*kosei*," or individual style. Her response was that this singer exaggerated his singing and moved too much for *nagauta*. I did get to know one amateur student who favored the display of emotion in *nagauta*, but she was not a member of Kikuoka's school. She told me that because she truly enjoyed singing she was not afraid to show this to the audience. In the one performance of hers that I attended, she maintained the appropriate *seiza* posture without extraneous movement, yet she smiled contentedly the entire time that she sang, which is an unusual site in concert *nagauta*. Not surprisingly, her *sensei* was not in attendance at that particular concert.

Nagauta teachers disapprove of displays of raw emotion because the works of *nagauta* are vehicles for conveying aesthetic emotion, conceived of as existing separately from ordinary life, and thus demands that the individual restrain from any sort of self-expression. According to Ueda:

> Emotions in the work of art are impersonal and unhuman; they are, in fact, not emotions but atmospheres and moods. Thus Bashō maintains that grief in actual life must turn into *sabi* in the poem. The whole point of tea ceremony is to create an artificial atmosphere where many of the life-feelings are sublimated. Zeami's highest aim in art, sublimity, exists in a sphere beyond the reach of ordinary life... For the medievalists, catharsis is not simply the letting out of emotions; it is rather a qualitative transformation of them. Thus in Zeami's aesthetics agonizing grief turns into serene sublimity, and in Bashō's it changes into unhuman *sabi*, as life is transformed into a work of art. (Ueda 1967:220)

As *nagauta* compositions and the lessons by which they are taught are designed according to these traditional aesthetics, the student is meant to be transformed through submission to these aesthetic emotions; from a raw, unrefined state of emotion into an "atmosphere" or "mood" of a smooth, calm state of body and mind. Self-transformation can only come about if the student does not impose the self on the material given, whether it is a song, a school of *nagauta*, a tea room, a Shinto shrine, a factory workplace or any other setting of Japanese culture.

NAGAUTA COMPOSITION: *SUKEROKU* AS AN ANALOG TO REFINEMENT OF THE INDIVIDUAL

On close analysis, the *nagauta* composition *Sukeroku* appears as both prescriptive of the process by which one learns the proper formulaic, stereotyped patterns of *kata* from one's *sensei* and descriptive of the "atmosphere" of aesthetic emotion as described by Ueda. As a typical *nagauta* composition, *Sukeroku* is made up of stereotyped patterns of standard vocal and *shamisen* phrases that Kikuoka teaches to students as precise forms of aesthetic emotion. While the student submits to the expression of this emotion as part of the shaping process of *nagauta* lessons, these standardized patterns "paint" the image of this dramatic legend of old Edo and shapes his character as well. As a work of concert *nagauta*, the short fragments of lyric imagery, which are ordinarily presented in short sections to support the kabuki play of the same name, are presented as a single, continuous piece. Lacking any storyline, the fragmented, lyrical imagery as rendered by the voice and *shamisen* makes this piece not a story, but a character study of the image, thoughts, actions and emotions of Sukeroku set in the pleasure quarters of Yoshiwara where he searches for his father's killer. More than just describe Sukeroku, the vocal and *shamisen* lines work together to depict a social transformation of this character from a violent, unruly and sexual character, into a peaceful, refined and elegant human being.

The lyrics to Sukeroku were written by Sakurada Jisuke III circa 1832 as part of the play "Sukeroku Yukari no Edo Zakura," which was first performed in March 1832. The first version of the play used a style of *shamisen* music known as *handayubushi*, but in 1839 a new version of the poem was set to *nagauta* music by Kineya Rokuzaemon X, one of the most well-known composers of the *nagauta* repertoire. Two versions of music for Sukeroku survive in kabuki today, one in *nagauta* style and another in *katōbushi* style. Depending on the performers of the play, one of these styles is employed for the annual performance of *Sukeroku* at the Kabukiza Theater in Tokyo's Ginza district, performed at the beginning of the season in January or February.

The lyrics of the *nagauta* piece are as follows:

<table>
<tr><td>Saki nioo sakura to hito ni yoi no kuchi
yabo wa momarete sui to naru
koko o ukiyo no Nakanocho
koi ni kogarete Sukeroku ga</td><td>The fragrant blooming of cherry blossoms
among the early evening crowds,
the crude Sukeroku becomes refined
here in Nakanocho, longing for his love.</td></tr>
<tr><td>Kasa sashite nure ni
kuruwa no yoru no ame
misesugagaki ni koe sōru
kane wa Ueno ka Asakusa ni
so no namo datena Hanakawado</td><td>With his umbrella, soaking wet,
he comes on a rainy night,
as voices from the windows and the sound of
temple bells in Ueno and Asakusa call to this
sophisticated man from Hanakawado.</td></tr>
<tr><td>Kono hachimaki no
murasaki wa yukarizo
kakaru fujinami no aroute
chiyo no iromasaru
matsu no hakesaki sukibitai
tsutsumi hachō
Emonzaka kayoi naretaru
nuribanao hitotsu inrō
hitotsumae
futaemawari no kumono obi
sashita shakuhachi samezaya wa
kore gozonji no detachibae</td><td>This purple bandana,
full of meaning,
washed by waves of purple,
has reigned superior for many generations.
With pine brush hair and shaved forehead,
he passes slopes and towns,
coming and going through Emonzaka.
Lacquer shoes and tobacco case,
kimono and undergarment together
with an obi of clouds wrapped twice around
and a shakuhachi tucked into it —
everyone knows his style.</td></tr>
<tr><td>Sekuna sekyaruna
sayoe ukiyowana kuruma
meguru tsukihi ga entonaru

meguru tsukihi ga entonaru</td><td>Do not hurry,
because life is a wheel,
as time passes the opportunity will
come to you,
as time passes the opportunity will
come to you.</td></tr>
</table>

Koi no yozakura	Night of love and cherry blossoms,
uwaki de kayō	he goes to his love affair.
mabu no natori no tōrimono	This lover's name is well known.
kenkajikakeya	He starts fights,
irojikake	uses sex to his advantage,
chikarazukunara	uses force and special techniques —
nani tekuda nara	such personal style.
ryūgi ryūgi de	He meets them face-to-face
mukōzura	without letting them pass through the gate
tada wa tōsanu ōmon o	and challenges them to crawl
mata kuguru to wa	through his legs, risking his life.
inochigake	
Dotebushi	To order a man to stop singing
yameyo amigasa o	Dotebushi,
totte nageru wa	throw away his straw hat,
kyoku ga nai	and dispose of him
kekon de mishō yakatabune	is not as interesting as
korya mata nan no kota	ramming a riverboat up his nose,
Edo no hana	what the hell… ?
Fuji to Tsukuba no yama ai no	This flower of Edo,
sodenari yukashi	between the mountains of Fuji and Tsukuba
kimi yukashi	in marvelous kimono sleeves,
shinzo inochi o Agemaki	you are extraordinary,
no kore Sukeroku ga maewatari	so devoted to Agemaki.
	Here comes Sukeroku.
Fuzei narikeru shidai nari.	And that is how it all came to pass.

Each stanza of the lyrics addresses a particular theme in this character portrait and the music follows this structure with accompaniment and interlude passages. After a brief, up-tempo instrumental introduction, the first stanza sets the scene and introduces the main character. This is followed by another up-tempo musical interlude leading to the next stanza depicting the character's experience of the sights and sounds of the pleasure quarters. A lengthy stanza follows which consists entirely of a detailed description of the character. After this character description of the hero, the mood of the piece shifts as the *shamisen* changes to a different tuning and the lyrics express a philosophical statement about life. The next two stanzas describe Sukeroku's actions, which are violent and sexual, as the music increases in density with the addition of a second *shamisen* part. The last five lines of the next to last stanza change suddenly from the violence of Sukeroku to an appreciation of the more refined qualities of his character, such as his love for the beautiful Agemaki.[7] The music also follows this change by slowing down the tempo and allowing for expressive passages of free meter vocal lines. The coda to this piece is a standard single line ending in *nagauta* which brings a feeling of closure to the piece.

PITCH CENTERS AND VOCAL PHRASING IN THE OPENING SECTION OF *SUKEROKU*

One of the most important features of *nagauta* melodic construction is the movement towards and away from pitch centers (see Malm 1986, 1978, and 1963). *Nagauta* melody typically consists of two pitch centers, a central pitch that corresponds to the center string of the *shamisen* and a secondary pitch that corresponds to the lowest string of the *shamisen* either a perfect fourth or a perfect fifth lower in pitch. The exact pitches are not absolute and vary with each performance, typically determined by the most suitable range for the vocalist. The instrumental opening of *Sukeroku* (measures 1–43) demonstrates this movement with pitch center B, announced at the beginning, shifting gradually towards an emphasis on pitch center E, eventually resolving with a double stop of E and B at the end of this section [see Appendix A for a complete transcription of the vocal and lead *shamisen* music of *Sukeroku*, based on Kikuoka's vocal and *shamisen* performance of the piece]. With the opening lyric section (measures 43–104) the scenery and character of Sukeroku are introduced as the vocal part and *shamisen* move between pitch centers. The opening line invoking the smell of fragrant blooming flowers is based on the two pitch centers B and E. Around these pitch centers is the melodic movement of leading tones one whole step below and one half step above these pitch centers, typical of *nagauta* and other styles of traditional Japanese music. For example, the vocal opening on A scoops up to B, followed by a similar scoop up from D to E at the end of the phrase.

The next vocal phrase (mm 52–65) continues to set the scene by describing the crowds of people typically seen gathering on a spring evening to view the blooming cherry blossoms of spring. The word "*sakura*" ("cherry blossom") is highlighted with the use of F-sharp and the rest of this phrase continues to work with the pitch centers and their upper and lower neighbors, ending on the main pitch center E. Tension is introduced both lyrically and melodically in the following phrase (mm 66–80) by working away from the pitch centers. Vulgarity is introduced with the word "*yabo*" ("crude") and melodic tension is created by beginning the first syllable on A and, instead of resolving up to B as one might expect, dropping to G on the second syllable. This tension is further increased on the next word "*sui*" ("taste or refined") which, according to Kikuoka, should be sung slightly sharp, almost as an A-sharp, to create a dissonance against the A of the *shamisen*. The phrase "*tonaru*" climbs briefly up to pitch center E, but drops back down to A with a tumbling vibrato embellishment. This single phrase, sounding tonally unstable by comparison to previous phrases, creates a tension between vulgarity and refinement, ending on an unresolved A.

The next phrase (mm 82–94) further describes the scene with the simple description of "*koko o ukiyo no Nakanochō*" ("here in Nakanochō"), which ends on a low B, the lowest pitch on the *shamisen*. This sets up a contrast with the beginning of the following phrase (mm 94–100) which features the highest pitches of this section. The word "*koi*" ("love") begins on a high G and the pitches of G-E-F-sharp-E in the vocal line contrast with a *shamisen* line of E-F-sharp-G-E creating an effect that is not so much dissonant as it is bright and outstanding. The phrase ends with the word "*kogarete*" ("fire, passion") which brings the melody back down to the pitch center E. The section ends with the final phrase (mm 101–104) of "*Sukeroku ga*," an introduction of the character who is the subject of the composition, rendered in a manner similar to this section's opening vocal phrase. The name of the character is given a dramatic emphasis with an extended, free-meter, vocal melisma on the main pitch centers of E and B, providing a typically strong kind of closure to this opening section. The opening section comes to a dramatic finish exactly at the point at which the character is introduced.

The entire opening section of this piece (mm 1–104) demonstrates how *nagauta* operates thematically. After a lively *shamisen* introduction exploring a wide range of pitches and wide intervals, a slow vocal section begins to paint pleasant scenery for the listener. Beginning and ending around the main pitches of B and E, the vocal section makes a departure midway through, introducing an unstable melodic line as the lyrics turn from merely descriptive to conceptual. The notion of a crude person is introduced with pitches away from the pitch centers. The word "love," indicating a way towards refinement, is introduced at the highest pitch level, followed by a return to the main pitch center and an introduction of the main character, setting the stage for the rest of the piece. The use of movement towards and away from pitch centers, coupled with subtle vocal techniques contrasting with the *shamisen* part, work together to word-paint a lyric depiction of an important process in Japanese art and Japanese society: the transformation from raw, unrefined and impure, to a state of refinement and purity. The key idea of refinement suggested in the opening passage of Sukeroku is developed in greater detail using similar techniques throughout the entire piece. The opening section functions very much like traditional Japanese poetry in its suggestive brevity, and is musically set off from the rest of the piece by a second and final instrumental interlude (mm 105–124). Following this instrumental, the character of Sukeroku is further developed for the remainder of the piece, uninterrupted by instrumental breaks.

SEX, VIOLENCE, AND REFINEMENT IN *SUKEROKU*

The next section (mm 125–245) is still in a scene-setting mode, describing Sukeroku as he experiences the sights, sounds and feeling of the pleasure quarters of Yoshiwara. In this section, the sexual nature of Sukeroku is introduced and sexual tension is created using similar techniques of pitch movement and vocal phrasing typical of *nagauta*. The sexual references are indirect and ambiguous through the common Japanese poetic technique of *kakekotoba* ("pivot words" conveying multiple meanings) employed by the lyricist. The music helps to develop the sensual atmosphere of the words through the use of sparse *shamisen* accompaniment in a slow tempo, leaving room for melismatic vocal passages on certain sexually charged words. As Sukeroku stands with his umbrella, soaked by the rain, the words "*nure ni*" ("wet") appear and, as in many *nagauta* pieces, the metaphor suggests the multiple meanings of being soaked from the rain, teary-eyed with sadness, and aroused by sex. Understandably, a word as charged with sensuality as "*nure*" receives a dramatic vocal dip down and up an octave (mm 135–142).

Another sexually suggestive vocal phrase that Kikuoka greatly emphasized was "*misesugagaki*," a word rich in meaning. *Misesugagaki* refers to the cross-hatched wooden window through which men peered to view prostitutes on display in the pleasure district of Yoshiwara. Misesugagaki is also the name of a *shamisen* pattern meant to be suggestive of prostitutes, many of whom were *shamisen* players during Edo. The poetry suggests that Sukeroku is hearing the sound of the prostitutes playing their *shamisen*, although the *misesugagaki* pattern is not played in this phrase. What is noticeable musically is how the word *misesugagaki* is phrased. Kikuoka spent a great deal of time with me on this one extended word (mm 166–178) that features dips down to indeterminate pitches (measure 169; measure 172), an unusual breath cut in the middle of the word (measure 173), and a leaping, arc-shaped phrase near the end, all of which seems to suggest the shortness of breath from sexual excitement. Similar sexual innuendoes can be found in other *nagauta* pieces such as *Azuma Hakkei* and *Yoshiwara Suzume*.

As the composition progresses the sexual nature of Sukeroku develops further, as well as the violence of Sukeroku's actions. After a lengthy description of all the details of Sukeroku's costume (mm 246–373), the mood changes with a tuning change in the *shamisen* from *honchōshi* (B-E-B) to *sansagari* (B-E-A) that occurs at about the halfway point of the entire piece. This section (mm 374–456) begins lyrically with some philosophical advice, perhaps addressed to Sukeroku and thus, to the audience as well, about the virtue of having patience in one's life and accepting one's fate. The message is that life is like a wheel and whatever is coming to you will eventually come around. This message is represented musically by melismatic vocal phrases that seem to meander as if it were some kind of spinning wheel.

The next section (beginning at measure 458) returns to sexual references and gradually begins to develop the violent, yet courageous, side of Sukeroku. Musically, the mood changes here with an increase in tempo and the addition of a second *shamisen* part based on the famous koto composition *Rokudan* (not included in this transcription) creating a denser, busier musical texture. In this section Sukeroku's sexuality takes on a less innocent character than earlier in the piece. Here he is described as intentionally using sex in a manipulative and forceful way to start fights with the intention of finding his father's killer. As the lyrics explain how Sukeroku also uses crass insults to start fights, his vulgarity is musically illustrated with subtle changes in vocal timbre. The vocal phrases of Sukeroku's aggressive refusal to let men pass ("*tada wa to sanu omon o*") without experiencing the insult of having to crawl through his legs ("*mata kuguru to wa*") are to be delivered with a harsher vocal timbre. The beginning of the phrase "*tada wa to*" is to be sung in a low-pitched, masculine growl (mm 553–555).

Sukeroku's threats become more violent in the lyrics in which he confronts a man who strolls through the pleasure quarters singing a popular song known as *dotebushi*, and knocks off his hat as an insult. The musical phrases of this section once again employ melodic tension around pitch centers. "*Dotebushi yameyo amigasa o*" emphasizes the half-step upper leading tone F without resolving to E, followed by "*totte nageru wa kyo ga nai*" which is sung in a rough, speech-like tone emphasizing B-flat. The flatting of the pitch center B is commonly used in *nagauta* compositions to emphasize peculiar word passages such as this one (Malm 1978:102). The melodic tension created here also heightens the dramatic conflict depicted in the lyrics of this passage. This entire section of sexuality and aggression comes to a resolution in measures 633–643 with a double-stop on the *shamisen* of pitch centers E and B followed by the vocal phrase describing Sukeroku as "*Edo no hana*" ("flower of Edo") delivered in a softer, delicate voice, and finally coming to rest on pitch center B.

The final section of the piece (mm 644–695) redeems Sukeroku from this crude display of violence. The lyrics praise Sukeroku for his devotion to his lover, Agemaki, which leads to his ultimate refinement. Three passages in particular are dramatically highlighted in this section with highly melismatic vocal phrases. An expression of praise, "*kimi yukashi*" (measure 665) is quietly intoned as the *shamisen* pauses, then builds an accelerating repetition of pitch center B. This is immediately followed by "*shinzō*" ("devotion") (measure 666) in which the *shamisen* drops out completely for the vocalist to sing each syllable in a free meter, separated by a breath cut, with the syllable "*-zō*" finishing with a delicately voiced high register arc-shaped phrase. The final vocal highlight is found in the word "Agemaki," the first two syllables of which are also melismatically drawn out during a pause in the *shamisen* accompaniment (mm 674–676). With the next to the last line "*… no kore Sukeroku ga mae watari*" ("here comes Sukeroku") the fully developed character has finally fully arrived at the end of the piece. The work ends in typical *nagauta* fashion with a relatively unimportant tag line ("and that is how it all came to pass") sung with a standard *shamisen* ending known as *dangire*.

The musical and lyrical development of the piece *Sukeroku* reveals a symbolic process of purification that also occurs in other *nagauta* pieces that take place in the city of Edo during the Tokugawa period (*Azuma Hakkei, Suehirogari, Yoshiwara Suzume* to name just a few). The purity of a scene-setting opening, usually an image of nature, is followed by the introduction of a character who then engages in some type of impure action, such as violence, sex or drunken revelry. The character is typically redeemed in the final section of the piece, which restores purity by invoking the emperor or a sacred place or spirit. Many *nagauta* pieces make this kind of lyrical journey into the sensual, at time almost lurid, floating world of the pleasure quarters of Edo, and end up as solemn prayers for prosperity or long life. The *nagauta* composition *Sukeroku* is just one such model of the spiritual path of *nagauta*, a path that begins in the profane space of the pleasure quarters, but leads to the spiritual goal of being shaped by the forms of the art.

The model character transformation of Sukeroku in *nagauta* presents a poetic example of a key aesthetic value of the Tokugawa era known as '*iki*' (refinement), a word that describes the ideal man of "taste" (*sui*) and "polish" (*tsu*) who is able "to comport oneself properly in the geisha quarters by dealing objectively with human emotions" (Heine 1991:169). Although the everyday use of the word *iki* may have been short-lived during the Tokugawa era (Nakano 1989:126) this Japanese notion of refinement in the face of the impurity of the pleasures quarters was further "refined" into a philosophical theory by twentieth-century philosopher Kuki Shūzō, as a spiritual process that unites mind and body:

> According to Kuki, *iki* must find continuous expression through 'physical statements' such as speech, posture, gesture, look, hairdo, and attire. *Iki* is composed of both body and spirit. Accordingly, *iki* should never be reduced simply to a 'phenomenon of consciousness.' It always requires a bodily expression. (Tanaka 2001:337)

As a philosophy that explicates a way of being for Japanese people, the ideal of *iki* as developed by Kuki was formulated into a kind of self-discipline in which one's emotions and desires are kept under control by recourse to the way of the warrior (*bushidō*) and the practice of Buddhist renunciation. Although the word is rarely used today, and seldom used in the present world of *nagauta*, the ideal of *iki*, as it developed from Tokugawa to the present, and continues to be manifested in works such as Sukeroku, is an ideal of the appropriate behavior of personal, emotional refinement that illuminates the shaping process of *nagauta*.

CONCLUSION

This chapter has shown how the shaping force of Japanese society as found in the social institution of *nagauta* is also manifested in the very structure of *nagauta*: from the musical components of its ensemble, to its concert staging, to the structure of musical compositions and the techniques employed to reproduce these compositions in performance. Examining the composition and performance of *Sukeroku,* a cultural document of *nagauta,* reveals a musical analog to the social institution of *nagauta.* At a purely interpretive level of symbolic analogy, the character Sukeroku is transformed from a raw, unruly, sexual and violent individual into a proper human being by the musical and lyrical techniques of an art form that also transforms its practitioners into appropriately behaving members of a social group. Just as the correct performance of *nagauta* as passed on from the *sensei* shapes the student of *nagauta,* it also poetically shapes the character of Sukeroku.

The composition and performance of *Sukeroku* also shows how *nagauta* music enhances the dramatic and emotional power of lyric poetry through stereotyped, predetermined musical phrases. These musical phrases operate as *kata,* the Japanese practice of predetermined, stereotyped patterns of behavior appropriate to a certain situation or artistic practice. The musical *kata* in *nagauta* compositions consist of stereotypical *shamisen* and vocal patterns that move melodically around tonal centers to create melodic tension. This tonal movement of *nagauta* works together with vocal techniques of subtle manipulations of timbre, microtones, and phrasing that are meant to express moments of emotional power of the music and highlight significant words in the text.

That these special techniques can only be learned through direct and careful imitation of the performance of one's teacher is an example of how emotional affect is controlled in traditional Japanese music. The emotional affect of *nagauta* music is not located in the raw emotional expression of the individual musician, but in the refined and proper execution of *kata* by individuals who have become shaped by the tradition. Although musical *kata* controls the manner of individual expression in the art of *nagauta,* such control should not be viewed negatively, but as a way of maintaining the aesthetic emotion that creates the atmosphere of beauty in this art form. The subtlety of expression of sexuality and violence in Sukeroku suggests that *kata* functions aesthetically as a safe and controlled way to express such powerful emotions without causing offense or polluting the purity of an art form in which grace and elegance are of the highest value.

Chapter Five

The Shape of *Nagauta* in the Twentieth Century: Two Compositions by Kikuoka

As was suggested in the previous chapter about *nagauta* composition, the stereotyped patterns that constitute *nagauta* compositions are not limitations of the art, but model forms that allow for the reproduction of elegance, grace and purity by singers, musicians and composers. As a musician who followed this *kata* of *nagauta*, Kikuoka was clearly a traditionalistic conservative of Japanese music, in spite of his progressive efforts at reforming *nagauta* social organization. Despite his challenge to the status quo of *iemoto*, Kikuoka's final goal was always to achieve purity, an ultimate value in Japanese art and society. In his own compositions, Kikuoka was a purist of *nagauta*. Although his compositions departed from typical *nagauta* enough to be recognized as twentieth-century works, Kikuoka's compositional choices were entirely motivated by the stereotypical forms of the tradition he inherited. While some of his works extensively feature modern techniques, Kikuoka never strayed from the appropriate *kata* of *nagauta* composition and was able to maintain the grace, elegance and purity essential to the music. This chapter shows how Kikuoka created within the prescribed boundaries of *nagauta* tradition by examining two works, one that stays fairly close to tradition, and another that incorporates modern techniques that are unconventional by *nagauta* standards. Examination of Kikuoka's compositions and his personal philosophy behind *nagauta* reveals an individual composer who simultaneously shaped, and was shaped by, the musical tradition of *nagauta*.

APPROACH TO MODERN COMPOSITION: THE IMPORTANCE OF "TRANSLATING THE PAST"

At the base of Kikuoka's conservative approach to *nagauta* was his self-perception, based on his musical lineage, in which he saw himself as an inheritor of a tradition that must be preserved in the modern world, yet must be reformed for the sake of its future survival. But for Kikuoka, the act of playing and composing *nagauta* music in the twentieth century was neither the rote repetition of music from the past, nor was it a revolution to reconfigure the structural properties of the music. Kikuoka claimed that his job was to "translate the past" into the present. This entailed as complete an understanding of the repertoire, techniques and form of *nagauta* as possible, which allowed him to "think like" the great composers and players of *nagauta* from the past, such as Kineya Rokuzaemon X, composer of *Sukeroku* and numerous other famous compositions.

Kikuoka's notion of translating the past into the present was his own way of confronting the quandary that confronts any composer striving to create a new work within a style as well-established and narrowly determined as *nagauta*. Unlike other *hōgaku* genres, such as those featuring *koto* and *shakuhachi*, which have a significant number of twentieth-century compositions in modern idioms and currently living artists dedicated to the creation of modern works, *nagauta shamisen* by comparison remains locked in the Edo period. The conventions of *nagauta*, the stereotyped patterns of *shamisen* passages and vocal phrasing, seem to function as a force of resistance against change. Malm described the limitations inherent in composing *nagauta* in the present with a grim assessment of the situation:

> The great problem that *nagauta* composers face today is how to separate the essentials of their music from the hackneyed elements and create a new music exploiting fresh ideas set within the matrix of these essentials.... At present there is no indication that anyone is deeply aware enough of the problem to struggle with it. Modern *nagauta* tend to be a mixture of traditional techniques and generally ineffectual imitations of the Western orchestral sound ideal. (Malm 1963:218–219)

Based on my interviews and observations, Malm's general dissatisfaction with modern *nagauta* was shared by many performers and listeners as well. Responses to questions about new *nagauta* performed in Tōonkai concerts during 1997–1998 ranged from complete lack of interest in any new compositions to complaints about specific compositions sounding "strange" or "unpleasant" in their departures from convention. As one listener put it, "It's not *nagauta* at all."

But the state of new *nagauta* in Japan is perhaps most revealing by looking at the Tōonkai concerts themselves. Ironically, part of Tōonkai's founding mission was to create and perform new works for *nagauta*. Although this was an important aspect of their concert programs during the 1960s, during the late 1990s, Tōonkai concerts had become much more conservative in choice of repertoire. The Tōonkai recitals that typically occur four times a year tended to follow a standard format of six or seven pieces, in which a well-known traditional piece would open the concert, followed by a new composition in the second slot on the program. The remainder of the pieces would be chosen from the standard repertoire of nineteenth-century pieces with a full-length, full ensemble work closing the performance. In interviews, Kikuoka described to me the formula for these concerts based on ways of maintaining audience interest, such as an "exciting opening piece," "a piece before intermission that entices the audience to stay," and "closing with a classic piece." In its number two slot in the Tōonkai concert programs, new compositions seemed to be treated more as oddities or "throw-away pieces" (*suteban*) than featured works. In this context the presence of new compositions seemed to be an obligatory act as part of the *kata* of contemporary Tōonkai performance.

In some cases, musicians expressed dissatisfaction with new *nagauta* not out of ambivalence, but out of a desire to hear something that truly sounded new. One professional Tōonkai performer I spoke with was dissatisfied with the state of new *nagauta* because most works failed to sufficiently break away from the past and as a result sounded all alike. This player was proactive, however, and composed a new composition of her own which stretched the conventional boundaries of *nagauta* with an interesting result. Her radical departure from convention was her specification that the vocal part should be sung in the vocal style of a Western soprano instead of in *nagauta* style. Ironically, she was dissatisfied by the more Westernized sound and after she reworked the vocal part to be sung in a conventional *nagauta* vocal style for subsequent performances she felt it was more successful. Even those *nagauta* musicians who seek new sounds feel the shaping force of proper compositional form in what sounds the most "natural" or coherent with appropriate *nagauta*. Maintaining this naturalness that marks the purity of *nagauta* in a new composition seems to be an impossible task if any "impure" modern elements are introduced.

Musicians who try to compose *nagauta* in the modern day are caught in a conflict between modern innovation as valued by Japanese scholars and traditional form as valued by *sensei*. Innovation has no place in the lesson process or in the concert hall of *nagauta*. This tension is addressed by Toyotaka (1956) in his history of Meiji era music that harshly criticizes the new compositions of the Kenseikai group that had a brief period of popularity in the early twentieth century. Although he acknowledged that "a new atmosphere was breathed into the world of *nagauta* as an independent musical form divorced from theatre," the experiments tried by the *shamisen* players in Kenseikai "could not surmount the limitations imposed by the musical instrument itself" (ibid.:52). Toyotaka's critical assessment of new *shamisen* composition also blamed the influence of vocal music:

> When the success of the *Nagauta* Study Group in achieving independence from the Kabuki marked the first step in the development of the *nagauta* as pure music, but at the same time one could not say that the possibility of true *shamisen* music had been taken in the direction of freeing the *shamisen* from the singing and making of it an independent instrumental music. (ibid.)

Toyotaka concludes that the conservatives of the *nagauta* world failed to Westernize their music, claiming that they "lacked the energy to stick their heads out of the hard shells in which they were enclosed and have a look at the outside world" (ibid.:53).

Similar values of Westernization are expressed in a comparison of two contemporary *hōgaku* composers from the early twentieth century by Katsumura (1986) who examines the reasons for the success of compositions by famed *koto* musician Miyagi Michio compared to the obscurity of compositions by *nagauta shamisen* player Kineya Sakichi IV. Whereas Miyagi succeeded by fully embracing Western idioms and notation, Sakichi IV "did not step outside of the bounds of traditional attitudes, and hence did not write scores as elaborate (in the Western connotation) as Miyagi" (ibid.:167). Katsumura attributes the limiting force of *nagauta* to its subordinate role as music for dance accompaniment in the music market which results in composers conforming to the demands of dance and, like Toyotaka, he cites the structural limitations of the *shamisen* itself which lacks the flexibility to employ new techniques (ibid.:167–168). The limitations imposed by the music market may have had an effect on Sakichi IV, but for Kikuoka who saw himself as a composer of pure concert *nagauta*, following form was dictated by the traditional aesthetics of accepting the materials given and respecting their essential characteristics (Saito 1997:383 and Saito 1998:550–551). Thus, the limitations of the *shamisen* cited by Katsumura, and the fidelity to vocal music as critiqued by Toyotaka are seen as the virtues of the *shamisen* in the traditional view of Kikuoka.

Kikuoka's compositional approach was to maintain the purity of what constitutes authentic *nagauta shamisen* music. He harshly criticized and dismissed many new works by composers who used the *shamisen* to compose in their own style. Composing a piece that could justifiably be described as a work of *nagauta shamisen* requires a thorough understanding of *nagauta*, which can only be achieved by an extensive amount of direct training required by the tradition. According to Kikuoka, without a thorough knowledge of the particularities of the instrument itself and how it is used in *nagauta*, a composer would fail to consider the many subtleties of the instrument, such as producing similar pitches at different fret positions that produces subtle differences in timbre of the same pitch. Even with a certain amount of training on the instrument, a modern composer would need the immense knowledge of repertoire and its conventions to attempt to compose something within the boundaries of the tradition.

The tradition-bound Kikuoka was highly critical of young Japanese composers who choose the *shamisen* simply as a tool for modern musical expression. In his opinion, many modern compositions are limited by the fact that composers focus too much on the technical aspects of the instrument and not enough on "song" (*uta*):

> It's not the case that new composers ignore the old ways. They just don't care. Their only concern is about the musical instrument, not *shamisen* music. Each musical instrument has a limit. The *shamisen* puts a limit on fingers, tone, and the sound of the *bachi* (plectrum). The *shamisen* has a limit. It is not a western musical instrument. Some players create new ways of playing such as using the smallest finger, using the thumb, or using the fingers instead of the *bachi*. These days some players are getting closer to Western music, but these new ways are difficult to express on the *shamisen*.

Kikuoka explained to me that the *shamisen*, because of its limitations in sound production, is inferior to Western instruments such as the piano or violin. For Kikuoka, the natural structure of the *shamisen* made it completely dependent on the voice and thus he viewed Toyotaka's call for freeing *shamisen* music from vocal music as impossible; *shamisen* music is by definition "*shamisen*-vocal music." Kikuoka emphasized that his role was not to compete with Western music, but to carry on within the conventions of the tradition as passed down by his artistic predecessors like Kenseikai. Although he acknowledged that there might be some value in the artistic experimentation of creating extended techniques on the *shamisen*, such music can never be thought of as *nagauta*. Kikuoka emphasized the point that *nagauta* is essentially a song which is the starting point for making a composition that can be called *nagauta*.

Using song as his starting point, Kikuoka claimed to always try to capture the "spirit" of the composers of *nagauta* that he admired. Kikuoka composed *nagauta* songs to existing lyric poetry, usually commissioned works by poets such as Ishikawa Tangetsu. He would begin by reading the poetry and imagining the lyrical scene before picking up the *shamisen*. His next step would be to pick up the *shamisen* and try out melodic ideas for both the *shamisen* and the vocal lines. Although *shamisen* and the voice are inseparable in his development of the work, Kikuoka did tell me that in his mind, the *shamisen* line is the most important. Although this may reflect the bias of a professional *shamisen* player, it is nevertheless a revealing comment coming from a musician equally skilled in *nagauta* singing and oriented towards the lyrical aspects of *nagauta*. If Kikuoka's music is based on song and the *shamisen* is of primary importance, then the relationship between the vocal part and the *shamisen* part holds the key to understanding his compositions. Rather than existing merely as background, the *shamisen* is intertwined with the voice in such a way that the sum of their parts makes up the entirety of the melody. Whereas a Western song can still maintain its function and be identifiable without accompaniment, the situation is different for *nagauta*. A *nagauta* song can be sung unaccompanied and the melody may still be recognizable, but the subtle heterophonic interplay between voice and *shamisen* that is central to all forms of *shamisen* music would be missing.

For this reason, Kikuoka sings his melodic ideas while simultaneously creating the *shamisen* line. He told me that without integrating voice and *shamisen* in this way it would be impossible to make a suitable melody. Furthermore, Kikuoka's method was firmly based in *nagauta*'s oral tradition in that when composing he did not commit any of the music to paper until he had worked it out orally and memorized both the *shamisen* and vocal lines. Only after the work seemed to be complete did he create a notated score.

YUKI MUSUME (SNOW MAIDEN): TELLING A TALE IN MODERN *NAGAUTA*

Kikuoka's *Yuki Musume* (Snow Maiden) is the first composition in a triptych of works titled *Setsugekka* (literally "snow, moon, and flower"), a commonly used thematic designation for groupings of three works in traditional Japanese art.[1] *Yuki Musume* is based on a northern folk tale and contains lyrics that, as is typical with *nagauta* based on stories, only obliquely allude to the story. More importantly *nagauta* lyrics offer poetic impressions of the story and the role of the music is to transform these impressions into vivid images that convey the feeling of the story without resorting to narrative storytelling. This technique of word painting, as seen in the previous chapter's analysis of *Sukeroku*, is one of the main functions of *nagauta* music and is necessary for understanding the meaning of *nagauta* compositions. Kikuoka's composition is an excellent example of *nagauta* word painting and musical imagery that, with the exception of some surprises at the end of the piece, stays within the rules of the tradition.

The folk tale that inspired this piece is one version of many about the snow maiden in Japan. In this version a young girl is lost on a snowy night in the mountains and comes upon a house, asking for shelter. The man lets the girl inside, warms her by the fire and gives her food. This makes her feel warm but the warmth is only temporary. She stays overnight in the house, but during the night the cold north wind begins to blow and she becomes cold again. She mysteriously turns to snow and vanishes into the air. Like other folk tales of the snow maiden, this one makes clear the metaphor of the fleeting moments of the warmth of love and life, and the inevitable cold of loneliness and death to which we all must return.

The poet Ishikawa Tangetsu was commissioned to write this work specifically for Kikuoka and so wrote the poem to suit the conventions of *nagauta*. True to *nagauta*'s lyrical form, Ishikawa does not tell the story directly, but creates suitable imagery to conjure up the feeling of the story. A translation of the entire piece is as follows:

Yuki Musume (Snow maiden)

1. *Yuki ore mo kikoete kuraki yo naru kana*	Branches broken by snow are heard in the night.
2. *mada fumi narenu michi nagara*	She has never before walked such a terrible road,
3. *koi no tsurara ni nuresomete*	wet from the melting of love's icicles,
4. *noki no shizuku no shinkirashi*	from the impatient dew on the eaves.
5. *fukete tomamoru tomoshibiya*	In the late night a door offers protection — a lamplight.
6. *koishi itoshimo hitofude ni*	I miss you dear, she writes
7. *usuzumi iro no chirashigaki*	in fading ink in a letter of love.
8. *shiku wa taetemo hakkume no*	She can barely stand the struggle,
9. *fude sute masu no yuki mochi ni*	throwing away her brush as snow falls.
10. *kimi wa kōri no hashigakari*	The bridge to you is made of ice.
11. *mukashi no tori wa kasasagi ya*	The bird of long ago, a magpie,
12. *itoshi itoshi to iu tori wa*	calls out "dear, dear,"
13. *medetaki koto ni ōdori yo*	with the happiness of a nightingale.
14. *onna gokoro wa hiwa irona*	A woman's heart is like a greenish yellow bird
15. *koi ji o kayō shirasagi no*	following the path of love — if the heron
16. *kokoro tsugenaba kōnotori*	confesses love, the stork will appear.
17. *nushi wa shōwaru Tagoto no tsukiyo*	You're like the cruel moon over Tagoto
18. *nantosho nantosho*	what shall I do?
19. *doko e makoto ga utsuru yara*	Where your true reflection is, I'm uncertain.
20. *doshōzoina doshōzoina*	I am afraid.
21. *Mata hito shikiri furu yuki wa*	Still the snow falls, more than before,
22. *otomo naku tsumoru koi goro mo*	silently piling up love for him.
23. *kaze ga motekuru kuru kuru kururi*	The wind is starting to twist and turn.
24. *Fubuki ni sode ya kijinuran.*	The freezing storm turns her sleeve to ice.

The actual story is only alluded to in the beginning and ending of the song with several lyrical asides to other situations. In the first section, which includes an introductory poetic *haiku* set off from the first full verse, the young girl comes to the house. The second verse consists of the girl writing a letter expressing unrequited love to a man. Her futility is expressed with the image of ice at the end of this verse. The third verse takes us away from the snow imagery and into a lyrical aside consisting of more general poetic musings on the nature of women and love. The fourth verse returns to the female character in which she expresses her personal feelings of confusion and fear towards her lover. The final verse returns to something resembling the original story with the return of snow that continues to fall, the piling up of cold white snow being a metaphor for unrequited love. The wind blows and "freezes" the girl, thus beginning her mythical transformation. The poem has a symmetrical arc-shaped structure in its development from the snowy setting of the beginning, to a woman's personal expression to her lover, to a centerpiece of poetic musing, back to the woman's personal expression, and finally a return to the snowy beginning of the story.

Kikuoka's knowledge of the conventions of *nagauta* allowed him to create a composition rich in musical imagery that develops the poem's main theme, human suffering from unrequited love, and its key symbol of snow. Kikuoka utilized traditional techniques of word painting and programmatic imagery commonly used in *nagauta* composition. Chief among these techniques are working with pitch centers and their upper and lower leading tones, which serves both to increase melodic tension and to resolve melodies. Throughout the piece he also judiciously employs the use of silence (*ma*), another key technique of *nagauta* and Japanese music, to evoke the image of snow. Following *nagauta*'s kabuki-influenced formal structure, the piece opens with a scene-setting section that establishes the main theme and the mood of the piece both lyrically and musically. *Ma* is used sparingly, yet effectively, in this opening section in well-placed one-beat rests, two-beat rests (mm 4–5; mm 10–11), and a three-beat rest that provides a dramatic opening for the vocalist's first phrase. A close look at the *shamisen* pitches used in the first twenty measures of instrumental leading up to the opening lyric reveals an unconventional, yet not without precedent, use of *nagauta* tonality (see Appendix B for a complete transcription of the *shamisen* and vocal parts of *Yuki Musume*).

The piece begins with the *shamisen* playing in a slow tempo in *san-sagari* tuning (the three strings tuned in two fourths) and is joined by "off-stage" (*geza*) musicians faintly playing gong and *shinobue* flute. A shifting tonality on the *shamisen*, together with *shinobue*, creates an effect of uncertainty suitable for depicting the young girl wandering in the snow. The *shamisen* phrases, all roughly four measures long, shift the tonal center several times during this brief introduction. The opening notes on A descend in typical *nagauta* fashion (A to F to E) to the main pitch center E, suggesting an *in* scale built on E (mm 1–4). However, the phrase ends in measure four with two notes of F-sharp, suggesting a new pitch center. After two beats of *ma*, the next *shamisen* phrase reveals the tonality to be an *in* scale built on B (mm 5–8).[2] The next *shamisen* phrase, like the opening phrase, shifts to a new tonality at the end of the phrase, this time with two notes of C-sharp (mm 10–11), followed by another well-placed two beats of *ma*. The next two notes of A suggest that the new tonality is an *in* scale built on F-sharp, but the final descending *shamisen* passage of this introduction (mm 14–19) clearly follows an *in* scale built on E.

Complimenting this slow tempo and wandering tonality are two sustained, unornamented notes on the *shinobue*. The first flute pitch A begins at measure 5 and supports the *in* scale built on B. This pitch overlaps with the new tonality of C-sharp of measures 10–11 and fades away by measure 12. The flute returns at measure 16 with pitch B, suggesting the new tonality to be introduced by the vocal line beginning in measure 21. This extended two-note flute phrase is a standard *nagauta* pitch resolution of leading tone A to pitch center B that occurs at key moments in *nagauta* pieces such as introductions or cadences. Kikuoka has cleverly disguised this standard phrase in the distant sounding flute allowing the *shamisen* an expressive passage of wandering tonality throughout a wide range that is somewhat unconventional in the openings of pieces.[3] The *shamisen,* together with the flute and the light punctuation of the gong, achieve a total thematic effect of uncertain wandering in the snow.

1. *Yuki ore mo kikoete kuraki yo naru kana*	Branches broken by snow are heard in the night.

The opening line of this piece, a *haiku* of 5-7-5 syllable structure, is a single poetic image of the sound of branches breaking from the weight of snow and is designed to set the mood of the tale. Just as the poet enriches his poem by describing the sound of branches bending and breaking, Kikuoka enriches this image by painting the breaking sound using shifts in tonal centers. Following the ambiguity of the introduction, the opening vocal line begins on A in an extended three-beat rest of *ma*. As heard in the earlier flute phrase, the opening of the vocal line on A resolves up to the pitch center B by measure 25. No sooner is the stability of pitch center B established than a dramatic shift occurs on the word "*kikoete*" ("can be heard") as the *shamisen* paints the breaking sound with a series of plucked eighth notes on pitch center B, followed by a flatting of this pitch to B-flat (mm 24–28) to express the heavy weight. This B-flat begins a new tonality of an *in* scale built on A and creates a darker mood for the next words "*kuraki yo*" (dark night) after another well-placed two-beats of *ma* (mm 29–33). As the singer completes the phrase, the tonality shifts back to an *in* scale on E and the B-natural returns.

2. *mada fumi narenu michi nagara*	She has never before walked such a terrible road,
3. *koi no tsurara ni nuresomete*	wet from the melting of love's icicles,
4. *noki no shizuku no shinkirashi*	from the impatient dew on the eaves.
5. *fukete tomamoru tomoshibiya*	In the late night a door offers protection — a lamplight.

After this opening statement the *shamisen* play a brief instrumental maintaining a stable tonality of an *in* scale built on B. This instrumental section increases the tempo with a denser *shamisen* passage utilizing eighth notes and serves to set apart the dramatic opening haiku image from the rest of the piece. As the vocals resume at another three-beat rest in measures 62–63, the character of the young girl first appears in the lyrics. The next two lines describe the plight of the young girl and, as is typical of the abstract, lyrical nature of *nagauta*, key words receive special emphasis through upper register pitches and vocal melisma. The key word "*koi*" (love) appears prominently on a high G, a fifth above the *shamisen* accompaniment and the forlorn romantic word "*nure*" (wet) with its connotations of tears and sexual love is drawn out melismatically, accompanied by a series of plucked eighth notes on *shamisen* which may also be a gesture of sexual excitement.

All four lines of this stanza focus on the image of snow melting, a poetic image with a complexity of meaning which is developed musically by Kikuoka. While melting suggests on one level a positive image of falling in love, the image here is darker and more negative: when one's purity (snow) is warmed by love, the melting means destruction of innocence and ultimate downfall. The image of a woman made of snow, destroyed by human warmth, calls for a mood that Kikuoka captures in the next two lines with lower register pitches in the voice and descending *shamisen* lines. The drops of snow melting from the eaves in line 4 become active metaphors as the word "*shizuku*" (jealousy, impatience) descends to an unusually low A in the vocal. With the word "*tomoshibiya*" (the torch outside the house) at the end of line 5, the *shamisen* illustrates the melting or falling with a brief passage downward in unusual intervals. The unusually close descending intervals of F-sharp to F-natural help accentuate this downward motion. Accentuating the descent of F-sharp-F-C-B, Kikuoka uses two-beat rests, indicating snow falling/melting, and hence the emotional state of the girl who is falling, ultimately to her destruction.

6. *koishi itoshimo hitofude ni*	I miss you dear, she writes
7. *usuzumi iro no chirashigaki*	in fading ink in a letter of love.
8. *shiku wa taetemo hakkume no*	She can barely stand the struggle,
9. *fude sute masu no yuki mochi ni*	throwing away her brush as snow falls.
10. *kimi wa kōri no hashigakari*	The bridge to you is made of ice.

The next section consists of a stanza that departs from the story in which the girl attempts to write a love letter, giving up in futility. This verse is differentiated from the previous section's low register phrases by a shift to an upper register vocal passage in a slower tempo as sung by the second vocalist of the ensemble. The vocal entrance begins as before within a three-beat *shamisen* rest as the opening line begins with the word "*koi*" (love) and ascends upward, using the upper register to great effect in lines 6 and 7 to describe the intensity of the girl's longing.

The next two lines taken up by the second singer utilize the upper register even more, but with the *shamisen* playing an octave below the vocal line to provide contrast. Line 8 has Buddhist implications not evident in the translation above: "*shiku*" refers to four sufferings of human life (age, sickness, death, daily living) and "*hakku*" refers to four more sufferings (separation from a loved one, jealousy, desire, suffering caused by others). The girl writes that although she can tolerate the more general sufferings of "*shiku*," she has to suffer with "*hakku*," the kinds of suffering related directly to love.

Her futility reaches a peak in line 9 in which she throws away her brush (*fude sutemasu*) and completion of the line is briefly suspended while the *shamisen* answers with another descending line infused with the *ma* of a two-beat rest (mm 193–200). This sets up the most important word of the piece, "*yuki*" (snow), which is given emphasis by extending it melismatically on upper register E and F during a fermata on the *shamisen* (mm 203–207). "*Mochi ni*" (falling) is also melismatically extended in a descending phrase and is accompanied by a descending, syncopated *shamisen* phrase that suggests falling snow fluttering down (mm 208–209). Both singers join in chorus for the first time in the piece to emphasize the woman's final frustration of this stanza, "the bridge to you is made of ice." This is clearly marked as a standard section ending with a *ritard* slowing to a stop on the main pitch center of B.

11. *mukashi no tori wa kasasagi ya*	The bird of long ago, a magpie,
12. *itoshi itoshi to iu tori wa*	calls out "dear, dear,"
13. *medetaki koto ni ōdori yo*	with the happiness of a nightingale.
14. *onna gokoro wa hiwa irona*	A woman's heart is like a greenish yellow bird
15. *koi ji o kayō shirasagi no*	following the path of love — if the heron
16. *kokoro tsugenaba kōnotori*	confesses love, the stork will appear.

A *shamisen* instrumental passage (*aikata*) of 25 bars serves as a bridge to the next section a kind of "bird song" (*tori uta*), in which the poet plays with images of several birds functioning as metaphors of love. The quick tempo instrumental explores the range of pitches of *in* scales based on E (mm 219–231) and B (233–240), finally returning to pitch center E. The *shamisen* interlude outlines the main tonalities used in the piece up to this point and sets up the contrast of the new section beginning on a pitch center not yet used in the piece. As the instrumental comes to an end on the primary pitch center E, the start of the next section is announced abruptly with a staccato A followed by a syncopated phrase containing the most important tones of the *in* scale built on A (B-flat, A, G and E), thus announcing the new tonality. The tonality shift is motivated by the change in mood of the poem and announces this section to be an interlude. This begins the *taikoji,* a section of the piece which includes the *nō hayashi* ensemble.

As foreshadowed by the last line of the previous verse, the singers begin this verse in chorus singing chant-like on pitch center A (mm 247–252). This syllabic style of singing on a single pitch is a common device in *nagauta* for declamatory statements, hearkening back to *nō* drama and ancient Buddhist chant, and is thus used appropriately in the opening line which begins an ancient story with "*mukashi*" (the Japanese equivalent to "once upon a time"). Coinciding with "*kasasagi*" (magpie) the *shamisen* evokes this bird image with a four-measure syncopated phrase typical of those used in *nagauta* to depict the walking and bobbing heads of birds. The spry rhythm continues after this line in the *shamisen* as the hayashi musicians play kabuki-derived patterns (named *chirikara* after the oral mnemonics by which they are learned). The magpie's call of "*itoshi itoshi*" ("dear, dear," an echo of the earlier use of this word in the verse about the girl's letter) is also animated by the *shamisen* line and a use of *ma* quite different from the earlier use of *ma*. In this case, the two-beat rests make room for responses from the drums, helping to enhance the rhythm.

As Malm has noted about pitch centers in *nagauta*, playing the secondary pitch center of A with its upper leading tone of B-flat is reserved for certain moments that are lyrically unusual or sad and its appearance does not last long before modulating back to one of the main pitch centers of B or E (Malm 1978:102). In this section of the piece, Kikuoka plays with the tension created by pitch A and its upper leading tone B-flat. The opening B-flat serves to clearly announce a new section in measure 245 and the next B-flat appears along with the B-natural in the syncopated "magpie" pattern (mm 251). Although lines 11 and 12 both end with a resolution to the main pitches E and B played as double-stops on the *shamisen* (mm 263 and mm 279), for the remainder of this section there is an increasing tension as the *shamisen* veers between A (the leading tone of B) and F (the upper leading tone of E) without resolution. The repetition of A and F and the occasional use of B-flat create a melodic tension throughout line 13. This tension creates an ironic contrast with the opening word of line 13, "*medetaki*" (happiness), which features the highest vocal pitch — and the brightest glimmer of hope — in the entire piece (mm 290).

Furthermore, the tension of this section is increased by two-beat and three-beat rests which allow for *hayashi* drum responses that provide a sense of rhythmic drive.

At the end of line 13, the tonal ambiguity is heightened with further use of the B-flat (mm 306 and 311) and without any final resolution to a pitch center. Line 14 continues the tension with both the *shamisen* and vocal line using pitches above and below pitch center B to describe a woman's heart and finally resolving with the vocal line ending on an upper register E. Line 15 again sets the opening word "*koi*" (love) in the upper register on G and the phrase gradually descends with the lyrics describing the "path of love" and the *shamisen* line descending in a stepwise motion of G-F-sharp-F to pitch center E. Line 15 ends with the word "*shirasagi*" (heron) delivered in a staccato manner and the two *shamisen* respond programmatically with an interlocking two-note phrase on G and F-sharp that suggests birds in flight or perhaps movement down some sort of path. The last line of this section depicts the heron's "confession of love" as the *shamisen* finally comes to a clear resolution with a *ritard* double-stop on E and B. Following this resolution in a slower tempo is a standard section ending phrase moving from B down to E and the final word "*konotori*" (stork) brings the section to a close, indicating what may be the woman's ultimate hope for happiness, the arrival of the stork, symbolic of maternity.

17. *nushi wa shōwaru Tagoto no tsukiyo*	You're like the cruel moon over Tagoto
18. *nantosho nantosho*	what shall I do?
19. *doko e makoto ga utsuru yara*	Where your true reflection is I'm uncertain.
20. *doshōzoina doshōzoina*	I am afraid.

After a brief *shamisen* interlude based on an *in* scale on E the next section begins in a quieter and very different mood. For the most intimate and emotional verse in the poem, Kikuoka creates a movement that allows the singers a little more rhythmic freedom. As a result, the emotional dilemma expressed by the female character contains the most expressive singing of this piece, although I do not know to what extent Kikuoka may have guided them, or left them to their own vocal interpretation. The pair of *shamisen* begins this section playing a four-note ostinato pattern built on E-A-B an octave apart. This ostinato accompanied by the long tones of the *shinobue* flute allow for a vocal line that exists independently from the *shamisen*. As the *shamisen* stays entirely within the *in* scale on E, the vocal line floats freely above the *shamisen* ostinato. While the main *shamisen* plays mostly quarter notes, the upper octave *shamisen* plays a more embellished version of the main *shamisen* melody using eighth notes.

With the *shamisen* remaining relatively stable tonally throughout this section, the interest is created entirely by the emotional singing of the vocal line in wide-ranging sweeps and extended phrase endings. Line 17 states that her lover is a womanizer (*showaru*) and evokes the image of the moonlight over Tagoto, an area in Nagano prefecture known for its picturesque terraced rice fields. The moonlight creates many different reflections on these wet rice fields and the woman feels panicked because she does not know which reflection truly represents her lover (line 19). Implicit in this metaphor is the notion that the many moons reflected in the rice fields suggest many mistresses. The opening word "*nushi*" (you; her beloved) begins on a high A and the vocal quickly descends down to E on "*showaru*" (womanizer). The *shamisen* then begins to create tension with the leading tones A and F as the voice sweeps back up again to a high B to describe the moon over Tagoto. The singers join together in chorus to express her dilemma in line 19, "*nantosho nantosho*" (what shall I do?), and this is followed by a *shamisen* passage with percussion that follows the *shamisen* rhythm. The first singer delivers line 20 about her futile search for truth in the reflection in an upper register passage with extended phrases. Parallel to line 19, the singers join together again in line 21 to express her fear, "*doshozoina doshozoina*" (I am afraid), as the vocal line descends from upper register A down to E. The *shamisen* returns to the *ostinato* phrase with which the section began.

21. *Mata hito shikiri furu yuki wa*	Still the snow falls, more than before,
22. *otomo naku tsumoru koi goro mo*	silently piling up love for him.
23. *kaze ga motekuru kuru kuru kururi*	The wind is starting to twist and turn.
24. *Fubuki ni sode ya kijinuran.*	The freezing storm turns her sleeve to ice.

The final verse of the poem returns to the original story announced immediately by an instrumental passage that depicts a snowstorm. At measure 511 the slow tempo of the previous section ends as both *shamisen* play a rapidly accelerating pattern on A and are joined by percussion. The large *taiko* drum begins to play a steady pulsation well-known in kabuki as an indication of a storm. The *nōkan* also plays a tuneless, tonally ambiguous, "windy" sounding pattern that is also easily recognizable as the sound of a storm. After the first two measures the second *shamisen* maintains this steady drone on A while the main *shamisen* begins to play rhythmic accent patterns based on B, C, E and A which gradually increase in density to depict the increasing power of a snowstorm. As the second *shamisen* drone on A continues insistently, there is an increasing tension for a resolution up to B. A descending glissando technique is played on the main *shamisen* in measures 531–532 to emphasize falling. As the *shamisen* reach top speed with dense, eighth note playing, the second *shamisen* stops the drone on A (mm 543). The two *shamisen* play in unison a two-note *ostinato* on D and A with an eighth note rest creating a rhythmic accent that prepares the listener for the vocal entrance.

Both singers enter in unison describing the dramatic increase in snowfall in a syllabic, chant-like vocal line on D resolving up to E. The *shamisen* follow with a syncopated phrase utilizing 16th notes. The word "falling snow" appears in the text but, unlike previous appearances of snow in the text (in the opening section and in the letter-writing section), which were treated with elongated, melismatic melancholy, the phrase has a much different character in the midst of the storm. "*Furuyuki wa*" is delivered flatly on E in rapid staccato eighth notes and the voices are accompanied by a dense flurry of sixteenth-notes on the *shamisen.*

Techniques of *ma* dramatically different from earlier in the piece occur in this section hearkening back to the early part of the piece in which snow and the silence of *ma* was prominent. Line 21 finishes on a single-beat rest on the *shamisen* that is followed by four measures of *shamisen* playing staccato B. These four measures steadily increase in volume and launch into rapid eighth notes. This volume surge is suddenly halted with four beats of rest as the singers begin line 22 singing a staccato "*otomonaku*" (silently), inserting silence into the midst of the raging storm. In immediate contrast, the word "*tsumoru*" (piling up) is elongated in a descending line that utilizes the B-flat, recalling the earliest snow image in the opening words of the piece.

The next vocal phrase, the end of line 22 and the beginning of line 23, is structured in a similar way. Again alternating rapid eighth-note singing with elongated lines, line 22 finishes with the rapid staccato singing of "*koi goro mo*" (love towards him, also a double meaning of the lover's clothes which may be evoked here out of the woman's need for warmth). This is followed immediately by an elongated "*kaze ga motekuru*" (wind starting) enhancing the windy feeling in a descending phrase again using the movement from B to B-flat. In the closing lines of the piece, just as in the beginning of the piece, the poet uses an image of sound and Kikuoka emphasizes this through word painting. In this case, the sound image is a sound in itself, "*kuru kuru,*" onomatopoeia for the sound of wind twisting and turning, so the vocal line for these words employs melismatic elongated tones and wide upward leaps. Another rapid *shamisen* passage follows this and ends with a one-beat rest for the onomatopoeia "*kururi*" to be sung again, this time in rapid staccato. The *shamisen* mimics the sound of "*kururi*" with a brief flourish, followed by four muted left-hand taps on the fingerboard that slows the piece down.

As the tempo slows down the last line appears at first to be delivered as a standard *nagauta* ending called *dangire.* But as the final image of the storm turning her kimono sleeves to ice is sung (the double meaning of the kimono sleeve suggested here is a loss of youthful innocence and vigor), the stormy sounds of the flute and the *taiko* continue faintly in the background. As is typical of the *dangire* ending, all instruments pause indefinitely for the singer to melismatically phrase the final word. However, the *shamisen* plays an unusual pair of sixteenth notes on B-flat for its final statement and, as the singer begins the last phrase "*kijinuran*" (freezing), the faint sound of the storm is heard in the pulsating *taiko.* On the final syllable the *shamisen* begins to play the accelerating *ostinato* again which began this final section at measure 511. The *shamisen* continue to play through the instrumental section again accompanied by the stormy sounds of the flute and percussion.

For the ending of this work on the studio recording for Crown Records, Kikuoka defies the normal expectations of *nagauta* by coming ever so close to a standard ending, but then returns to the snow imagery by repeating from measure 511. Instead of a final resolution to the story, the listener is left with a storm that seems to continue indefinitely as a studio fade-out is employed on the recording during this *shamisen* instrumental depiction of a snowstorm. However, the repeat and studio fade-out was only intended for the recording as there is no repeat indicated in the original score. The unresolved feeling of the studio-enhanced ending suggests that the story has not fully ended in that there are two more sections of this *nagauta* triptych that follow, even though the following pieces are each completely unrelated. Except for its unusual finish on the recording, *Yuki Musume* is a very conventional *nagauta* composition in its use of programmatic *shamisen* music to paint lyric imagery. Kikuoka fully exploited standard *nagauta shamisen* techniques of creating melodic tension with movement towards and away from pitch centers within a typical *nagauta* formal structure. The next work examined in this chapter is *Sakura Emaki* (Flower pictures), the third part of his *nagauta* triptych featuring much bolder departures from the conventions of *nagauta*.

SAKURA EMAKI: CONFLICTS OF MODERNITY IN A TRADITIONAL SETTING

Kikuoka's composition *Sakura Emaki* (*sakura* or "blossom" pictures) is the third part of his trilogy called *Setsugekka*, of which *Yuki Musume* is the first part.[4] Like *Yuki Musume*, this piece draws heavily upon *nagauta* tradition, but involves a different structure, a contrasting mood and a greater degree of assimilation of modern musical ideas. However, Kikuoka maintains such an adherence to the techniques and structure of *nagauta* that the music is clearly identifiable as belonging in the *nagauta* tradition. Furthermore, the modern elements employed, such as vocal harmony and the dissonant tones found in the multi-part *shamisen* sections, are seamlessly integrated into the work and motivated by the lyric poetry of Ishikawa Tangetsu. As the subject matter of the poem is the revelry of spring flower viewing, a common theme in many Japanese artworks, Kikuoka draws inspiration from a previous model, describing this work as a modern version of *Hanami Odori* (Flower viewing road), a well-known *nagauta* composition from the nineteenth century. Although he draws a great deal of inspiration from this earlier work, his composition is nevertheless a completely different piece, original in its structure and its *shamisen* and vocal techniques.

The music is set to another poem by Ishikawa Tangetsu. A translation is as follows:

Sakura Emaki (Sakura pictures)

1. *Hana no kinu, Hana no kinu*	Clothes of flowers, clothes of flowers,
2. *kasumi no koromo uchi tsuranu*	misty robes lined up like
3. *itonoyanagi ni haru ya kazaran*	wispy willow spring decorations.
4. *Omoshiroya hitoeda o kosode ni inoraba*	View of one branch, blessed by a short
5. *hanra to chirinuru hana wa sakari no*	sleeve, falling leaves, falling flowers in full bloom
6. *nagame yo no nagame yo no*	look at them, look at them.
7. *iyoyo iyoyo no onorimono*	At last the *onorimono*,
8. *are are mairu*	look, look, it's coming,
9. *okoshi mo mairu*	the *okoshi* is also coming,
10. *suzuite mairu hana no shitaeda ni*	one after another passing underneath the branches.
11. *icho nicho sancho yonchome no kago wa*	One, two, three, four carriages
12. *satemo kirara no*	so glittery
13. *kirara kayo no*	and shining.
14. *asagi murasaki shōjōhi kogane wakakusa*	Yellow, purple, red, gold, and green,
15. *ironi dete nioi medetaki*	many colors coming out, the scent of happiness,
16. *hanakatsura*	a wig made of flowers.
17. *saita sakura ni taga kinu kakeru*	On the fresh blossoms, someone's clothes
18. *eda wa kakururu hana wa chiru*	hanging on the branch, hiding the flowers that fall.
19. *ina ina mazu wa hana ikusa*	Never mind; first is the flower battle.
20. *hana no zuishin hana no tomo*	The flower's protector and the flower's
21. *tagai ni tawamure*	friend are playing with each other
22. *arasoite*	and fighting.
23. *omote ni honnori akezakura*	Red-faced, vermillion blossoms,
24. *youte tamoto no nunobikizakura*	drunken, sleeve-pulling blossoms,
25. *kumoizakura no ayaukuba*	cloudy Imperial blossoms endangered,
26. *naka o torano o izazakura*	intimate tigertail blossoms troubled,
27. *rachi mo ariyakezakura to narite*	order becomes blossoms of dawn,
28. *sareba medetaku narazakura*	and at last Nara blossoms of happiness.
29. *utai sōrae haya sōzu*	Let's sing and make loud music.

30. *some wake tazuna nana iro no*	The seven-colored banner held by a rope
31. *maku ni soyoto yamakaze wa*	flapping in the mountain breeze.
32. *hana o mamori no taenaru suzu no ne*	Protecting the flowers is the sound of a bell tree.
33. *hibiki ni yōte yugasumi*	Pealing in the drunken evening mist,
34. *iriai no kane sora somete*	the sunset bell in the tinted sky.
35. *hana mo hajirau utage kana*	Even the flowers are embarrassed by this feast.
36. *hana mo hajirau utage kana*	Even the flowers are embarrassed by this feast.

From the beginning Kikuoka wanted this piece to be purely lyrical in style and he requested that Ishikawa write these lyrics in a more abstract style without any narrative. This was in conscious emulation of his model piece, *Hanami Odori*, which is also non-narrative. The lyrics in this work, according to Kikuoka, are "only images" and as such are "not as important as the music." The complexity of the *shamisen* parts and the atmosphere created by the unusual mix of men's and women's voices are the essence of this piece.

Nevertheless, *Sakura Emaki* stays true to Kikuoka's philosophy of song as the basis of *nagauta* in that he still composes music that enhances the mood of the poetry. Thus, all of the elements we can identify as modern, such as vocal harmony or dissonant *shamisen*, are motivated by the song lyrics. Like *Hanami Odori*, these lyrics depict the cherry blossom season in Japan and the mood is one of fullness, liveliness, color and activity. In contrast with *Yuki Musume*, in which Kikuoka used *ma* to create an austere feeling of emptiness, loneliness, and isolation of the human in nature, in *Sakura Emaki* Kikuoka uses a busy, dense sound to create a celebratory feeling of fullness, togetherness and unity of the human in nature. Like an early April afternoon in any blossom-filled park or meadow in Japan where one encounters dense hordes of people engaged in annual flower viewing, *Sakura Emaki* is also crowded with sound. Not only does the piece use a full ensemble, complete with *hayashi* and *geza* accompaniment, but both male and female chorus are also used.

The imagery of a crowded celebration is depicted from the opening section (*maebiki*) that opens with a bell sound from the geza musicians resembling a rhythmic motif from *Hanami Odori*. The bell proceeds to play a steady repeated note on the first beat of each measure throughout the entire *maebiki* section. The lively atmosphere of a crowded flower viewing spot is created by a trio of *shamisen*, including one low register bass *shamisen*, that seem to be engaged in lively conversation. As this use of a trio with a bass *shamisen* is a modern development not found in pre-twentieth-century *nagauta* compositions, the modern sound of the opening is easily recognized by the listener. The trio of *shamisen* allows Kikuoka to create dense clusters of sound, enhancing the melodic tension and creating a crowded feeling. More traditional *shamisen* techniques such as altering tonality and double-stops are used as well.

The interchange of the three *shamisen* in the opening measure accentuates their differences as they enter one at a time and explore different ranges and tonalities. *Shamisen* 1, which plays predominately in the upper register during the trio sections throughout most of the piece, enters first with a phrase that emphasizes the high pitch center E. *Shamisen* 2, which plays predominately middle register, dovetails after the last note of the first phrase with a phrase built around middle pitch center B. The contrast appears in *shamisen* 3 which overlaps with *Shamisen* 2 at measure 8 with an unusual descending scale of F-E-D-C-sharp-B-E. As *shamisen* 1 begins another phrase based on an *in* scale on E, *shamisen* 3 clashes with this by repeating its unusual opening phrase. *Shamisen* 2 joins in again at measure 14 and all three instruments create contrasting phrases that overlap throughout the first 35 measures of the piece. The overall sound texture becomes progressively thicker as double-stops are used first by *shamisen* 1, then joined by *shamisen* 2, as they begin an interlocking melody in measure 36. Tonality changes on all the *shamisen* with the introduction of an F-sharp at measure 40, but then tonalities clash in measures 46–47 as all three *shamisen* synchronize rhythmically to form unusual triads built from their different tonalities. Following this peak of dissonance, the *shamisen* trio resolves to pitch center E and the section repeats from the beginning.

This opening section sets the mood for the entire piece and is the initial development of an overall theme of man, nature and society in conflict. The trio of *shamisen* is introduced here and reappears in several later sections of the piece. It includes the unusual bass *shamisen*, which plays a percussive role in the overall sound. In fact, Kikuoka described the bass *shamisen* as an extension of the *geza* offstage percussion section. The dissonance of mm 46-47 is but a small sample of the clustered *shamisen* sound to appear in later passages. The crowded sound is also enhanced by the use of double stops. The percussive, dissonant cluster of sounds develops further as the piece progresses and the poetry begins to suggest competition and conflict, yet all the while using a pleasant kind of flower imagery. These decorative and colorful, yet boisterous and competitive, flowers in this imaginative musical work are metaphors for Japanese people who are connected to nature and society, and are in conflict with both.

1. *Hana no kinu, Hana no kinu*	Clothes of flowers, clothes of flowers,
2. *kasumi no koromo uchi tsuranu*	misty robes lined up like
3. *itonoyanagi ni haru ya kazaran*	wispy willow spring decorations.

Man's belonging to nature is established from the beginning in the scene-setting section. The opening line, which twice states "*Hana no kinu*" (clothes of flowers or flowered kimono), is a most important scene-setting image as it unifies the people in the scene with the flowers, expressing the unity of man and nature that is central to this piece. As the *shamisen* trio continues from the *maebiki*, the opening line "*hana no kinu*" is sung first by the men with a phrase built on pitch center E followed by the female chorus response with a phrase built on the B a fifth above. Although the appearance of the mixed group here is a clear sign of the modern, as the use of mixed gender choruses in *nagauta* is generally avoided, Kikuoka takes advantage of the different timbre and vocal ranges to express the diversity of humankind and the flowers of nature. Throughout this piece both male and female "flowers" are represented in wide-ranging, mixed gender, vocal choruses.

Humanity fills the frame of this opening scene-setting section as the throng of blossom-viewers expresses the fullness that is a central theme in this piece. Line 2, which suggests many people lined up (*tsuranu*), is accompanied by a series of dense *shamisen* double-stops from the trio which end with an unresolved feeling in the upper register F against the pitch center E. This is followed by a quiet and unusual passage consisting only of a bass *shamisen* two-note ostinato as the female chorus sings "*ito no yanagi ni*" (thin or "wispy" willows), extending the last syllable melismatically as if to express the drooping branches. Tension is introduced as the female chorus continues with "*haru ya*" (springtime) accompanied by *shamisen* 1 and 2 playing an interlocking pattern of double-stops on E and F. As the *shamisen* resolve to E, both male and female choruses sing the phrase "*kazaran*" (decorate) in octaves, vocal intervals that are undesirable in traditional *nagauta*, but quite effective as a cadence here. The repeat of the line "*haru ya kazaran,*" (spring decorations) features an even more radical departure from tradition as "*kazaran*" features the female chorus singing in harmony a fourth above the men. The last syllable is elongated as the women sing pitch center E with the men singing B, a reversal of the opening male and female vocal phrases. The opening vocal phrases return as the entire opening section is repeated. In this poetic fashion, using simple harmonies, dense *shamisen* chords, and the tension and release of tonality, springtime is decorated, not only with flowers, but also with the crowds of men and women who inhabit nature.

4. *Omoshiroya hitoeda o kosode ni inoraba*	View of one branch, blessed by a short sleeve,
5. *hanra to chirinuru hana wa sakari no*	falling leaves, falling flowers in full bloom
6. *nagame yo no nagame yo no*	look at them, look at them.

Kikuoka follows the dramatic opening section by setting lines 4–6 in a more intimate song setting. He calls this section a *kouta* (short song), referring to the genre of short Japanese *shamisen* songs associated with geisha in an intimate teahouse setting. Although *kouta shamisen* is traditionally played by plucking the strings with the fingernails, this *kouta* is plucked quietly in *nagauta* style using a plectrum. The main *shamisen* is joined by an upper register *shamisen* playing embellishments and together they decorate the text in a brisk tempo with eighth notes and syncopation. The text easily lends itself to a short song setting as it is consists of only three lines expressing a single image that serves the main overall theme of the piece. The conflict of the shared world of man and nature is expressed in this verse depicting a single branch, which is breaking from the weight of a "sleeve" (perhaps someone's resting arm) as the leaves and flowers fall off. On another level, this image also expresses the conflict of male and female relationships as flowers in full bloom (*hana wa sakari no*) symbolizes women in their youth and the short sleeve (*kosode*) that is doing the breaking refers to a man's kimono, as young women traditionally wear long sleeve kimono.

Between the lines of text, Kikuoka places appropriate *shamisen* embellishments that paint the poetic imagery. Just before the line "*hanra to chirinuru*," an onomatopoeic phrase for falling leaves and flowers, the *shamisen* utilizes a special technique that appears in *Hanami Odori* and many other *nagauta* pieces called *urahijiki*, in which the fingernails of the left hand are flicked rapidly across the top string. This technique is utilized on B and followed by a drop down to E, creating a sense of something delicate breaking or falling. After the phrase "*hanra to chirinuru*" the voice and *shamisen* "fall" from the upper pitch center E down to C, as the *shamisen* begin to create a melodic tension with an interlocking phrase built on C, the upper leading tone of B. The brighter sound of a *yo* scale built on E appears at measure 170, accompanying the line about the flower in full bloom.[5] The *shamisen* and vocal phrase ascend to a high B on "*sakari*" (blooming) which is immediately followed by a descending phrase on the imperative "*nagame yo no*" (look at them). The closing phrase means not just looking at a scene or landscape but also implies looking with love and desire. The *kouta* section closes with the two *shamisen* playing a transition to the next section making use again of the double stops.

7. *iyoyo iyoyo no onorimono*	At last the *onorimono*,
8. *are are mairu*	look, look, it's coming,
9. *okoshi mo mairu*	the *okoshi* is also coming,
10. *suzuite mairu hana no shitaeda ni*	one after another passing underneath the branches.

Although the next three stanzas of Ishikawa's poem comprise a continuous scene in which a festival procession approaches and passes by, Kikuoka musically separates these stanzas into two distinct, but connected, musical sections. Lines 7–10 consist of the distant approach of the procession and so Kikuoka sets these lines in a quiet *kudoki* (lyric section) which transitions into a section of lively music suitable for the procession in lines 11–16. The *kudoki* passage of lines 7–10 contrasts with all of the previous sections in that it is the first single-line *shamisen* accompaniment of the entire piece. This quiet, lyrical passage with sparse *shamisen* has none of the tension that characterized the previous sections. Although the quietness of this passage seems to go against the excitement expressed by the speaker in the poem, this section features highly expressive, melismatic vocal phrases that express the emotional anticipation of the arrival of the procession. As the procession features a "noble carriage" (*onorimono*), the double stops in the brief *shamisen* melody that follows this phrase is a melodic type known as *gaku* or *kangen*, which is sometimes used in reference to court nobles or the aristocratic Heian era.[6] The final vocal phrase on the last line of this section expresses the excitement of the arrival of the floats with an ascending upper register vocal line accompanied by double stops on *shamisen* that resolve up to a high B.

11. *icho nicho sancho yonchome no kago wa*	One, two, three, four carriages
12. *satemo kirara no*	so glittery
13. *kirara kayo no*	and shining.
14. *asagi murasaki shōjohi kogane wakakusa*	Yellow, purple, red, gold, and green,
15. *ironi dete nioi medetaki*	many colors coming out, the scent of happiness,
16. *hanakatsura*	a wig made of flowers.

The final high B vocal phrase that ends the *kudoki* section extends and overlaps with the beginning of this new section with the return of the bass *shamisen* playing a rhythmic pattern based on the main pitches B and E. This bass ostinato, along with the off-beat double-stops in the upper register *shamisen* create the lumbering sound of large, rolling carriages as the singer continues, counting the floats one by one ("*icho nicho sancho*"). With the arrival of the fourth float ("*shichome*") the scene becomes crowded once again as both male and female choruses join in, singing in octaves. The choruses then alternate singing two similar lines, both expressing shining or glittering ("*kira*") which is followed by the sound of festival-style flute and drum accents.

In line 14 the male chorus begins to list various colors ("*asagi murasaki shojohi*") and Kikuoka follows this with an appropriately colorful passage of three descending *shamisen* lines producing a kaleidoscopic dissonance of conflicting tone colors all presented in a homophonic rhythm of quarter notes (mm 311–320). After the men's chorus finishes the listing of colors, the *shamisen* trio becomes sparse and exchanges short phrases with each other and with the rhythm section (mm 324–328). This is followed by another striking use of vocal harmony and octaves as the male and female chorus sing "*ironi dete*" (colors coming out). The octave singing continues with the phrase "*nioi medetaki*" describing the wonderful scents in the air. For the final line about a flower piece for the hair, a different tonality is suggested only momentarily in all three *shamisen* playing G and F-sharp. The trio then close the section with a passage progressing from a dense series of double-stops to single notes resolving on pitch center E.

17. *saita sakura ni taga kinu kakeru*	On the fresh blossoms, someone's clothes hanging
18. *eda wa kakururu hana wa chiru*	on the branch, hiding the flowers that fall.

The next stanza of the poem is another isolated image similar to a *haiku* but with a structure of 7+7+7+5 syllables. Similar to lines 4–6, humans disturb nature again with this image of a person's clothes destroying a newly bloomed flower. Kikuoka sets this section as a brief *jiuta* piece that features only a solo *shamisen* in the most sparse section and slowest tempo of the entire composition. The delicacy with which this passage is played and sung contributes to the power of this brief poetic image. An *in* scale built on E sets the scene in line 17, followed by the *shamisen* moving to the upper register and the gentle surprise of an unusual F-sharp-A-B-flat phrase. Line 18 also goes to the upper register and again the bright image of the blooming *sakura* (as was seen at measure 170) is treated with the brightness of a *yo* scale built on E (mm 397–403). The vocalist finishes line 18 by extending the word "*chiru*" (fall) on a high upper leading tone F and the *shamisen* illustrates the fall with two parallel phrases made of eighth notes that move gently downward back to finish at pitch center E.

19. *ina ina mazu wa hana ikusa*	Never mind; first is the flower battle.
20. *hana no zuishin hana no tomo*	The flower's protector and the flower's friend
21. *tagai ni tawamure*	are playing with each other
22. *arasoite*	and fighting.

The quiet sound of the previous section is suddenly broken by a brisk, up-tempo *aikata* instrumental on the *shamisen*, which transitions into the next section, beginning a gradual build-up to the climactic ending of the composition. The stanza of lines 19–22, sung by the female chorus, sets the scene for the next stanza in which flowers will do battle. The *hayashi* percussion is used in this section, which also increases the build-up of tension. Kikuoka makes clever use of the B-flat in this section, first appearing on the word "*ikusa*" (battle or competition), but then appearing rather unexpectedly appearing on the word "*tomo*" (friend, or possibly lover), which is elongated on the low-pitch A by the female chorus. This subtle irony is complete when the B-flat occurs again on the last word "*arasoite*" (fighting) and the preparation for battle is complete. The *shamisen* play a strong 4-measure phrase made of the main pitches E and B using wide octave leaps (mm 506–509). Then a four-measure rest is left open for the *kotsuzumi* and *ōtsuzumi* drums to respond with kabuki-style *chirikara* patterns (mm 510–513). The *shamisen* and percussion continue this competitive exchange through the remainder of this section. After the *shamisen* resolves on an E-B double-stop, the *kotsuzumi* plays a brief solo consisting of a rapid acceleration and a slow deceleration. This drum interlude creates a break in the standard duple rhythm of *nagauta*, allowing for the contrasting triple rhythm of the next section.

23. *omote ni honnori akezakura*	Red-faced, vermillion blossoms,
24. *youte tamoto no nunobikizakura*	drunken, sleeve-pulling blossoms,
25. *kumoizakura no ayaukuba*	cloudy Imperial blossoms endangered,
26. *naka o torano o izazakura*	intimate tigertail blossoms troubled,
27. *rachi mo ariyakezakura to narite*	order becomes blossoms of dawn,
28. *sareba medetaku narazakura*	and at last Nara blossoms of happiness.

The stanza of lines 23–28 features a poetic device that would be described here as *sakura-zukushi* (blossom display) because the poetry is dominated by words for different kinds of blossoms.[7] This poetic litany of blossoms features actual flowers, such as *torano o zakura* (tiger tail blossom), and blossoms created through imaginative word-play, such as *nunobiki zakura* (sleeve-pulling blossom). These metaphors for people, perhaps young girls, depict flowers that are drunk and disorderly. The flowers of this stanza are anything but gentle and peaceful as the flower images continue to operate as metaphors for humanity and the theme of conflict continues to develop musically. Kikuoka thus employs his most radical departure from traditional *nagauta* by setting the entire section in triple rhythm and features extended vocal harmony accompanied by several dissonant chord passages.

Triple rhythm is hardly a new invention in the predominately duple *nagauta* genre. Because of its use in the famous *Hanami Odori*, triple rhythm has adopted the musical connotation of drunkenness. Whereas in *Hanami Odori*, triple meter occurs only briefly in a *shamisen aikata* instrumental that is otherwise predominately duple, in *Sakura Emaki* Kikuoka extends the triple meter for an entire section. Kikuoka exploits triple meter for its drunken connotations, which make it suitable for the drunken battle section of the poem.

The section begins in triple meter with two *shamisen* playing phrases using an *in* scale based on E. In the introduction Kikuoka makes use of contrary motion in mm 554–557 as the lower *shamisen* moves upward from A resolving to B while the upper *shamisen* plays a descending passage F-E-C resolving down to B as the vocals begin. With each vocal phrase the *shamisen* tonality is altered to create contrast with each line of the poem and create the tension necessary for this scene of drunken conflict. The tension is increased further by the vocal harmonies sung on the last syllable of each vocal phrase and extended across the shifting *shamisen* tonalities. As the vocalists sing "*honnori*," at the end of the first phrase in line 23, the last two syllables are harmonized in fourths on A and D, the two leading tones for the main *nagauta* pitches B and E. The following *shamisen* phrase then emphasizes leading tone A as well as upper leading tones C and F. The second half of line 23, "*akezakura*," features vocal harmony that resolves to B and E on the last syllable which is accompanied by a similar resolving phrase on the *shamisen*.

Each line of text is treated in a similar fashion in this section, featuring an unresolved vocal harmony in the middle, followed by a resolution to the main pitches B and E sung in harmony. The first half of line 24 ends without resolution as the upper voice ends on E with the lower voice holding the leading tone D. The *shamisen* then plays an unusual sequence of notes, F-E-A-D-sharp-D-A, which becomes resolved as line 24 ends on the stable tones of B and E heard in the vocal harmony and *shamisen*. Line 25 features a particularly dissonant passage as the first half ends with a vocal harmony of A and E against the unusual descending scale of A-sharp-G-sharp-F. Line 25 similarly ends on the stable tones of B and E in the vocal harmony and *shamisen*. The music of this entire section repeats for the setting of lines 26–28 and ends abruptly with an accelerating A ostinato on all the *shamisen*.

29. *utai sōrae haya sōzu*	Let's sing and make loud music.
30. *some wake tazuna nana iro no*	The seven-colored banner held by a rope
31. *maku ni soyoto yamakaze wa*	flapping in the mountain breeze.
32. *hana o mamori no taenaru suzu no ne*	Protecting the flowers is the sound of a bell tree.
33. *hibiki ni yōte yugasumi*	Pealing in the drunken evening mist,
34. *iriai no kane sora somete*	the sunset bell in the tinted sky.
35. *hana mo hajirau utage kana*	Even the flowers are embarrassed by this feast.
36. *hana mo hajirau utage kana*	Even the flowers are embarrassed by this feast.

The final section of the piece begins with the single line stanza of line 29 set as a conventional *chirashi*, a climactic movement that signals the approaching end of a *nagauta* composition. This is signaled by the *hayashi* percussion section that begins with two strong *taiko* strokes followed by a rhythmic pattern known as *kami-mai* (god dance). But the modern sound of the bass *shamisen* reappears at measure 806 with an unaccompanied ostinato on the low B string and the *shamisen* trio resumes its dense playing style as heard in earlier sections of the piece. As in earlier sections, double-stops on the *shamisen* are used to create a dense texture as in the interlocking passage in measures 837–850. Tonality is also altered in this section to enhance the build-up of tension. Starting in measure 856 the *shamisen* plays a 10-bar passage using B-flat-C-D-E which suggests an *in* scale built on A, but the sequence of notes never resolves to A, nor does it even use the pitch A. This emphasis on the B-flat which happens to appear in conjunction with the word "*yamakaze*" (mountain breeze) could be a subtle reference back to the first piece of the trilogy, *Yuki Musume*, in which the B-flat was an important pitch in creating the imagery of snow and suffering.

The male and female choruses sing line 32 together, featuring the brighter sound of octaves. The most extended harmony of the entire piece occurs in the second half of line 33, "*sora somete*" (tinted sky), the only phrase in the piece in which every note is harmonized. This is followed by another clashing passage from the *shamisen* trio in which all three lines are in different tonalities (mm 927–937). This dissonant passage resolves and sets up the final vocal phrase which is sung twice, emphasizing both the main pitch centers E and B, finally resolving on an extended upper register E. After the vocals finish, the *shamisen* trio continues until the end to generate the rhythmic and harmonic density, and melodic tension that illustrates the song's theme of conflict. Following the last vocal line is another trio passage of clashing tonalities and dense eighth notes (mm 967–974). This dissonant passage resolves into a contrasting *shamisen* passage that adds strongly to the rhythm with double-stop accents on main pitches (mm 975–982). Another contrast occurs as this is followed by more tonal ambiguity (mm 983-986). The piece comes to a sudden finish with a final passage of dense eighth notes finally resolving to B, a fifth above pitch center E.

Although the piece does resolve, it is a highly unconventional *nagauta* ending. The ending on the fifth above pitch center B is similar to the end of a *chirashi* section, leaving the listener to expect to hear the final ritard of a *dangire* section to follow. Kikuoka's elimination of the *dangire* denies the work a feeling of closure in the conventional *nagauta* sense and, like the studio fade-out of *Yuki Musume*, suggests a continuation of the final movement. The unresolved feeling of *Sakura Emaki* implies that the competitions and conflicts, between man and nature, and between human beings in their everyday social relationships, are all part of an eternal struggle.

Mixing both conventional and unconventional word painting techniques to depict the idea of conflict central to the lyric poetry, *Sakura Emaki* is a truly modern work that seems to struggle with the limits of *nagauta* tradition. Kikuoka has created a work that depicts a violent modernity invading Japanese music, but softens it, maintaining elegance and avoiding roughness in accordance with traditional Japanese aesthetics of restrained beauty. Beneath a surface of fragrant blossoms and joyful flower-viewing imagery lies an expressive composition with the theme of conflict that is accentuated by the clash of tradition and modernity in the work. In this sense, Kikuoka has created a harmony of dissonant parts that is one of the central organizing principles of *nagauta*.

A SUMMARY OF TEXT-PAINTING DEVICES IN *NAGAUTA*

After examining *nagauta* compositions in detail in chapters four and five, a set of standard text-painting devices can be identified. Most text-painting in compositions by Kikuoka involved the development of tonality in a manner consistent with classic *nagauta* pieces of the 18th and 19th centuries. Other text-painting techniques such as the use of *ma*, timbral effects on voice and *shamisen*, and extended melismatic vocals, typically work in conjunction with the development of tonality to create the total effect of text-painting that is central to *nagauta*. The following is a summary of text-painting techniques employed in *Sukeroku*, *Yuki Musume* and *Sakura Emaki*.

Tonality and Melodic Tension

Development of tonality in *nagauta* is based on the use of central pitches as "pillar tones whose upper or lower leading tones become important sources of tension" (Malm 1978:92–93). The predominant pillar tones in a given piece are built from a central pitch as agreed upon by the performers, and its fifth degree. Most melodic movement in a *nagauta* piece moves between these two pitch centers, represented in transcriptions in this book as pitches E and B. Secondary pitch centers are also commonly developed on the major second (F-sharp) and the perfect fourth (A) above the central pitch. At any given moment in a *nagauta* composition, there is the sense of a pitch center towards which melodic movement is gravitating. Melodic tension is created by movement away from the pitch center and resolved by a return to this pitch center. The following lists a number of ways in which tonality contributes to text-painting in *nagauta*.

1. Leading Tones. The most common melodic movement in *nagauta* is the use of two kinds of leading tones: a half step above and a whole step below the pitch center. Melodic tension can be created by extending these leading tones without immediately resolving to the pitch center. This kind of unresolved leading tone heightens the drama of a snowstorm in *Yuki Musume* and extends through the end of the piece to give an unresolved quality to the entire work. A clear example of this can be found in the repeated A that begins at measure 511 in *Yuki Musume*.

2. Change of tonal center. New sections are often introduced by changing tonality. The shift to one of the secondary pitch centers (F-sharp or A) can signal a change of mood or introduce a new section of the composition. The shift to pitch center A is particularly noticeable as it emphasizes the upper neighbor tone of B-flat.

3. Flatted tonal center. This effect involves the sudden use of B-flat in *shamisen* passages dominated by pitch center B. Rather than suggesting a new tonal center on A, the immediate use of B-flat can be used to create a darker, tonal effect. Measures 27–30 in the opening section of *Yuki Musume* feature the sudden appearance of B-flat following B-natural to depict the bending and breaking of a branch.

4. Avoidance of tonal center (tonal ambiguity). The use of pitch centers is so dominant throughout *nagauta* compositions that the avoidance of establishing a pitch center in a given section can be used for effect. Kikuoka makes use of such tonal ambiguity in the opening measures of *Yuki Musume* (mm 1–20). Although employed before any lyrics are introduced, the absence of clear tonal centers with upper and lower leading tones creates a wandering feeling that foreshadows the opening verse about the woman's wandering.

Ma *(Silence or Interval)*

Ma, silence or an interval of rest, is an important technique used by Kikuoka and is featured prominently in *Yuki Musume* where it functions as an important text-painting device. While *ma* is used as a symbolic device to indicate snow, the use of two-beat and three-beat rests supports the development of tonality as well. The following is a list of some of the ways in which *ma* is used.

1. *Ma* as a symbolic device. Kikuoka used *ma* to create the denotative meaning of snow in *Yuki Musume.* Although there are actual musical patterns that indicate snow in kabuki such as the *jiuta shamisen* piece *Yuki* and accompanying pattern on the *ōdaiko* (large drum) (see Malm 1963:112), snow is thought of by Kikuoka and many other Japanese musicians as being silent.[8]

2. *Ma* as a device to develop melodic tension. In the opening measures of *Yuki Musume*, Kikuoka uses *ma* to help enhance the sense of tonal ambiguity by pausing immediately following the introduction of pitches that appear to shift the tonality to a new central pitch. Later in this opening verse, a series of two-beat rests of *ma* (mm 132–137) help to elongate a slow, melodic descent that eventually resolves on pitch center E (mm 144).

3. *Ma* as a transitional device. *Ma* is an effective device for making a transition from one section to the next, especially two sections in sharp contrast with each other. An example of this is the transition between the opening section of *Sakura Emaki* with its depiction of a raucous crowd of people and flowers and the quiet section that follows. A few beats of *ma* create the quiet mood in the following section with its depiction of a single sleeve on a single branch (mm 114–115).

Increase in Density

At the opposite end of the spectrum from the silence of *ma* in *nagauta* is density of sound. Density is created through increased use of 8th and 16th notes, faster tempo, *shamisen* double-stops, and multiple parts for *shamisen* and highly syllabic vocals. *Yuki Musume*, a piece about snow and characterized by the use of *ma* in the beginning, gradually employs these techniques of density to depict the chaos of a snowstorm in the final section. *Sakura Emaki*, however, is a scene that is crowded and full, thus it utilizes a dense sound organization from the very beginning of the piece. The piece features several sections of multiple *shamisen* parts played at fast tempo with extensive use of double-stops. One modern technique of increasing density employed by Kikuoka is the use of multiple-voice vocal lines which paints the scenery of *Sakura Emaki* with the voices of men and women singing in octaves and harmony.

Syncopation in the Shamisen

Syncopated patterns in the *shamisen* parts may be employed to create special effects. The brief syncopated passage in *Yuki Musume* (mm 251–253) depicts the bobbing motion of a magpie that appears in the lyrics. Kikuoka employs syncopated *shamisen* at the end of this same piece to rhythmically drive the force of a snowstorm in the final section of this piece (mm 551–555).

Changes in Meter

Nagauta is traditionally set in duple meter with only rare appearances of triple meter. The brief use of triple meter in *Hanami Odori* is a text-painting device used to indicate drunkenness that was adopted by Kikuoka and extended for an entire section in *Sakura Emaki.*

Timbral Manipulations of the Shamisen

A common feature of many *shamisen* passages is the pizzicato pluck by the left hand without the use of the plectrum. These plucks are ubiquitous in *nagauta* and only occasionally serve a text-painting function. For example, in the opening verse of *Yuki Musume,* Kikuoka exploits the use of a succession of rapid 8th note plucks to depict the image of a bending branch about to break. The more delicate timbre of pizzicato is more effective in depicting this image of a frail branch than regular plectrum strokes. In *Sakura Emaki* another image of a delicate branch breaking is created using another left hand technique (*urahijijki*) in which the fingernails of the fifth, fourth and third finger are gently brushed across the surface of the string.

Vocal Techniques (Melismatic and Syllabic Singing)

1. Melismatic vocal style. Melismatic extension of particular syllables is found throughout virtually any *nagauta* compositions and is not always necessarily connected to text-painting. However, in certain passages melismatic vocal style powerfully expresses the emotional content of the lyrics. *Yuki Musume* features one section in which the tonally stable *shamisen* accompany a highly melismatic vocal part in which the woman expresses her most intimate thoughts about her lover in elongated tones (mm 422–499). Broad sweeps ranging from upper register, as on the word "*nushi*" (you, my beloved), cascading melismatically down to lower register, as on "*showaru*"

(womanizer), are used to paint an image of love leading to disappointment. Melisma is also used to create the atmosphere of sexuality that is often subtly suggested in *nagauta* poetry. The word "*nure*" (wet) is often depicted musically by vocal melisma. *Sukeroku* features an extended melisma on "*nure*" (mm 135–141) in a passage that takes place in the brothel district and is charged with sexual suggestiveness. In a somewhat less erotic passage of *Yuki Musume*, a more subtle use of melisma on the word "*nure*" is heard (mm 87–89).

The sudden, brief drop of the voice to a much lower, indeterminate pitch is heard in erotic passages as well. The melismatic treatment of the word "*nure*" in Sukeroku, as mentioned in the previous paragraph, ends with a dramatic dip downward, sounding almost as if the singer is gulping excitedly before proceeding to the next word. Later in this same section the suggestion of sexuality on the word "*misesugagaki*" is enhanced with another sudden drop of indeterminable pitch (measure 170). Breath cuts are another feature used in erotic passages as heard in this same melismatic treatment of the word "*misesugagaki*" from Sukeroku. Sexual excitement is subtly suggested by an unusual breath cut after "*-ga*" in the middle of the word, followed by a sharp, upward arching melisma on "*-ki*" (mm 167-179).

2. Syllabic vocal style. The sensuality suggested in some of these melismatic passages contrasts with more syllabic treatments of the vocal line that sometimes suggests a more pious musical mood. *Nagauta* typically features passages sung in a highly syllabic style with emphasis on the tonal center and occasional lower and upper leading tones. This style derives from the chant-like singing of *nō* and is sometimes used as a text-painting device to suggest something from a *nō* drama or from antiquity. Kikuoka used this chanted style in *Yuki Musume* to signal the beginning of a new section telling the ancient story of a bird. The phrase "*mukashi no tori wa kasasagi ya*" (the magpie of long ago) sung primarily on pitch center A, suggests the chant-like style of *nō* (mm 247–252). Syllabic vocal style can also be combined and contrasted with melismatic voice or elongated vocal tones for text-painting purposes. Kikuoka uses this kind of contrast in vocal lines to depict the shifting winds of a snowstorm in the final section of *Yuki Musume*. Vocal delivery in this section alternates between rapid syllabic style, as on the word "*otomonaku*" (silently) and elongated tones, as on the word "*tsumoru*" (piling up) (mm 565–573).

CONCLUSION: NEW MUSIC IN THE *NAGAUTA* TRADITION

In spite of the bleak outlook described by scholars regarding new compositions for *nagauta*, Kikuoka's compositions demonstrate a great degree of success as a composer working within the confines of the tradition. Although Kikuoka's compositions will most likely remain obscure in a tradition as resistant to innovation as *nagauta*, the works examined in this chapter show a mastery of both conventions and subtle innovations without breaking the established form that makes these legitimate works of *nagauta*. His modern extensions of *nagauta*, such as the use of lower pitched instruments, triple rhythms in the *shamisen* parts, and harmonized vocal lines, were all motivated entirely by the demands of the poetry which is in keeping with *nagauta*'s musical function as lyric song. The lower pitched instruments, which Kikuoka described as similar in function to the off-stage instruments, served to expand the range of traditional instruments to express the imagery of crowdedness and conflict. Triple rhythm actually derives from *nagauta* tradition and as such is an extension of depictions of drunkenness in earlier compositions, such as the triple rhythms employed in *Hanami Odori*. To depict variety and color appropriate for the setting, male and female voices were used together, sometimes singing in harmonies of fifths and fourths which, although unconventional, is in keeping with the common use of pitch centers in *nagauta* music. Furthermore, the use of vocal harmony was a convenient solution to differences in register between male and female voices. In this last sense, Kikuoka modernized *nagauta* for a gender-egalitarian society without straying too far from the gender-segregated sound ideal. As a composer, Kikuoka may not have revolutionized music for a free and independent *shamisen*, but considering his modern adaptations for *nagauta* without breaking its form, his work has been successful in his goal of "translating the past" into the present day. Perhaps the success of *nagauta* composition is to be found in this kind of continuity and purity that Kikuoka maintained.

Conclusion: Shaped by Japanese Music

This ethnography of an individual in a particular setting of Japanese traditional music has shown how music is embodied in the lives of individuals through a training and socialization process that is driven by deeply embedded cultural values such as harmony, nature and purity. The five chapters of analysis that have centered around one individual, Kikuoka Hiroaki, were directed at trying to understand how a traditional genre of music such as *nagauta* is maintained in modern Japan and what kinds of dynamic forces are at work in a particular context at a particular time. Recounting the career of Kikuoka, a prominent musician of concert *nagauta*, in chapter one showed how one individual helped to shape, and was shaped by, historical developments in the tradition during the second half of the twentieth century. The ethnographic account of chapter two focused on the centrality of the teaching process in *nagauta* and how the relationship between Kikuoka and his students directly imposed appropriate behavior as a fundamental aspect of *nagauta* in his lesson place. Chapter three outlined the broader forces of social control that operated through this musical tradition, as well as the cultural values that allowed the perpetuation of such coercive forces in the lives of musicians. Shifting from social analysis to musical analysis, chapter four examined some of the ways this shaping process in the social institution of *nagauta* is evident in the cultural documents of *nagauta*, particularly in the structure of musical composition and performance ensembles. Returning to Kikuoka in chapter five, my analysis of two representative examples of his musical compositions in detail demonstrated how his creative works were also shaped by the strict conventions of the tradition as he "translated the past" of *nagauta* music to suit the present.

Although I have taken these five interrelated "views" of Japanese music (to borrow Malm's term) and created a theme of a "shaping process," it has not been my intention to create an essentialist model of how Japanese musical culture operates generally. Depicting culture as a set of control mechanisms for ordering behavior as I have done here is quite common in anthropology and is by no means limited to studies of Japan (Geertz 1973:44–45). This particular subculture socially constructed around an individual who embodies a Japanese traditional art is only one of many innumerable settings that exist in Japanese music. It is my hope that other researchers of Japanese music will produce ethnographic studies of particular individuals in specific locations that can support, modify or refute any of the themes I have developed in this study.

Most importantly, the five aspects of *nagauta* examined here were directed towards answering fundamental questions of ethnomusicology that are often overlooked in research on Japanese music. What cultural values and social processes are present in musical practice, performance and composition? How do Japanese musical practices symbolize, as well as reinforce and generate, cultural values and social organization? In what ways do musicians support or challenge social organization or cultural values through musical practices? As such broad questions invite generic answers for a culture that has experienced more than its share of cultural stereotypes, I intentionally narrowed my focus on how cultural values and social processes operate in the career strategies, teaching practices, and compositional approaches of a single performing musician and other musicians within the domain of his school. Kikuoka's experience with the world of music in which he lived can help ethnomusicologists understand some of the ways in which traditional music is historically constructed, socially maintained and individually created in modern society. This concluding chapter describes the ways in which this ethnography has examined music as a field of discourse, as a social process, as a cultural metaphor, and as an individual creation.

MUSIC AS A FIELD OF DISCOURSE: VALUES IN *NAGAUTA*

This book's focus on an individual *nagauta* musician and his domain illuminates a discourse of cultural values prevalent in *nagauta* music in late-twentieth-century Japan. At the center of this discourse among musicians of *nagauta* was a concern for proper form. Proper form, referred to here as *kata*, includes the appropriate form of musical structure and execution, the appropriate form of the body of the individual, and the appropriate form of social interaction, all of which connote cultural values of harmony and purity for many musicians. Although the obligation to maintain proper form in all aspects of musical and social interactions was both an external and internalized coercive force in the *nagauta* world of this study, what was perceived to be proper form often varied according to individuals and depended on one's position in the field of *nagauta*, that is, one's belonging to a particular school, one's status as professional or amateur, one's gender or economic level. In spite of the coercive forces behind maintaining proper form, *nagauta* musicians here were not mere passive recipients of culture. As cultural values were invoked in different ways by different musicians, individuals were actively involved in shaping, as well as being shaped by, a musical tradition. As such, proper form is less easily schematized into abstract, objectivist models of behavior or cognition than it is examined from the point of view of individuals and their strategic use of proper form in particular situations at particular times.

As a professional performer, composer, teacher, and founder of a music organization, Kikuoka occupied a central and influential position in shaping the discourse concerning the tradition of *nagauta* in the twentieth century. Discourse about musical tradition, as Rice points out, is a conscious, reflexive practice found in modern societies, as opposed to traditional societies in which what is considered tradition may be beyond discourse (Rice 1994:14). In a modern society, tradition is brought to life, taking on "the appearance of an objective existence, as if it were a being with life and therefore demands of its own" (ibid.:15). For Kikuoka and other musicians in the Tokyo location examined here, the discourse of *nagauta* was a conscious, reflexive practice as they invoked a range of different cultural values in service of the "tradition" of *nagauta* music.

The orthodox position in this modern discourse on *nagauta* is exemplified by *iemoto*. From this perspective the proper form of *nagauta* social organization is the *ie*, a group traditionally marked by stage names that identify musicians as belonging to a school. In this conception, the social organization of musicians is rooted in deeply embedded cultural concepts of purity/pollution that legitimize boundary distinctions between the inside (*uchi*) and the outside (*soto*) of the school. If these distinctions are maintained by the exclusive membership in, and loyalty to, the *ie*, then the *nagauta* it produces maintains its purity. Kikuoka's notion of purity was a heterodoxy that was opposed to the orthodoxy of *iemoto* and drew on a different interpretation of values. His own notion of pure *nagauta*, as exemplified by Tōonkai and his own school of teaching, was an extension of the growing autonomy of the art form begun in the early twentieth century that had been initiated by the Kenseikai group. This group's goal at the turn of the century of creating *nagauta* that could exist independently of dance, followed by *Nagauta* Kenkyukai's mission in the 1940s of purifying *nagauta* of corrupt *iemoto*-like business practices, set the stage for Kikuoka's efforts to create an autonomous form of *nagauta* with similar values. Pitting the modern value of merit in Western education against the value of name in Japanese family life, Kikuoka's purification of *nagauta* was an effort to reduce or eliminate the influence of that which he believed was extrinsic to the art form in order to create a more autonomous *nagauta*.

As an advocate of an autonomous art, Kikuoka is akin to Bourdieu's "independent intellectual who does not recognize nor wish to recognize any obligations other than the intrinsic demands of his creative project" (Bourdieu 1971:163). The "creative project" of *nagauta* undertaken by Kikuoka in the 1950s with his new organization formed in opposition to *iemoto* can be described in Bourdieu's words as:

> the place of meeting and sometimes of conflict between the intrinsic necessity of the work of art which demands that it be continued, improved and completed, and social pressures which direct the work from outside. (ibid.:166–167)

In Kikuoka's view, *nagauta* was an art that should be purified of decadent economic interests that are extrinsic to the art. Although the *iemoto* system had long been associated with the tradition of *nagauta*, an autonomous art of *nagauta* in the twentieth century should not tolerate business practices perceived of as extrinsic to the art, such as the buying and selling of stage names. Such practices are extrinsic to a pure form of the art conceived strictly in terms of transmitting the proper *kata* directly from teacher to student.

But debate over proper form was not simply a matter of modern values in opposition to traditional values. Even orthodox positions in defense of *iemoto* were expressed by musicians invoking similar notions of extrinsic forces impinging upon the purity of the art form, such as the singer from a *nagauta* family mentioned in chapter one who refused to join Tōonkai. He criticized the modern university approach advocated by the Tōonkai group as a tragic standardization of the art of *nagauta*, forcing musicians to conform to a standard that was legitimized by the university. Denying any comparison of his family to an *iemoto*-like system, the singer objected not to the educational institution's challenge to his family's traditional way of singing, but rather to the challenge to his own individual way of singing. In his opinion, the standardization of Tōonkai's approach took away the freedom of the individual to interpret the music according to the performance situation. In this case, the orthodoxy of *iemoto* practice was being defended by claims to individual freedom of expression. As was demonstrated here, debates over traditional forms of music in modern society may involve a combination of both traditional and modern values that may be invoked by different individuals in unpredictable ways.

Regardless of how they are constructed, both heterodox and orthodox positions are conceived within the larger realm of doxa that exists beyond the level of discourse and is beyond critique (See Bourdieu 1977:164–171). In the autonomous field of *nagauta* in the late twentieth century, the intrinsic artistic value of the music was central to the discourse among musicians, while its economic value, perceived of as extrinsic to the art, existed outside the discourse. This was true even of Kikuoka's heterodox position criticizing the decadence of an artistic practice that was too "business-like." Kikuoka's full financial disclosure of his *benkyōkai*, which was a response to the secretive financial transactions of *iemoto*, could not nullify the fact that he too was dependent on the economic value of *nagauta*. Although he favored the artistic ideal of his *benkyōkai*, Kikuoka felt obligated to maintain the *osaraikai* as a source of income for his fellow *nagauta* musicians. While Tōonkai worked to raise musical standards and reduce *iemoto* power, the survival of the organization was always at stake in the concert marketplace. As the demands of the "creative project" of an autonomous field of music are that it be "continued, improved and completed," the economic value of *nagauta* must remain hidden in any discourse on the music, especially one seeking to purify the art of the "decadent" focus on making money. The economic necessity of adopting stage names for the Tōonkai group in order to continue its project of promoting high quality *nagauta* must have seemed inevitable even to Kikuoka by the 1990's.

Kikuoka was not only the living embodiment of *nagauta* tradition, but he embodied its economic value as well. Although Kikuoka pitted the economic value of *nagauta* against the artistic value of *nagauta*, as a high-ranking expert of the music he was able to command substantial lesson fees and secure stable university employment, both necessary sources of income given his purist rejection of lucrative concerts accompanying dance. Although critical of the business practices of *nagauta*, Kikuoka was inescapably part of the *nagauta* business and his high profile position was perhaps a point of personal conflict. The high standards of pure *nagauta* set by Kikuoka were ultimately unattainable given the social and economic pressures that he considered extrinsic to the art. For Kikuoka, the social pressures impinging upon the art of *nagauta* consisted not only of economic survival for himself and members of the Tōonkai organization, but it included survival and perpetuation of his own school of teaching, which depended on a form of succession that he opposed.

As the living embodiment of a tradition, Kikuoka had no successor to carry on his tradition of pure *nagauta* that ended with his death. For all his efforts to develop a pure and autonomous *nagauta*, he chose not to adopt a successor. Choosing a successor for his school would have been the ultimate move towards the kind of *ie* system that he worked against, but it could have allowed him to continue his ideal, provided the right student was chosen. It appeared that he had been grooming a successor in K, his top *deshi*, but K's betrayal put an end to that possibility and perhaps soured Kikuoka on the possible worthiness of anyone else within his school. Perhaps Kikuoka's perfectionist idealism caused him to dismiss all *nagauta* players as unfit for the job. Although it meant the end of his school, the absence of a named successor was consistent with his philosophy of independence of players from any sort of *ie* system. Nevertheless, Kikuoka still derived the legitimacy for his school from a musical lineage, although the lineage was more ideological than biological and the continuity of transmission from master to pupil that is so essential to *nagauta* eluded Kikuoka in the end. Kikuoka's case demonstrates the fragility of musical lineage in Japan, especially in the modern era. As a result of his personal strategies for creating pure *nagauta*, Kikuoka's legacy survives not in the continuity of a school based on his own performance style in the manner of an *iemoto*, but in the existence of Tōonkai, even in its compromised form, that raised performance standards within the field of *nagauta*.

MUSIC AS A SOCIAL PROCESS: TRANSFORMATION THROUGH *KATA*

In spite of the rise and fall of individual schools such as Kikuoka's, or the shifting dynamics of organizations such as Tōonkai, the music of *nagauta* continues to survive through the transmission of *kata*. Although the social process of *kata* in the arts is not thought of as an art form itself and is not a part of ordinary discourse, its function and purpose has been addressed by some artists and scholars. Ooms reveals a history of positions on the instilling of "norms through forms" centered on a tension between external forms of *kata* and the inner self (Ooms 1998:35). At least three views of the relationship between external *kata* and inner self can be identified: 1) forms of *kata* require an interaction with the inner self in order to create art that is meaningful, as theorized by Zeami;[1] 2) forms of *kata*, as fixed by ritual, produce in the individual a properly formed or refined inner self, as rooted in Confucianism and articulated by Sorai; and 3) forms of *kata* demand only that the individual conform to the external practice, regardless of any influence or affect on one's inner self, as argued by Sorai's student, Dazai Shundai (ibid.).

The first view of *kata*, suggesting the possibility of individual expression, was the only one of these three perspectives to enter everyday discourse in Kikuoka's school, and even then only rarely. Kikuoka told me that his teacher, Yamada Shotaro, claimed to be able to judge a person's true personality simply by hearing their performance of the *nagauta* standard *Aki no Irokusa* (1845), one of the early classic concert pieces composed for *shamisen* and voice without drum accompaniment. Although Kikuoka never isolated a single piece as a tool for such psychological divination, he did claim that Yamada's humanity and his comic side were clearly evident in his playing, but not in any way that he could describe. Judgment of other players by Kikuoka and some of his students was more commonly an evaluation of the execution of the formal techniques of *nagauta*, such as "his *ma* is no good" or "she uses *umiji* (melisma) well." But some players, including Kikuoka, distinguished between players who were merely "skillful" (*gijutsuteki*) and those who were "artistic" (*geijutsuteki*). As in Kingsbury's study of a Western conservatory of music (1988), sometimes judgements of the quality of art were expressed in ways that became judgements of personality. One veteran professional *shamisen* player in the Tōonkai group was dismissed by some listeners as sacrificing musical quality for showing off his technical speed, thus earning him the pejorative nickname of *denki mashin* ("electric machine"). From this perspective, the ideal performer of *nagauta* should possess both skill and artistry. Kikuoka described his teacher Yamada as the first performer he had met who possessed the highest degrees of both skill and artistry, qualities Kikuoka believed were equally necessary for *nagauta*. Kikuoka said that prior to meeting Yamada he had been simply memorizing and practicing pieces, and that Yamada had finally taught him to play real music.

The second view of *kata* as an external form that refines or transforms the personality of the student was also a part of Kikuoka's philosophy about music. The artistic process was described by Kikuoka using his metaphor of tea and teacup, which encompasses a notion of an outer form and an inner state of the individual. According to this metaphor, making the proper vehicle or teacup (the musically, socially informed body of the musician) is necessary for the proper tea (the music/the self).

The human life in the music valued by Kikuoka was ideally a merging of the outer physical form of individuals with their inner state through a process in which the student is transformed.[2] The third view of *kata* as an external state of artistic perfection or social harmony completely separate from inner selves had no place in Kikuoka's pure *nagauta*. Kikuoka had no interest in an art that was only a set of surface practices without a process of self-transformation.

Locating this research of *nagauta* practice in a specific place has helped to demonstrate how this process of personal development and social transformation takes place. Learning *nagauta* is a social process that takes place in a specially created environment by teachers such as Kikuoka. The environment of the lesson place (*okeiko*) as described in detail in chapter two, is one which is clearly marked as an inside (*uchi*), thus creating a social world that is separate from the outside world. The student enters into this environment, a special lesson place built around the teacher and delineated by social activity within a group, and undergoes a transformation of external social behavior and, ideally at least, internal artistic sense. The learning of musical *kata*, such as the appropriate execution of melody, rhythm, and embellishment is combined with the learning of social *kata*, such as the appropriate manner of bowing and manners in relation to others, to create a total learning environment. Ikuta Kumio, in her study on the transmission of *waza* (artistic skill) in the arts (1997), focuses on this situated, transformative social process in an effort to explain the differences in the execution of the same *kata* by two different dance groups. The student's entrance into, and participation within, the community of the teacher and fellow students is a crucial part of the transformation of the individual, changing the individual's identity as well as the community itself. In her view, Japanese art is not something that lives within any single individual, but rather is a separate entity that lives and develops in the social process itself and evolves through transmission between people.

As a social process of shaping individuals that is linked to Japanese cultural values, *nagauta* bears a resemblance not only to other domains of art guided by *kata*, but also to other domains of daily life in Japan. As a source of deeply embedded cultural values, it is not surprising to find Japanese religious practices guided by a similar social process. Shinto-Buddhism exists in the daily lives of most Japanese people more as a ritual practice than as a doctrine of belief. Describing Japanese religion as a religion of action, Ian Reader demonstrates how appropriate social action, or correctly performed ritual, substitutes for doctrine (1991). One example cited by Reader is in the series of actions involved in the practice of honoring the souls of the dead. Formal actions such as going to temple, having a priest perform the appropriate rituals, enshrining the deceased soul on the family altar, and making offerings to the altar, constitute a kind of *kata* to be executed in the proper manner. These actions are so formalized that Buddhist sects publish handbooks that detail not only the correct procedures to be followed, but also the proper frame of mind in which they should be done (ibid.:15). Crucial to the efficacy of *kata* is the notion that if the proper form is executed on the surface (*tatemae*), the proper frame of mind (*honne*) will be achieved.

Ritual displays of group belonging and interdependency among members of Kikuoka's school such as the *benkyōkai* and *osaraikai* student recitals find their equivalent in more common everyday rituals in Japan. Edwards's research of modern Japanese weddings (1989) demonstrates the importance of the socializing process of these rituals and how the various ritual actions of the ceremony have symbolic meaning about the future lives of the couple. Important components of the ceremony express not only the bond between the bride and groom, but also their need to rely on parents and the community around them. The proper execution of the ritual both symbolizes and helps create a network of future relations necessary for a successful marriage and for the healthy existence of the *ie.*

The *ie* is not merely a feudalistic remnant of the Tokugawa era that only survives in traditional arts such as *nagauta*. In many Japanese families, social life is still structured by, or at least heavily influenced by, the traditional *ie* family structure. The pressure of the continuation of the *ie* remains a vital force in the small, family-owned businesses studied in an ethnography by Dorinne Kondo (1990). The tension and conflict that led to the dissolution of Kikuoka's *ie* is similar to Kondo's depictions of the threat of modernity to these traditional structures in Japanese life. Young would-be successors' conflicts between choosing lucrative, stable employment in large companies outside the family over the inheritance of a struggling, uncertain future as a small shop owner pose a threat to the continuation of *ie* structures. Kondo's research suggests that the agony of the discontinuation of *ie* is a regular occurrence in modern Japan.

MUSIC AS A CULTURAL METAPHOR: READING THE "MAPS" OF *NAGAUTA*

The focus in this book on *nagauta* as a social process that instills cultural values in individuals does not minimize the importance of musical composition and performances within the genre. These cultural documents of *nagauta* practice are the results of *kata* and serve as artifacts that the ethnomusicologist can study to learn how *kata* operates musically. As mentioned in this book's Introduction, one objective of my research was to avoid merely creating an essentialized "map of Japanese music" and instead utilize a person-centered approach to give a sense of "what it's like to live there." Such an approach is opposed to an essentialist top-down imposition of deterministic social theories on the music and instead proceeds by collecting data from the bottom-up in a particular place and at a particular time. However, it is still useful to step back and see what can be discovered on the "maps" that already exist, such as the standard *nagauta* ensemble and individual works of music. An examination of *nagauta* in this way reveals how these musical products are also shaped by the same social process and cultural values that shapes individuals in musical practice. As a musical tradition that is itself "shaped" by society, *nagauta* music emerges as a metaphor of Japanese culture.

The *nagauta* ensemble onstage exists as a cultural metaphor in its visual display of the social order. As a product of the Tokugawa era, it is not surprising that the standardized seating arrangements on the *nagauta* stage clearly display the hierarchical relationships of musicians. Important to the control of society by the Tokugawa military government, as Ooms points out, was the tactic of making the social order visible through various types of display. The government dictated visible signs of status, such as types of clothing, so that status symbols became a kind of "social tattoo" indicating an individual's place in society (Ooms 1998:25–26). The social order of the Tokugawa era was also visually displayed through the elaborate processions of *daimyo* (leaders of fiefdoms) that "presented to society gigantic moving and movable tableaux vivants of its ordered self" (ibid.:26). Society's "ordered self" is evident to observers of *nagauta* performances through seating arrangements and costumes that display group hierarchy, as well as the anonymity that unifies and equalizes the group. By reducing all possibility of extraneous individual movement, the rigid order of the *nagauta* performance insures that no protruding "nails" will need to be "hammered down."

The sound of *nagauta* metaphorically represents this shaping process as well. An analysis of the classic composition *Sukeroku* reveals the shaping process metaphorically embedded in the music. Evidence of the process is found in the manner in which music paints the textual imagery in the poetry, which is the most basic function of music in *nagauta*. Text painting techniques reinforce the underlying theme of the piece in which a rough and unruly character is metaphorically refined and formed into a properly socialized individual. The dramatic, emotional power of the piece lies in the stereotyped patterns of *kata*. Such musical phrases are learned directly and meticulously from teachers such as Kikuoka and are intended to be reproduced with the precision necessary to generate the proper emotion. Through extensive repetition of the proper *kata* modeled by the teacher, the student of *nagauta*, like the character of Sukeroku, becomes shaped by tradition.

This analysis of *nagauta* as both a visual and sonic metaphor suggests the notion of music as iconic of culture as developed in ethnomusicology (Becker 1981, Feld 1988, Turino 1989). A *nagauta* concert can be described as iconic to the degree that it "creates a sense of coherence between behavior and forms in different fields of activity," and through its perceived "naturalness" appears to viewers to be a true representation of the world (Turino 1989:1). While players can provide detailed explanations of the way *nagauta* is supposed to look and sound, any visual or sonic resemblance to the social order of Japanese culture is beyond discourse. Whether performed by an established *iemoto* group, an "alternative" group such as Tōonkai, or even by groups of young musicians organizing their own performances, the performance of *nagauta* appears fixed and predictable in its standardized presentation. The orderly display of *nagauta* appears natural to performers and audiences because of its coherence with the social process by which it was created. *Nagauta* appears coherent with Japanese society visually in its fixed patterns of performance and aurally in its fixed vocal patterns of emotional display.

MUSIC AS INDIVIDUAL CREATION: UNDERSTANDING THE HUMAN LIFE IN THE MUSIC

Perhaps the most important aspect of a person-centered approach in ethnomusicology is the way in which musical choices are made by individuals. Analysis of modern *nagauta* compositions revealed how Kikuoka's art is shaped by the tradition into the proper form, yet his compositional choices while working within the restrictions of proper form allowed him to give a modern shape to tradition. Kikuoka's music demonstrates the extent to which the musical boundaries of a genre as resistant to expansion as *nagauta* can be stretched, while simultaneously maintaining the proper form. Kikuoka achieved this by preserving the primacy of the song lyric as the sole motivation behind all compositional decisions and maintained the basic musical function of word-painting that is central to the appreciation of *nagauta*. Employing standard *nagauta* techniques such as the creation of melodic tension around tonal centers and vocal melisma, Kikuoka's compositions are traditional musical *kata* in a modern mode. In addition to the song lyric, Kikuoka acknowledges the structure of the *shamisen* itself to be fundamental to *nagauta* composition and thus his experiments with the genre were never attempts to break away from the inherent limitations of the instrument by employing extended techniques. The *shamisen*, the voice, the composition, and the artist himself, maintain the proper shape of *nagauta*.

The proper shape of a composition, however, is not the ultimate goal of the art of *nagauta*. It is rather the proper shape of the self. This study has shown how *nagauta* is an experiential process of music, involving a process of the student's embodiment of behavior appropriate to the tradition, which is embodied not in any one piece of music, but in a teacher who is the living carrier of the tradition. This is why many Japanese musicians will say that the most important thing needed in order to make Japanese music is a teacher. Only a *sensei* can provide a musician access to the process of embodiment of *kata*, to shape the musician in the appropriate way. The goal in *nagauta*, as in other Japanese arts, is to shape the self in the way of the art form. Although meaning in *nagauta* may be sought in the external products of expression or interpretation created by its artists, its real significance is embodied in the artists themselves who have been shaped into the pure form of the art. Following my teacher Kikuoka and paraphrasing William Malm, who described *nagauta* as "the heart of kabuki music," I propose that at the heart of *nagauta* is the human life in the music.

Appendix A

TRANSCRIPTION: *SUKEROKU*

Notes on the Transcription

As the fundamental pitch of *nagauta* varies with each performance and is subject to the preference of the performers, I have chosen to transcribe all of the following works with the starting pitch of B below middle C, which corresponds to the open pitch of the lowest string on the *shamisen*.

Because the focus of this study is on Kikuoka's music, the following transcriptions include only the vocal and *shamisen* parts as sung and played by Kikuoka. Additional instruments such as *kotsuzumi*, *ōtsuzumi*, *taiko*, *fue* and others that appear in performances and recordings are not included here as they are not fixed in composition and vary according to the school of musicians that provide the accompaniment.

The transcription of *Sukeroku* is based on my own lessons from Kikuoka in his school. The transcriptions of *Yuki Musume* and *Sakura Emaki* are based on the Crown Records recording *Setsugekka* CRCM 60005.

Special characters used in transcriptions

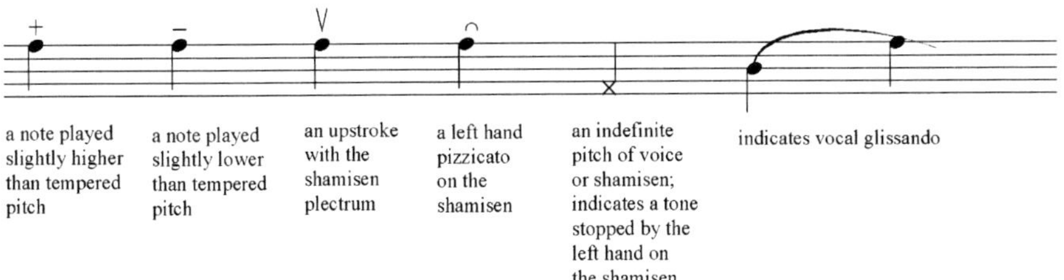

Sukeroku

45
v.
ni
o
45
sh.
49
v.
o
49
accel.
sh.
50
Moderato
v.
Sa
-
ku
50
sh.
54
v.
ra
to
54
sh.
57
v.
hi
-
to
ni
yo
57
sh.

61
v.
i no ku chi
61
sh.
65
v.
Ya - bo wa
65
sh.
69
v.
mo - ma - re - te
69
sh.
73
v.
su - i to na -
73
sh.
77
v.
ru
77
sh.

81
v.
ko
-
ko
o
81
sh.
85
v.
u
-
ki
-
yo
no
85
sh.
89
v.
Na
-
ka
-
no
-
cho
89
sh.
93
v.
ko
-
i
ni
93
sh.
97
v.
ko
-
ga
-
re
-
te
97
sh.

101
v.
Su - ke - ro -
101
sh.
104
v.
ku ga
104
sh.
accel.
105 Allegro
sh.
113
sh.
121
v.
Moderato
Ka - sa sa -
121
sh.
rit.
129
v.
Lento
shi - te mu - re
129
sh.
rit.

137
v.
ni
ku
-
137
sh.
145
v.
ru
-
wa
no
yo
-
ru
no
145
sh.
153
v.
a
-
me
Andante
153
sh.
161
v.
mi
-
se
-
su
-
161
sh.
169
v.
ga
-
ga
-
ki
ni
169
sh.

177
v.
rit.
ko - e so-
177
sh.
rit.
Allegro
185
v.
o - ru
185
sh.
193
v.
ka - ne wa
193
sh.
rit.
Moderato
201
v.
U - e - no ka A - sa - ku - sa
201
sh.
accel.
209
v.
ni so no na - mo da - te -
209
sh.

217
v.
na
Ha - na -
217
sh.
rit.
225
v.
225
sh.
accel.
233
v.
ka - wa - do
233
sh.
241
v.
Ko - no ha -
241
sh.
rit.
249
v.
chi - ma - ki no mu - ra - sa - ki
249
sh.
Lento

257
v.
wa yu - ka - ri - zo ka ka -
257
sh.
265
v.
ru fu - ji - na - mi no a - ro -
265
sh.
273
v.
o - te chi - yo no
273
sh.
281
v.
i - ro - ma - sa -
281
sh.
289
v.
ru ma - tsu no ha -
289
sh.

297
v.
ke - sa - ki su - ki - bi -
297
sh.
accel.
305
v.
ta - i tsu - tsu - mi cho E - mo-n-
305
sh.
rit.
accel.
313
v.
za - ka ka - yo - i
313
sh.
Allegro
321
v.
na - re - ta - ru
321
sh.
329
v.
nu - ri - ba - na - o hi -
329
sh.

337
v.
to - tsu i - n - ro hi - to - tsu - ma - e
337
rit.
sh.
345
v.
fu - ta - e - ma - wa - ri no ku-
345
Moderato
sh.
358
v.
mo - no o - bi sa -
353
sh.
361
v.
shi - ta sha - ku - ha - chi sa - me - za - ya wa ko - re go - zo-
361
sh.
370
v.
n - ji no de - ta - chi -
370
sh.

373
v.
ba - e
373
sh.
rit.
accel.
374
v.
Se - ku - na
374
sh.
Andante
382
v.
se - kya - ru -
382
sh.
390
v.
na sa - yo - e u -
390
sh.
398
v.
ki - yo - wa - n - na -
398
sh.

406
v.
a - a - ku - ru - u -
406
sh.
414
v.
ma sa - yo - e
414
sh.
422
v.
422
sh.
430
v.
me - gu - ru tsuki - hi ga e - n - to - na - ru
430
sh.
438
v.
me - gu - ru tsuki - hi ga e - n - to - na -
438
sh.

446
v.
a - a - ru
446
sh.
454
v.
Ko - i
454
sh.
Allegro
462
v.
no
yo - za -
462
sh.
470
v.
ku - ra
u -
470
sh.
478
v.
wa - ki
de
ka - yo
478
sh.

486
v.
486
sh.
494
v.
ma - bu no na - to - ri
494
sh.
502
v.
no to - ri - mo - no ke-
502
sh.
510
v.
n - ka - ji-ka - ke - ya
510
sh.
518
v.
i-ro - ji - ka - ke chi - ka -
518
sh.

526
v.
ra - zu - ku - na - ra na - ni te -
526
sh.
534
v.
ku - da na - ra ri - yu - gi ri - yu -
534
sh.
542
v.
gi de mu - ko - zu - ra
542
sh.
550
v.
ta - da wa to - sa - nu o -
550
sh.
558
v.
mo - n o
558
sh.

566
v.
ma - ta ku - gu - ru
566
sh.
574
v.
to wa i - no -
574
sh.
582
v.
chi - ga - ke
582
sh.
590
v.
Do - te - bu - shi ya - me -
590
sh.
598
v.
yo a - mi - ga - sa o
598
sh.

606
v.
to - t - te na - ge - ru wa kyo-ku
606
sh.
614
v.
ga na - i ke - ko - n de mi - sho ya-
614
sh.
3
622
v.
ka - ta - bu - ne ko - rya
622
sh.
630
v.
ma - ta nan no ko - ta E - do no ha -
630
sh.
3
638
v.
na Fu - ji
638
sh.
rit.
a tempo

646
v.
to Tsu - ku - ba no ya - ma - a -
646
sh.
654
v.
i no so - de - na - ri
654
sh.
662
v.
yu - ka - shi
662
rit.
sh.
665
v.
ki - mi yu - ka - shi
665
accel.
sh.
666
v.
shi - n - zo
666
sh.

667
v.
667
sh.
accel.
i - no -
670
v.
chi o
670
sh.
3
674
v.
A - ge - ma - ki
674
sh.
accel.
678
v.
no ko - re Su - ke - ro - ku ga ma - e - wa - ta - ri Fu - ze - i
678
sh.
686
v.
rit.
na - ri - ke - ru shi - da - i na -
686
sh.
rit.

694
v.
ri
694
sh.

Appendix B

TRANSCRIPTION: *YUKI MUSUME*

19
v.
Yu - ki o - re mo ki - ko -
19
sh. 1
25
v.
e - te ku - ra -
25
sh. 1
31
v.
ki yo na - ru ka -
31
sh. 1
37
v.
na
37
sh. 1
43
sh. 1

49
sh. 1
55
sh. 1
61
v.
ma
-
da
61
sh. 1
67
v.
fu
-
mi
na
-
re
-
nu
67
sh. 1
73
v.
mi
-
chi
na
-
ga
-
ra
73
sh. 1

79
v.
ko - i no tsu - ra -
79
sh. 1
85
v.
ra ni nu - re - so -
85
sh. 1
91
v.
me - te
91
sh. 1
97
v.
97
sh. 1

103
v.
no - ki
103
sh. 1
109
v.
no shi - zu - ku no shi -
109
sh. 1
115
v.
n - ki - ra - shi
115
sh. 1
121
v.
fu - ke - te to - ma - mo -
121
sh. 1

127
v.
ru
to - mo - shi - bi -
sh. 1
133
ya
139
ko -
145
i - shi i - to -
a tempo

151
v.
shi - mo hi - to - fu - de
151
sh. 1
157
v.
ni u - su - zu - mi
157
sh. 1
163
v.
i - ro no
163
sh. 1
169
v.
chi - ra - shi - ga - ki
169
sh. 1

175
v.
175
sh. 1
181
v.
shi - ku wa ta - e - te - mo
181
sh. 1
187
v.
hak - ku - me no
187
sh. 1
193
v.
fu - de su - te - ma - tsu no
193
sh. 1

199
v.
yu - ki
199
sh. 1
205
v.
mo - chi
205
sh. 1
Moderato
211
v.
ni
ki - mi wa ho - ri no ha - shi -
211
sh. 1
217
v.
ga - ka - ri
217
rit.
Presto
sh. 1
223
sh. 1

229
sh. 1
235
sh. 1
241
rit.
Allegro
sh. 1
247
v.
mu-ka - shi no to-ri wa ka - sa - sa -
247
sh. 1
253
v.
gi ya
253
sh. 1
259
sh. 1

265
v.
i - to - shi
i - to - shi to
265
sh. 1
271
v.
i - u
to - ri
271
sh. 1
277
v.
wa
277
sh. 1
283
v.
283
sh. 1

289
v.
me - de - ta - ki -
289
sh. 1
295
v.
ko - to ni
295
sh. 1
301
v.
o - u to - ri
301
sh. 1
307
v.
yo
307
sh. 1

313
v.
on -
313
sh. 1
319
v.
na
go - ko - ro
319
sh. 1
325
v.
wa
325
sh. 1
331
v.
hi - wa i - ro - na
331
sh. 1

337
v.
sh. 1
343
ko - i
349
ji
o
ka - yo
355

361
v.
shi - ra - sa - gi no
361
sh. 1
367
v.
ko -
367
sh. 1
367
sh. 2
373
v.
ko - ro tsu - ge - na - ba
373
sh. 1
373
sh. 2

379
v.
sh. 1
385
rit.
391
ko - no - to -
a tempo
397
ri
rit.
Presto
403
sh. 2

409
sh. 1
sh. 2
415
rit.
Adagio
421
v.
nu - shi wa sho -

427
v.
wa - ru
sh. 1
sh. 2
433
Ta - go - to no tsu - ki -
439
yo

445
v.
na - n - to - sho na - n -
sh. 1
sh. 2
451
to - sho
457

463
v.
do -
463
sh. 1
463
sh. 2
469
v.
ko
e
ma - ko - to
469
sh. 1
469
sh. 2
475
v.
ga
475
sh. 1
475
sh. 2

481
v.
u - tsu - ru ya - ra
sh. 1
sh. 2
487
do - sho-
493
zo - i - na do - sho - zo - i - na

499
v.
499
sh. 1
499
sh. 2
505
sh. 1
rit.
505
sh. 2
511
sh. 1
accel.
Presto
511
sh. 2
517
sh. 1
517
sh. 2

523
sh. 1
523
sh. 2
529
sh. 1
529
sh. 2
535
sh. 1
535
sh. 2
541
sh. 1
541
sh. 2

547
v.
Ma - ta hi - to shi - ki - ri
547
sh. 1
553
v.
fu - ru yu - ki wa
553
sh. 1
559
sh. 1
565
v.
o - to - mo na - ku tsu - mo - ru
565
sh. 1
571
v.
ko - i go - ro mo ka -
571
sh. 1

577
v.
ze
ga
mo - te - ku - ru
577
sh. 1
583
v.
ku - ru
ku - ru
583
sh. 1
589
v.
ku - ru - ri
589
rit.
sh. 1
595
v.
Fu - buki
ni
so - de
ya
Moderato
595
sh. 1

601
tempo ad lib
v.
hi - ji - nu - ra - n
sh. 1
accel.
sh. 2
607
Presto
613
619

625
sh. 1
625
sh. 2
631
sh. 1
631
sh. 2
637
sh. 1
637
sh. 2

Appendix C

TRANSCRIPTION: *SAKURA EMAKI*

13
sh. 1
13
sh. 2
13
sh. 3
19
sh. 1
19
sh. 2
19
sh. 3
25
sh. 1
25
sh. 2
25
sh. 3

31
sh. 1
31
sh. 2
31
sh. 3
37
sh. 1
37
sh. 2
37
sh. 3
43
sh. 1
43
sh. 2
43
sh. 3

49
sh. 1
rit.
Moderato
sh. 2
sh. 3
55
(male chorus)
v.
Ha - na no ki - nu
sh. 1
sh. 2
sh. 3

(female chorus)
61
v.
Ha-na no ki - nu
sh. 1
sh. 2
sh. 3
67
(male chorus)
ka-su-mi no ko - ro -

73
(tutti)
v.
mo
u - chi tsu - ra -
sh. 1
sh. 2
sh. 3
79
ne

85
(female chorus)
v.
i - to - no - ya - na - gi
sh.1
sh. 2
sh. 3
91
ni
(tutti)
ha -

97
v.
ru ya
ka - za -
sh. 1
sh. 2
sh. 3
103
ra - n
ha - ru ya
ka -

109
v.
za - ra - n
109
sh.1
109
sh. 2
109
sh. 3
115
v.
(male solo)
O - mo - shi -
115
sh.1
Moderato
121
v.
ro - ya hi - to - e - da
121
sh.1

127
v.
o
127
sh.1
133
v.
ko - so - de
133
sh.1
139
v.
ni
o - ra - ba
139
sh.1
145
v.
ha - n -
145
sh.1

151
v.
ra
to
chi - ri -
sh.1
157
nu - ru
163
ha - na wa
169
175
sa - ka - ri no na - ga -

181
v.
me
yo
no
na - ga - me
181
sh.1
187
v.
yo
no
187
sh.1
193
sh.1
199
v.
i - yo - yo
199
rit.
Adagio
sh.1
205
v.
i - yo - yo
no
o - no -
205
sh.1

211
v.
ri - mo - no
211
sh.1
217
sh.1
223
v.
a - re a - re
223
sh.1
229
v.
ma - i - ru o - ko -
229
sh.1
235
v.
shi mo ma - i - ru
235
sh.1

241
v.
su - zu - i -
241
sh.1
247
v.
te ma - i - ru
247
sh.1
253
v.
253
sh.1

259
v.
ha-na no shi-tzu - e ni i -
sh.1
Moderato
sh. 2
sh. 3
265
cho ni - cho san - cho

(female chorus)
v.
sh. 1
sh. 2
sh. 3
271
shi - cho-
277
me no ka - go wa

283
(male chorus)
v.
sa - te - mo ki - ra - ra no
sh.1
sh. 2
sh. 3
289
(female chorus)
ki - ra - ra ka - yo

295
(male chorus)
v.
no
a - sa - gi
sh.1
sh. 2
sh. 3
301
mu-ra - sa - ki
sho - jo -

307
v.
hi
sh. 1
sh. 2
sh. 3
313

319
(tutti)
v.
ko - ga - ne wa - ka -
sh.1
sh. 2
sh. 3
325
kusa

331
v.
i - ro - ni de-
sh. 1
sh. 2
sh. 3
337
te

343
v.
ni - o - i me - de -
sh. 1
sh. 2
sh. 3
349
ta - ki ha - na - ka - tsu -

355
v.
ra
sh.1
sh. 2
sh. 3
361

367
v.
sh. 1
rit.
Solo shamisen
Lento
sh. 2
sh. 3
373
(Male solo)
sa - i - ta sa - ku -
379
ra ni ta - ga ki -

385
v.
nu
ka - ke - ru
385
sh.1
391
v.
e -
391
sh.1
397
v.
da
wa
ka - ku - ru - ru
397
sh.1
403
v.
ha - na
wa
chi - ru
403
sh.1

409
v.
409
sh.1
415
rit.
421 Presto
427
433
439
445
(female chorus)
i - na i - na - i - na
445 rit.
Allegro

451
v.
ma - zu wa ha -
451
sh.1
457
v.
na i - ku - sa
457
sh.1
463
v.
ha - na no zu - i - shi - n ha -
463
sh.1
469
v.
na no to - mo
469
sh.1

475
v.
475
sh.1
481
sh.1
487
v.
ta - ga - i
487
sh.1
493
v.
ni ta - wa - mu - re
493
sh.1
499
v.
a - ra - so - i - te
499
sh.1

505
v.
505
sh.1
511
sh.1
517
sh.1
523
sh.1
529
sh.1
(kotsuzumi solo break)
Moderato
529
sh. 2
535
sh.1
535
sh. 2

541
sh. 1
541
sh. 2
547
(male chorus)
v.
o - mo - te ni ho - n -
547
sh. 1
547
sh. 2
553
v.
no - ri
553
sh. 1
553
sh. 2

559
v.
a - ke -
559
sh.1
559
sh. 2
565
v.
za - ku - ra
565
sh.1
565
sh. 2
571
v.
571
sh.1
571
sh. 2

577
sh. 1
577
sh. 2
583
v.
yo - u - te ta - mo - to
583
sh. 1
583
sh. 2
589
v.
no
589
sh. 1
589
sh. 2

595
v.
nu - no -
595
sh.1
595
sh. 2
601
v.
bi - ki - za - ku - ra
601
sh.1
607
v.
607
sh.1
607
sh. 2

613
v.
ku - mo - i
613
sh. 1
613
sh. 2
619
v.
za - ku - ra no
619
sh. 1
619
sh. 2
625
v.
625
sh. 1
625
sh. 2

631
v.
a - ya u - ku -
631
sh.1
631
sh. 2
637
v.
ba
637
sh.1
637
sh. 2
643
sh.1
643
sh. 2

649
sh. 1
649
sh. 2
655
sh. 1
655
sh. 2
661
sh. 1
661
sh. 2
667
v.
na - ka o to - ra - no
667
sh. 1
667
sh. 2

673
v.
o
673
sh.1
673
sh. 2
679
v.
i
-
za
-
679
sh.1
679
sh. 2
685
v.
za
-
ku
-
ra
685
sh.1
685
sh. 2

691
sh. 1
691
sh. 2
697
sh. 1
697
sh. 2
703
v.
ra - chi mo a - ri - ya -
703
sh. 1
703
sh. 2

709
v.
ke
-
709
sh. 1
709
sh. 2
715
v.
za
-
ku
-
715
sh. 1
715
sh. 2
721
v.
ra
to
na
-
ri
-
te
721
sh. 1

727
v.
sh.1
sh. 2
733
sa - re - ba
739
me - de - ta - ku

745
v.
sh. 1
sh. 2
751
na - ra - za - ku - -
757
ra

763
sh. 1
sh. 2
769
accel.
(Taiko break)
775
v.
(male chorus)
u - ta - i
Allegro
781
so - ra - e

787
v.
ha - ya so -
sh.1
793
zu
799
805
sh. 2
sh. 3

811
v.
sh.1
sh. 2
sh. 3
817
(tutti)
so - me wa - ke ta -

823
v.
zu - na
sh.1
sh. 2
sh. 3
829
na - na i - ro no

835
v.
sh.1
sh. 2
sh. 3
841
to - ba - ri ni

847
v.
so - yo - to
sh.1
sh. 2
sh. 3
853

859
v.
ya - ma - ka - ze wa
sh. 1
sh. 2
sh. 3
865
ha -

871
v.
na o ma - mo - ri no ta - e - na -
sh.1
sh. 2
sh. 3
877
ru su - zu no ne

883
v.
hi - bi - ki ni yo -
sh. 1
sh. 2
sh. 3
889
u - te

895
v.
yu - ga - su - mi
sh. 1
sh. 2
sh. 3
901
i -

907
v.
ri - a - i no ka - ne
sh.1
sh. 2
sh. 3
913
so -

919
v.
ra
so - me
-
te
919
sh. 1
919
sh. 2
919
sh. 3
925
v.
925
sh. 1
925
sh. 2
925
sh. 3

931
v.
sh.1
sh. 2
sh. 3
937
ha - na mo ha - ji - ra - u u -

943
v.
ta - ge ka - na ha - na
sh.1
sh. 2
sh. 3
949
mo ha - ji - ra - u u -

955
v.
ta - ge ka - na
sh. 1
sh. 2
sh. 3
961
v.
sh. 1
sh. 2
sh. 3

967
sh. 1
967
sh. 2
967
sh. 3
973
sh. 1
973
sh. 2
973
sh. 3
979
sh. 1
979
sh. 2
979
sh. 3

985
sh. 1
985
sh. 2
985
sh. 3
991
sh. 1
991
sh. 2
991
sh. 3
997
sh. 1
997
sh. 2
997
sh. 3

sh. 1
sh. 2
sh. 3

Notes

NOTES TO THE INTRODUCTION

1. Dewoskin's overview of the aesthetics of the artistic traditions of China and Japan provides a useful comparison of East and West: "East Asian traditions are rich in the achievements of artistic geniuses, yet there is little premium put on individuality and the expression of individual, personal feeling. In contrast to post-Romantic interests in the West, there is little mention of originality in the traditional discourse. Excellence resides in perfection of skills, mastery of principles of an art genre, and submission to the inner order of the world" (Dewoskin 1992:69). Dewoskin describes the ideal Asian artist as follows: ". . . the concept of innovation resides more in the personality and life of the artist than in his art. This reflects a general sense that the artists and their efforts are a more crucial locus of the aesthetic than the outcome—that is, the performance or objects themselves. Hence, the focus of much writing on aesthetics is on innate endowments, inner self-cultivation, reclusive lifestyles and the interactions between the artist and his media and between the artist and the outside world" (ibid.).
2. For a biographical sketch and analysis of the works of Kikuoka's teacher, *nagauta shamisen* performer and composer, Yamada Shōtarō, see Malm 1999.
3. William Malm was also a student of Kikuoka during the late 1950s, appearing in the first student recital of Kikuoka's school. I participated in Kikuoka's final student recital.
4. See Dale 1986 for an analysis of the *nihonjinron* phenomenon.
5. Geertz, however, argues for the importance of including both experience-distant and experience-near concepts in ethnography. Both experience-distant concepts (such as "social stratification" or "phobia") and experience-near concepts (such as "love," "caste," or "nirvana") are necessary if we are to avoid interpretations that may be "systematically deaf to the distinctive tonalities" of existence or depict people as "imprisoned in their mental horizons" (Geertz 1983:57).
6. Rice has more recently called for ethnomusicologists to capture the particularity of individual musical experience in "subject-centered musical ethnography" for the purpose of addressing increasingly perplexing problems of understanding musical experience in a more complex, unbounded world of interacting cultures (Rice 2003:151–152).

7. Within the Japanese traditional performing arts it is common practice for notable performers, in particular those bestowed with honorable titles from the government, to publish autobiographies, although none exists for Kikuoka.
8. Bakan, however, sees no reason for ethnomusicologists to necessarily limit their role to that of "bit player," arguing that the experiences of the ethnomusicologist are no less relevant in ethnography than those of whom the ethnomusicologist is studying (Bakan 1999:16–17).
9. Donald Keene (1995), based on Kenkō's *Essays in Idleness*, renders the aesthetics of Japanese art in four basic categories: "suggestion," "irregularity," "simplicity," and "perishability." Although, "experience-distant" concepts may be helpful for the appreciation of Japanese art forms, artists themselves may resist such essentializing terms. Japanese artists have a long tradition of resistance to formal aesthetic theories as is evident in common sayings such as "If you have time to think about theory, you should use that time for practice" (Shimosako 2002:545).

NOTES TO CHAPTER ONE

1. This attack from the teacher's *shamisen* plectrum is remarkably similar to an incident told in Tanizaki Junichirō's 1933 short story "Shunkinshō ("A Portrait of Shunkin"). Tanizaki tells of several incidents of teacher brutality, including the famous singer Koshiji-dayū II, who had a scar on his forehead from his teacher's plectrum (see English translation by Hibbett 1963:28–29).
2. Kikuoka's officially registered birthdate is January 12, 1928. At that time children born close to the end of the year were sometimes given false birthdates in the new year for good luck. Kikuoka's name change was due to the influence of his stepmother, who also changed her own name after her religious conversion to one of Japan's many new religions, Seichō no ie. Although he followed his stepmother's lead, Kikuoka was not active in this religion.
3. Malm speculates that the subsequent structural changes that led to the development of the modern *shamisen* were probably due to the influence of *biwa* performers. The replacement of the snakeskin covering for the more durable cat or dog skin was probably due more to the lack of large snakes in Japan than to the damage caused by the heavy plectra of *biwa* players. However, the creation of a special cavity at the top of the neck to create the characteristic buzzing timbre of the lowest string on the *shamisen* is most likely an imitation of the buzzing sound found on the lowest string of the *biwa* (Malm 1963:56–57). The substitution of small finger picks with much larger-sized plectra is another likely influence from *biwa* musicians (ibid.: 58).
4. For a listing of the surviving pieces in the standard *nagauta* repertoire see Asakawa (1974: 22).
5. See Malm 1994 for a study of the predominance of nineteenth-century *nagauta* pieces in modern concert performances.
6. An example of one such ranking of an *iemoto* system can be found in Read and Locke 1983.
7. It must be pointed out that, in spite of their idealism in creating new *nagauta*, Rokushirō and Kosaburō were not anti-*iemoto* as they were deeply involved in power struggles over lineage succession. In fact, these two pioneers of concert *nagauta* were forced out of kabuki because of a power struggle over lineage with Kineya

Rokuzaemon XII, who became chief musician of the new Kabukiza theater which opened in 1889 (Machida 1956:410–412). This feud eventually led to a new version of the name Kineya in 1908 when Rokushirō's father, Kineya Saburōsuke VI, changed the two Chinese characters of the name Kineya to read "rare-sound-house" while keeping the same pronounciation (Malm 1999:37). At the same time, he created the name Jōkan, becoming Jōkan I, with his son, Rokushirō, becoming Kineya Jōkan II in 1926 (ibid.).

8. This refers to number notation commonly used in *nagauta* today. During the Edo era, all *nagauta shamisen* patterns were memorized without the use of notation, which was a twentieth-century development. Even today *shamisen* players typically do not use any notation on stage. See the appendix in Malm 2000 on notation in Japanese music.
9. No longer needing any validation through traditional *nagauta* credentials, Kikuoka appeared on NHK in the 1960s as the host of a program of *shamisen* instruction in which he brought the Tōonkai style to a national audience of television viewers.

NOTES TO CHAPTER TWO

1. Kurokami is unusual in that it belongs also to the *jiuta* repertoire of music for *koto, shamisen,* and *shakuhachi.* It seems likely that the work was originally a *jiuta* piece based on a comparative study of the two versions by Miyazaki (1984).
2. This sort of reaction from him did not seem unusual considering that informants often suspect that the researcher may be exercising a round-about method of getting information and will often confront the researcher directly (Bernard 1994:213).
3. Japanese students often apply imitative learning strategies in Western music as well. See Fujita (2002:767) and Harich-Schneider (1973:548).
4. This prioritization of the way one executes music over the resultant sound of the music is cited by Fujita (2002) as a paradox of traditional Japanese music: "the accuracy of the process for producing a sound is crucial whereas the resultant sound is less rigorously defined. This problem often arises in discourse about the spirit of performance. For example, one will often hear comments such as "the sound wasn't good, but the timing was correct" or "the breathing was right." Such evaluations arise because each performance is considered a form of *keiko* in preparation for the future" (ibid.:770).
5. Although silent imitation in learning is valued, in actual modern-day practice, many teachers verbalize extensively during the lesson period. Questions and discussions during lessons have been identified as a modern development in traditional Japanese music (Fujita 2002:772). Such verbalization may be helpful, but is sometimes more of a distraction in learning as some students are heard to complain that their *sensei* is not teaching because he is "talking too much."
6. *Kata* are evident in virtually any extensive musical analysis of many genres of Japanese traditional music. See Malm 2000 for a survey that demonstrates the presence of stereotyped, named patterns in several genres of Japanese music. See Komparu 1983 for an analysis of patterns in *nō* music and Yano 2002 for a study of *kata* in popular music. Patterned forms can also be found in studies of everyday social behavior Henshall 1999, and religious practices, Reader 1991.

7. Malm provides an example of the shameful consequences of awkward or ungraceful behavior from his own early performance experience (1999:35).
8. In a similar story, Blasdel (2001) writes of a beginning student of *tokiwazu* who had at first misunderstood her teacher's emphasis on stage manner as she nervously prepared for a performance, believing that the sound of her voice required the most development. As a result of learning the proper *kata*, she managed to find her confidence and the proper voice that ensured her success in her first recital. Blasdel notes that even if she had not been able to sing a note, "adhering to the form would save her from losing face and preserving her dignity on stage" (ibid.).
9. The tea ceremony is described by Ōhashi (2002) as a way in which a pure space, separated from the ordinary world, reveals the aesthetics behind everyday actions with religious implications: "The ceremonial teahouse is separated from the secular world by a path. Known as the 'roji,' a 'pure and innocent place,' this path leads to the other world into which the soul of the faithful believer will enter. Those who pass through this place on their way to participate in the tea ceremony are, according to the tea-way, cleansed of the dust of the secular world. The events in the tea ceremony room are confined everyday actions. In the teahouse, which the 'roji' separates from ordinary life, commonplaceness is reproduced in such a way that the concealed dimensions of everyday life—for example, the inherent mortality and the 'once-ness' of individual life—are specifically expressed" (ibid.:30).
10. There is the potential for embarrassment and confusion if a mistake is made, such as the case of one student who had once forgotten to put money in an envelope and gave her teacher an empty envelope.
11. An analogue to the movements toward the "spiritual center" of Kikuoka's lesson place can be found in the "advances" within the space of a Shinto shrine that make up the *kata* of approaching a sacred spirit (Nelson 2000: 38–40).
12. This 3-step method of the teacher performing a phrase, followed by teacher and student together, and finishing with the student performing alone with corrections by the teacher, closely resembles the teaching process documented by Fujie (1986:223).
13. For an analysis of this kind of heightened spatial awareness in the tea ceremony, see Izutsu 1981.
14. Hendry (1995) analyzes the co-existence of equality and hierarchy within groups in kindergarten. In this setting the enforcement of equality through school uniforms and alternating shared chore duties prevents the abuse of a hierarchical system based on age. Ideally, equality and hierarchy are meant to work together to maintain social harmony (45–46).
15. The large sums of money spent by students in *osaraikai* can also be a corrupting influence, compromising the teacher-student relationship. As one veteran amateur student reported, he had heard of many instances of teachers having their students "stolen" by other teachers who offer lower rates for *osaraikai.*

NOTES TO CHAPTER THREE

1. The "consensus" myth of social harmony in Japan eventually led to the development of a "conflict" model that sought to dismantle and re-examine the previous paradigm (see Krauss, Rohlen, and Steinhoff 1984).

2. As Hsu (1975) points out, an *iemoto* system is defined by belonging to, or residing in, the actual household or *ie*. Thus adopted individuals unrelated by kinship or marriage may be much closer to the people with whom they reside than biological relatives who live outside the *ie* (ibid.:33).
3. Detailed analysis of the levels of government bureaucracy and control of educational policy can be found in Sugimoto (1997). Even those patient enough to go through such a process, such as approval of textbooks, are faced with direct forms of censorship (ibid.:120–121).
4. Liza Dalby's research on *geisha* demonstrates the degree to which the *shamisen* is an indispensable part of geisha life (see Dalby 1998:251–260).
5. Today's OL or "office ladies" who do find time for hobbies seem more inclined to study English. That the conversational English lesson market has a much greater number of females than males is perhaps because the OL typically has fewer responsibilities in her work than a company's male employees and thus more time to pursue hobbies such as foreign language study. Males who are occupied with greater responsibilities are more likely to study English in company classes as the need to learn foreign language arises from the demands of the job.
6. De Ferranti (2000) identifies endurance over time as a key value in Japanese traditional arts. Such endurance is important in the validation of its authenticity.
7. Tanaka (2002) argues that Japanese descriptions of nature are directly related to Japanese conceptions of human relations such as order, interaction and hierarchies, and as such, form Japanese conceptions of the political economy and the nation-state (ibid.:133).
8. Purification is found in the story in the ancient mythological text, *Kojiki*, in which the sun goddess hides herself away in a cave, plunging the world into darkness, following the insult of pollution caused by her brother, the storm god. Nature had to be put back into balance by the human intervention of luring the Sun Goddess out of her cave through the entertainment of song and dance (Varley 1984:11). This act of restoring nature through the purifying force of music and dance has been ritually recreated for centuries in the performance of *kagura*. Detailed descriptions of *kagura* ritual as a mythical re-enactment are found in Honda (1966) and Brinkman (1996:39–54). See Garfias (1968) and Keister (1995) for articles addressing the music of *kagura*.
9. *Nagauta*, as well as many other forms of Japanese music, can be used for ritual purification at Shinto shrines. The Meiji Shrine in Tokyo, for example, features annual performances of *gagaku*, *nō*, *koto*, *shakuhachi* and *shamisen* music with the intention of entertaining the *kami* spirits. Although an audience may be present, such performances are directed solely at the gods and, before any performance begins, performers and audience alike are purified by the waving of a priest's paper wand. The stage manner of musicians and dancers of such ritual performances for the *kami* is essentially the same as secular performances in a theater for an audience.

NOTES TO CHAPTER FOUR

1. The complexities of these multiple identities in *Sukeroku* are the subject of a study by Barbara E. Thornbury (1982).

2. See Malm's *Six Hidden Views* (1986:65–66) for a comparison of *nō* versus *nagauta* style of declamatory singing.
3. Malm (1986) analyzes the various interpretations of *nagauta* as performed by different schools (123–150) and discusses the communal nature of *nagauta* composition/performance (49–51).
4. A recent study by Masato and Toshinori (1998) examines melodic patterns in *nagauta* compositions in an attempt to determine consistent lengths of patterns.
5. Tokumaru refers to the importance of two kinds of memorization utilized by *shamisen* players: memorization of individual works and stylistic memorization of the global characteristics of a particular style. Such stylistic memorization can only be obtained through working closely with a teacher (Tokumaru 1986:123).
6. See Kakinoki (1975) for an analysis of melismatic ornamentation in a performance of the *nagauta* composition *Ninin Wankyu*.
7. Ironically, the love that refines Sukeroku is his love of Agemaki, a prostitute. However, the play itself glorifies the setting of the pleasure quarters, transforming the prostitute underworld into a noble, elegant and courtly display of beauty.

NOTES TO CHAPTER FIVE

1. Musical analysis of the pieces in this chapter is based on the Crown Records recording *Setsugekka* CRCM 60005.
2. The most common scale form in *nagauta shamisen* music is the *in* scale: E-F-G-A-B-C-D.
3. Such an unconventional beginning can be seen, however, in the piece *Shiki no Yamamba* as analyzed by Malm 1978.
4. The second work in Kikuoka's *Setsugekka* triptych, *Kyō no Tsuki* (Moon over the Capitol) is not included in my analysis. Although the piece is another impressive work of modern *nagauta* with a mood perfectly suited to fit between the first and third parts, the more traditional techniques of this piece are similar to those of *Yuki Musume*, and the purpose of my analysis in this chapter is primarily to contrast the more traditional work *Yuki Musume* with the more modern work *Sakura Emaki*.
5. The *yo* scale is another common scale type in Japanese music: E-F-sharp-G-A-B-C-sharp-D.
6. See Oshio (1999) for an analysis of how *gaku* patterns are used in *nagauta*. Although the term *gaku* refers to the aristocratic court music of *gagaku*, there appears to be no musical similarity between these *shamisen* patterns and court music.
7. This poetic device can take many forms in *nagauta*, such as "*yama-zukushi*," (mountain display), which is heard in the classic *nagauta* composition Musume Dōjōji, listing the names of several famous mountains in Japan.
8. In demonstrations of kabuki drum patterns by living national treasure percussionist Katada Kisaku, his demonstration of the sound of snow routinely begins by *not* playing the drum, eliciting laughter from audiences.

NOTES TO THE CONCLUSION

1. Zeami distinguished between the "ordinary way" (technical practice) and the "real way," (inner spirituality). See translation and analysis of Zeami's "The Nine Stages" by Izutsu (1981:37).
2. The transformation of a student through proper musical technique, as well as linking execution of musical technique, with personality attributes, was a belief held by Shinichi Suzuki, founder of the Suzuki method of violin instruction (see Peak 1996:363-364).

Bibliography

Asakawa, Gyokuto. 1974. *Nagauta no kiso kenkyū* (a basic study of *nagauta*). Tokyo Hōgakusha.

_______ . 1991. *Nagauta meikyoku yosetsu* (an explanation of famous *nagauta* pieces). Tokyo: Hōgakusha.

Bachnik, Jane M. 1983. "Recruitment Strategies for Household Succession: Rethinking Japanese Household Organization." *Man* 4:160–182.

_______ . 1998. "Time, Space, and Person in Japanese Relationships." In *Interpreting Japanese Society: Anthropological Approaches* 2nd edition, edited by Joy Hendry, 91–116. London: Routledge.

Bakan, Michael B. 1999. *Music of Death and New Creation: Experiences in the World of Balinese Gamelan Beleganjur.* Chicago: University of Chicago.

Becker, Judith and Alton. 1981. "A Musical Icon: Power and Meaning in Javanese Gamelan Music." In *The Sign in Music Literature*, edited by Wendy Steiner, 203–215. Austin: University of Texas Press.

Benedict, Ruth. 1977. *The Chrysanthemum and the Sword.* London: Routledge and Kegan Paul.

Bernard, H. Russell. 1994. *Research Methods in Anthropology: Qualitative and Quantitative Approaches.* Walnut Creek, CA: Altamira Press.

Blasdel, Christopher Yohmei. 2001. "Killing the Buddha: Form vs. Content in *Hōgaku*." *The Japan Times*, April 22.

Bourdieu, Pierre. 1971. "Intellectual Field and Creative Project." In *Knowledge and Control: New Directions in the Sociology of Education*, edited by M. F. D. Young, 161–188. London: Collier-Macmillan.

_______ . 1977. *Outline of a Theory of Practice.* Cambridge: Cambridge University Press.

Bourdieu, Pierre and Loic J. D. Wacquant. 1992. *An Invitation to Reflexive Sociology.* Chicago: University of Chicago.

Brinkman, John T. 1996. *Simplicity: A Distinctive Quality of Japanese Spirituality.* New York: Peter Lang.

Brandon, James R. 1975. *Kabuki: Five Classic Plays.* Cambridge, MA: Harvard University Press.

Clammer, John. 1994. *Difference and Modernity: Social Theory and Contemporary Japanese Society.* London: Kegan Paul International.

Cowan, Jane K. 1990. *Dance and the Body Politic in Northern Greece.* Princeton, NJ: Princeton University Press.

Dalby, Liza Crihfield. 1998. *Geisha.* Berkeley: University of California Press.

Dale, Peter N. 1986. *The Myth of Japanese Uniqueness*. London: Croom Helm Ltd.

De Ferranti, Hugh. 2000. *Japanese Musical Instruments*. New York: Oxford University Press.

Dewoskin, Kenneth J. 1992. "Chinese and Japanese Aesthetics." In *A Companion to Aesthetics*, edited by David Cooper, 68–73. Oxford, UK: Blackwell.

Dunn, Charles J. and Bunzō Torigoe, trans. 1969. *The Actors' Analects* (*Yakusha Rongo*). New York: Columbia University Press.

Edwards, Walter. 1989. *Modern Japan Through Its Weddings: Gender, Person & Society in Ritual Portrayal*. Stanford, CA: Stanford University Press.

Feld, Steven. 1982. *Sound and Sentiment*. Philadelphia: University of Pennsylvania Press.

_______ . 1988. "Aesthetics as Iconicity of Style; or 'Lift-up-over-Sounding': Getting into the Kaluli Groove." *Yearbook for Traditional Music* 20:74–113.

Fitzgerald, Timothy. 1993. "Japanese Religion as Ritual Order." *Religion* 23(4):315–341.

Frisbie, Charlotte J. and David P. McAllester, ed. 1978. *Navajo Blessingway Singer: The Autobiography of Frank Mitchell, 1881–1967*. Tucson: University of Arizona.

Fujie, Linda. 1986. "The Process of Oral Transmission in Japanese Folk Performing Arts: The Teaching of *Matsuribayashi* in Tokyo." In *The Oral and the Literate in Music*, edited by Tokumaru Yoshihiko and Yamaguchi Osamu, 231–238. Tokyo: Academia Music.

Fujita, Takanori. 2002. "Continuity and Authenticity in Traditional Japanese Music." In *The Garland Encyclopedia of World Music, Volume 7, East Asia: China, Japan, and Korea*, edited by Robert C. Provine, Yoshihiko Tokumaru, and J. Lawrence Witzleben, 767–772. New York: Routledge.

Garfias, Robert. 1968. "The Sacred *Mi-Kagura* Ritual of the Japanese Imperial Court." *Selected Reports in Ethnomusicology* 1(2):150–178.

Geertz, Clifford. 1973. *The Interpretation of Cultures*. New York: Basic Books.

_______ . 1983. *Local Knowledge: Further Essays in Interpretive Anthropology*. New York: Basic Books.

Gerstle, C. Andrew. 2002. "Flowers of Edo: Eighteenth-Century *Kabuki* and Its Patrons." In *A Kabuki Reader: History and Performance*, edited by Samuel L. Leiter, 88–111. Armonk, NY: East Gate.

Groemer, Gerald. 1999. *The Spirit of Tsugaru*. Warren, MI: Harmonie Park Press.

Hare, Tom. 1996. "Try, Try Again: Training in *Noh* Drama." In *Teaching and Learning in Japan*, edited by Thomas P. Rohlen and Gerald K. LeTendre, 323–344. Cambridge: Cambridge University Press.

Harich-Schneider, Eta. 1973. *A History of Japanese Music*. London: Oxford University Press.

Hendry, Joy. 1986. *Becoming Japanese: The World of the Pre-school Child*. Honolulu: University of Hawaii Press.

_______ . 1992. "Individualism and Individuality: Entry into a Social World." In *Ideology and Practice in Modern Japan*, edited by Roger Goodman and Kirsten Refsing, 55–71. London: Routledge.

_______ . 1995. *Understanding Japanese Society*. London: Routledge.

Henshall, Kenneth G. 1999. *Dimensions of Japanese Society: Gender, Margins and Mainstream*. New York: St. Martin's Press.

Hibbett, Howard. 1963. *Seven Japanese Tales by Junichirō Tanizaki*. New York: Alfred A. Knopf.

Honda, Yasuji. 1966. *Kagura*. Tokyo: Makujisha.

Hsu, Francis L. K. 1975. *Iemoto: The Heart of Japan*. New York: Schenkman Publishing Company.

Hughes, David W. 1993. "Japan." In *Ethnomusicology: Historical and Regional Studies*, edited by Helen Myers, 345–363. New York: Norton & Company.

Ikeda, Kōichi. 2002. *Nagauta Biiki* (*Nagauta* favorites). Tokyo: Seiabō.

Ikuta, Kumiko. 1997. "Waza: 'tsutaerareru' sonzai kara 'tsutawaru' e." *Edo no Shiso* 6:118–129.

Izutsu, Toshihiko and Toyo Izutsu. 1981. *The Theory of Beauty in the Classical Aesthetics of Japan*. Boston: Martinus Nijhoff Publishers.

Ivy, Marilyn. 1995. *Discourses of the Vanishing*. Chicago: University of Chicago Press.

Jenkins, Richard. 1992. *Pierre Bourdieu*. New York: Routledge.

Kakinoki, Gorō. 1975. "Music Analysis of a Traditional Song: Meaning and Function of 'Kobushi.'" *Ongakugaku* 21(2):78–88.

_______. 1978. "*Nagauta* Kokaji nimiru ryūhasei." *Geinō no kagaku* 9:154–204.

Katsumura, Jinko. 1986. "Some Innovations in Musical Instruments of Japan during the 1920s." *Yearbook for Traditional Music* 157–172.

Kawatake, Toshio. 1982. *Japan On Stage: Japanese Concepts of Beauty as Shown in the Traditional Theater*. Tokyo: 3A Corporation.

Keene, Donald. 1995. "Japanese Aesthetics." In *Japanese Aesthetics and Culture: A Reader*, edited by Nancy G. Hume, 27–41. Albany: State University of New York Press.

Keister, Jay. 1995. "Japanese *Mi-Kagura* Ritual as Embodied Performance." *Pacific Review of Ethnomusicology* 7: 17–29.

Kikkawa, Eishi. 1997. *Shamisen no bigaku to Geidai hōgakuka tanjobiwa* (Aesthetics of the *Shamisen* and a Secret Story of the Birth of the Development of Japanese Traditional Music at the Tokyo University of Fine Arts and Music). Tokyo: Shuppangeijutsusha.

Kineya, Eizō. 1932. *Nagauta no utaikata* (The singing of *nagauta*). Osaka: Sogensha.

Kingsbury, Henry. 1988. *Music, Talent, and Performance: A Conservatory Cultural System*. Philadelphia: Temple University Press.

Kleinman, A. and J. Kleinman. 1991. "Suffering and Its Professional Transformation: Towards an Ethnography of Interpersonal Experience." *Culture, Medicine, and Psychiatry* 15:275–301.

Komparu, Kunio. 1983. *The Noh Theater: Principles and Perspectives*. New York: Weatherhill.

Kondo, Dorinne K. 1990. *Crafting Selves: Power, Gender, and Discourses of Identity in a Japanese Workplace*. Chicago: University of Chicago Press.

Krauss, Ellis S., Thomas P. Rohlen and Patricia G. Steinhoff, eds. 1984. *Conflict in Japan*. Honolulu: University of Hawaii Press.

Lebra, Takie Sugiyama. 1992. "Self in Japanese Culture." In *Japanese Sense of Self*, edited by Nancy R. Rosenberger, 105–120. Cambridge: University of Cambridge.

LeVine, Robert A. 1982. "The Self in Culture." In *Culture, Behavior, and Personality*, 291–304. New York: Aldine.

Machida, Hirozō. 1924. *Nagauta keiko tebikigusa* (*Nagauta* practice guide). Tokyo: Hōgaku Kenkyūkai.

Machida, Kashō. 1956. "Japanese Music and Dance." In *Japanese Music and Drama in the Meiji Era*, compiled and edited by Komiya Toyotaka, translated and adapted by Edward G. Seidensticker and Donald Keene, 329–448. Tokyo: Ōbunsha.

Malm, William P. 1963. *Nagauta: The Heart of Kabuki Music*. Westport, CT: Greenwood Press.

_______. 1978. "Four Seasons of the Old Mountain Woman: An Example of Japanese *Nagauta* Text Setting." *Journal of the American Musicological Society* 31(1):81–117.

_______ . 1986. *Six Hidden Views of Japanese Music*. Berkeley: University of California Press.

_______. 1994. "The Rise of Concert *Shamisen* Music." In *Recovering the Orient*, edited by A. Gerstle and A. Milner, 293–315. Chur, Switzerland: Harwood.

_______. 1999. "Yamada Shōtarō: Japan's first *shamisen* professor." *Asian Music* 30(1):35–76.

_______. 2000. *Traditional Japanese Music and Musical Instruments*. Tokyo: Kodansha International.

Maraldo, John C. 2002. "Between Individual and Communal, Subject and Object, Self and Other: Mediating Watsuji Tetsurō's Hermeneutics." In *Japanese Hermeneutics: Current Debates on Aesthetics and Interpretation*, edited by Michael F. Marra, 76–86. Honolulu: University of Hawaii Press.

Matsushima, Shōjuro, ed. 1967. *Tōonkai junen* (Tōonkai 10 year anniversary). Tokyo: Tōonkai.

Matthews, Gordon. 1994. *What Makes Life Worth Living: How Japanese and Americans Make Sense of Their Worlds*. Berkeley: University of California Press.

Merriam, Alan P. 1964. *The Anthropology of Music*. Evanston, IL: Northwestern University Press.

Miyazaki, Mayumi. 1984. "Concerning the Piece 'Kurokami' of the Jiuta and *Nagauta* Repertoires." (Summary in English) *Toyo Ongaku Kenkyu* (Journal of the Society for Research in Asiatic Music) 49(2), September.

Mori, Barbara Lynne Rowland. 1996. "The Traditional Arts as Leisure Activities for Contemporary Japanese Women." In *Re-Imaging Japanese Women*, edited by Anne E. Imamura, 117–134. Berkeley: University of California.

Moriya, Takeshi. 1984. "The History of Japanese Civilization through Aesthetic Pursuits." In *Japanese Civilization in the Modern World: Life and Society*, Senri Ethnological Studies No. 16, edited by Tadao Umesao, et al. 105–116. Osaka: National Museum of Ethnology.

_______. 1994. "The Lesson Culture." In *The Electric Geisha: Exploring Japanese Popular Culture*, 43–50. Tokyo: Kodansha International.

Mouer, Ross and Yoshio Sugimoto. 1986. *Images of Japanese Society: A Study of the Structure of Social Reality*. London: Routledge and Kegan Paul.

Myers, Helen. 1992. "Ethnomusicology." In *Ethnomusicology: An Introduction*, edited by Helen Myers, 3–18. New York: Norton.

Nakane, Chie. 1970. *Japanese Society*. Berkeley: University of California Press.

Nakano, Mitsutoshi. 1989. "The Role of Traditional Aesthetics." In *Eighteenth-Century Japan: Culture and Society*, edited by C. Andrew Gerstle, Richmond, 124–131. UK: Curzon Press.

Nelson, John K. 2000. *Enduring Identities: The Guise of Shinto in Contemporary Japan*. Honolulu: University of Hawaii.

Nelson, Steven G. 2002. "Historical Source Materials." In *The Garland Encyclopedia of World Music, Volume 7, East Asia: China, Japan, and Korea*, edited by Robert C. Provine, Yoshihiko Tokumaru, and J. Lawrence Witzleben, 585–590. New York: Routledge.

Ōhashi, Ryōsuke. 2002. "The Hermeneutic Approach to Japanese Modernity: 'Art-Way,' 'Iki,' and 'Cut-Continuance.'" In *Japanese Hermeneutics: Current Debates on Aesthetics and Interpretation*, edited by Michael F. Marra, 25–35. Honolulu: University of Hawaii Press.

Ooms, Herman. 1998. "Forms and Norms in Edo Arts and Society." In *Edo, Art in Japan 1615–1868*, exhibition catalogue, 23–47. Washington DC: National Gallery of Art.

Ortolani, Benito. 1969. "*Iemoto*." *Japan Quarterly* 16(3):297–306.

Oshio, Satomi. 1993. "A Tonal Structure in *Nagauta*." *Ongagakugaku* (Journal of the Musicological Society of Japan) 38(2):85–97.

_______. 1999. "The Concept of '*Gaku*' in *Nagauta*." *Tōyō Ongaku Kenkyū* (Journal of the Society for Research in Asian Music) 64:1–2. (English summary of Japanese original.)

_______. 2002. "Gender Roles in the Performing Arts in Japan." In *The Garland Encyclopedia of World Music, Volume 7, East Asia: China, Japan, and Korea*, edited by Robert C. Provine, Yoshihiko Tokumaru, and J. Lawrence Witzleben, 763–766. New York: Routledge.

Peak, Lois. 1994. "The Suzuki Method of Music." In *Teaching and Learning in Japan*, edited by Thomas P. Rohlen and Gerald K. LeTendre, 345–368. Cambridge: Cambridge University Press.

Pelzel, John C. 1970. "Japanese Kinship." In *Family and Kinship in Chinese Society*, edited by Maurice Freeman. Stanford: Stanford University Press.

Read, Cathleen B. and David L. Locke. 1983. "An Analysis of the Yamada-ryu Sokyoku Iemoto System." *Hōgaku* 1(1):20–52.

Reader, Ian. 1991. *Religion in Contemporary Japan*. London: MacMillan.

Reischauer, Edwin O. 1977. *The Japanese*. Cambridge, MA: Harvard University Press.

Rice, Timothy. 1987. "Toward the Remodeling of Ethnomusicology." *Ethnomusicology* 31(3):469–488.

_______. 1994. *May It Fill Your Soul: Experiencing Bulgarian Music*. Chicago: University of Chicago.

_______. 2003. "Time, Place, and Metaphor in Musical Experience and Ethnography." *Ethnomusicology* 47(2):151–179.

Rohlen, Thomas P. and Gerald K. LeTendre, eds. 1994. *Teaching and Learning in Japan*. Cambridge: Cambridge University Press.

Rosenberger, Nancy R. 1992. *Japanese Sense of Self*. Cambridge: Cambridge University Press.

Said, Edward. 1979. *Orientalism*. New York: Vintage.

Saito, Yuriko. 1997. "The Japanese Aesthetics of Imperfection and Insufficiency." *The Journal of Aesthetics and Art Criticism* 55(4):377–385.

_______ . 1998. "Japanese Aesthetics: Historical Overview." In *Encyclopedia of Aesthetics* Volume 2, edited by Michael Kelly, 545–553. New York: Oxford University Press.

Sapir, Edward. 1958. *Selected Writings of Edward Sapir*. D. G. Mandelbaum, ed. Berkeley: University of California Press.

Seeger, Anthony. 1987. *Why Suya Sing: A Musical Anthropology of an Amazonian People*. Cambridge: Cambridge University Press.

Shimosako, Mari. 2002. "Philosophy and Aesthetics." In *The Garland Encyclopedia of World Music, Volume 7, East Asia: China, Japan, and Korea*, edited by Robert C. Provine, Yoshihiko Tokumaru, and J. Lawrence Witzleben, 545–555. New York: Routledge.

Shively, Donald H. 2002. "Bakufu versus Kabuki." In *A Kabuki Reader: History and Performance*, edited by Samuel L. Leiter, 33–59. Armonk, NY: East Gate.

Simeda, Takasi. 2002. "Music Scholarship in Japan." In *The Garland Encyclopedia of World Music, Volume 7, East Asia: China, Japan, and Korea*, edited by Robert C. Provine, Yoshihiko Tokumaru, and J. Lawrence Witzleben, 591–595. New York: Routledge.

Smith, Robert J. 1983. *Japanese Society: Tradition, Self, and the Social Order*. Cambridge: Cambridge University Press.

Stock, Jonathan P. J. 1996. *Musical Creativity in Twentieth-Century China: Abing, His Music, and Its Changing Meanings*. Rochester, NY: University of Rochester Press.

_______ . 2001. "Toward an Ethnomusicology of the Individual, or Biographical Writing in Ethnomusicology." *The World of Music* 43(1):5–19.

Sugarman, Jane. 1997. *Engendering Song*. Chicago: University of Chicago.

Sugimoto, Yoshio. 1997. *An Introduction to Japanese Society*. Cambridge: Cambridge University Press.

Sugimoto, Yoshio and Ross Mouer. 1982. *Japanese Society: Stereotypes and Realities*. Melbourne: Japanese Studies Centre.

Tanaka, Stefan. 2002. "Nature — the Naturalization of Experience as National." In *Japanese Hermeneutics: Current Debates on Aesthetics and Interpretation*, edited by Michael F. Marra, 127–141. Honolulu: University of Hawaii Press.

Thornbury, Barbara E. 1982. *Sukeroku's Double Identity: The Dramatic Structure of Edo Kabuki*. Ann Arbor, MI: University of Michigan Center for Japanese Studies.

Titon, Jeff Todd. 1997. "Knowing Fieldwork." In *Shadows in the Field: New Perspectives for Fieldwork in Ethnomusicology*, edited by Gregory F. Barz and Timothy J. Cooley, 87–100. New York: Oxford University.

Tokumaru, Yoshihiko. 1986. "The Interaction of Orality and Literacy in Structuring *Shamisen* Music." In *The Oral and the Literate in Music*, edited by Yoshihiko Tokumaru and Osamu Yamaguchi, 110–129. Tokyo: Academia Music.

_______ . 1991. "Intertextuality in Japanese Traditional Music." In *The Empire of Signs: Semiotic Essays on Japanese Culture*, edited by Yoshihiko Ikegami, 139–155. Amsterdam and Philadelphia: John Benjamins.

Toyotaka, Komiya. 1956. "Japanese Music." In *Japanese Music and Drama in the Meiji Era*, compiled and edited by Komiya Toyotaka, translated and adapted by Edward G. Seidensticker and Donald Keene, 49–53. Tokyo: Ōbunsha.

Tsuge, Gen'ichi. 1983. "Raiment of Traditional Japanese Musicians: Its Social and Musical Significance." *The World of Music* 25(1):55–67.

Turino, Thomas. 1989. "The Coherence of Social Style and Musical Creation among the Aymara in Southern Peru." *Ethnomusicology* 33(1):1–30.

_______ . 1991. *Moving Away from Silence*. Chicago: University of Chicago.

Ueda, Makoto. 1967. *Literary and Art Theories in Japan*. Cleveland, OH: The Press of Western Reserve University.

Valentine, James. 1998. "Models of Performance: Space, Time, and Social Organization in Japanese Dance." In *Interpreting Japanese Society: Anthropological Approaches*, edited by Joy Hendry, 259–281. New York: Routledge.

Vander, Judith. 1988. *Songprints: The Musical Experience of Five Shoshone Women*. Urbana: University of Illinois.

Varley, H. Paul. 1984. *Japanese Culture*. Honolulu: University of Hawaii Press.

Yakō, Masato and Toshinori Araki. 1998. "An Analysis of *nagauta-shamisen* Melody by Blocking." *Toyo Ongaku Kenkyu* (Journal of the Society for Research in Asiatic Music) 63, August, 37–76.

Yano, Christine R. 2002. *Tears of Longing: Nostalgia and the Nation in Japanese Popular Song*. Cambridge, MA: Harvard University Asia Center.

_______ . 1995. "Shaping Tears of a Nation: An Ethnography of Emotion in Japanese Popular Songs." Ph.D. dissertation, University of Hawaii.

Yuasa, Yasuo. 1987. *The Body: Toward an Eastern Mind-Body Theory*. Edited by Thomas P. Kasulis, trans. by Shigenori Nagatomo and Thomas P. Kasulis. Albany: State University of New York Press.

Index and Glossary

F

G

H

I

J

K

Y

Z